THE FUTURE CONDITIONAL

THE FUTURE CONDITIONAL

Building an English-Speaking Society
in Northeast China

Eric S. Henry

CORNELL UNIVERSITY PRESS   **ITHACA AND LONDON**

First published 2021 by Cornell University Press

Library of Congress Cataloging-in-Publication Data

Names: Henry, Eric S., author.
Title: The future conditional : building an English-speaking society in northeast
    China / Eric S. Henry.
Description: Ithaca [New York] : Cornell University Press, 2021. |
    Includes bibliographical references and index.
Identifiers: LCCN 2020034865 (print) | LCCN 2020034866 (ebook) |
    ISBN 9781501754906 (hardcover) | ISBN 9781501755163 (paperback) |
    ISBN 9781501754913 (epub) | ISBN 9781501754920 (pdf)
Subjects: LCSH: English language—Social aspects—China. | English language—
    Study and teaching—Social aspects—China. | English language—Study and
    teaching—Chinese speakers. | Group identity—China.
Classification: LCC P40.5.G762 C45 2021 (print) | LCC P40.5.G762 (ebook) |
    DDC 428.0071/051—dc23
LC record available at https://lccn.loc.gov/2020034865
LC ebook record available at https://lccn.loc.gov/2020034866

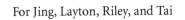

For Jing, Layton, Riley, and Tai

Contents

Preface

I first arrived in Shenyang in the bitingly cold winter of 2001 as an English teacher. Snow covered everything, and, driving in from the airport in a taxi with Pony, the school representative sent to meet me, we passed legions of students bundled against the weather; classes were canceled, and students had been organized into work details to chip at the layer of ice on the ground with shovels. A truck driver lay on the road beneath his vehicle, carefully passing a scrap of burning newspaper under his fuel line to defrost it. Everywhere people wrapped themselves in as many layers as possible, and the taste of coal dust from the overworked heating plants was thick on my tongue. Pony was the foreign teacher coordinator for a large private English school offering classes for children, beginning in preschool and often continuing straight through until high school. I had answered an advertisement on the internet only a month previously and, after confirming that I really did speak English, was offered a job to teach twenty hours of classes each week, mostly to children just beginning to learn the language.

For some, this may read as a confession. A renowned historian of China once told me to keep my original employment a secret, presumably lest whatever words that followed be tainted by this corrupting fact. Being an English teacher in China does appear to place one firmly in the camp of young, carefree adventure seekers who strike a kind of Faustian bargain in their new home—they work at a job where the only requirement is acquired in infancy, make scads of money in local terms, and spend all of it on travel and booze before returning home a year or two later. The very nature of the English teacher's transience weighs against developing any kind of deep understanding of the local culture, and most teachers, even if they end up staying years in the same place, acquire only a limited vocabulary of beer- and taxi-related terms, living in a bubble manufactured by language barriers and ethnocentrism.

But I had just finished a master's degree in anthropology and, with some debts to pay off and the desire to immerse myself in the language, being an English teacher seemed a way to profitably anchor myself in a foreign place, doing all the preparatory work before I started my "real" research later on. My goal was to continue ethnographically the largely archival and library-based research of my master's degree on the confluence between personal and institutional relationships in Chinese business practices. I had argued, in perhaps overly simplistic and prosaic terms, that the transition from a socialist to a market economy encouraged new forms of cooperation between entrepreneurs and government gatekeepers. The overall thesis was sound, but, as I was soon to discover, it was a topic that resisted ethnographic inquiry (although see Osburg 2013). The exercise of personal influence on bureaucratic systems, involving the back and forth flow of gifts and favors, is a sensitive topic. The gray nature of many of these transactions precluded easy investigation through simply interviewing people about them.

Instead, in a story familiar to many anthropologists, my attention was gradually drawn to a topic that people were not only willing to talk about but about which it was difficult to get them to stop talking. Thus, my temporary teaching arrangement, in which I traded my evening and weekend hours as a teacher for an apartment and Mandarin-language classes, became a research topic in itself. People wanted to ask me about English. A lot. And not just in the classroom—in restaurants, in homes, and on the street, people would stop me in midsentence (or sometimes would not even let me start) and ask me about the language. "How do I learn it?" they wanted to know. "Is it hard? What is the best age to begin study? Do you know any tricks or shortcuts to become fluent?" The last question often stumped me, not because I didn't know any tricks (at the time, I thought I knew everything about learning English, and so did most of the other foreign teachers), but because it appeared to equate native linguistic acquisition with pedagogical expertise. Did speaking a language really make me an expert in teaching it? And why was this such an important topic to bring up in the first place?

I slowly came to realize that to treat English acquisition in China as merely a linguistic or educational phenomenon forecloses the possibility of placing it within a broader theoretical frame, one that includes a host of other issues. Viewing English in isolation from China's other ongoing forms of transformation obscures the connections among them. For instance, in this book I will argue that understanding the use of foreign languages necessitates a discussion of urban renewal and the physical transformation of the city, which further implicates the way Chinese people understand processes of modernization and the logic of the racialized body. By developing this fuller understanding, the choice to speak English becomes one full of signification. An act of performance in a long genre of self-representation in China, English asserts a cosmopolitan and global identity for the speaker, as opposed to a marginalized local one. We can also discern how these performances and identities, although they draw on transnational imagery and ideas, are distinctly Chinese.

The original research for this book, undertaken in 2005, was generously supported by the Wenner-Gren Foundation and Social Sciences and Humanities Research Council of Canada (SSHRC). Subsequent fieldwork in 2010 was supported by a postdoctoral fellowship from SSHRC and in 2013 by Saint Mary's

University. I am deeply indebted to a range of colleagues and scholars who have read and commented on various parts of this manuscript, but a short list would include Elana Chipman, Marcie Middlebrooks, Jessica Falcone, Matt Erie, Kimberly Couvson-Liebe, and Jen Shannon. The overall direction my research has taken was due to advice and input from Andrew Lyons, Harriet Lyons, Tiantian Zheng, Paul Festa, Chantelle Falconer, Pauline McKenzie Aucoin, Ruanni Tupas, Shirley Hall, and Nicole Hayes. P. Steven Sangren, Andrew Willford, and Vilma Santiago-Irizarry shaped my development as an anthropologist, and I am grateful to all of them for the careful attention they paid to my work. I would also like to thank the many other scholars at Cornell who offered advice and guidance: Terry Turner, Magnus Fiskesjö, Frederic Gleach, Kathryn March, David Holmberg, and Jane Fajans, among many others. Tania Li and Jesook Song graciously hosted a doctoral retreat at the University of Toronto that afforded time to write and a critical engagement. I have enjoyed the intellectual kinship offered by colleagues at Carleton University, including Peter Gose, Donna Patrick, Xiaobei Chen, and Zhiqiu Lin; similarly, at Saint Mary's University I have benefited from the collegiality of Rylan Higgins, Paul Erickson, Marty Zelenietz, Jonathan Fowler, Tanya Peckmann, Michelle MacCarthy, Laura Eastham, Bill Sewell, and Elissa Asp. The editorial team at Cornell University Press, particularly Jim Lance, worked diligently to facilitate the editing and publishing process and deserve my thanks, along with the two anonymous readers who provided generous encouragement and feedback. I am grateful for the time afforded me by Carleton University and Saint Mary's University to conduct this work in addition to my teaching responsibilities. Finally, I would like to thank the many people who assisted my research in Shenyang, including the many teachers and students who sat for interviews or allowed me to watch their classes.

Readers will notice that a lot of the people I talk about in this book have English names like Charles and Sophia. The choice of which name to use was a deliberate one made by the people I interviewed, and even in interactions with other Chinese they often used English names. Other people have Mandarin names like Liu Xiaohua or Zhang Wen. Again, the choice of name, and language, was deliberate. All of these are pseudonyms, but in picking those pseudonyms I attempted to match the speaker's chosen language and term of address. The same is true of the schools I describe: all have been given pseudonyms, but ones that reflect the spirit of the originals. In China, surnames precede given names, and I follow this convention in the book when referring to individuals by their Chinese names and to Chinese scholars whose work I discuss.

Two chapters in this book are revised versions of papers previously published elsewhere. Chapter 5 is an improved version of the paper "Interpretations of 'Chinglish': Native Speakers, Language Learners and the Enregisterment of a Stigmatized Code," published by *Language in Society* 39 (5): 669–88, while chapter 6 is significantly revised from "Emissaries of the Modern: The Foreign Teacher in Urban China," published by *City & Society* 25 (2): 216–34. Both chapters are included here with the permission of the publishers. Unless otherwise noted, all figures and illustrations are my own.

Note on Transcription

The focus of this book is on discourse and the meaning of one or more types of language in conversation. I have therefore adopted a relatively straightforward transcription system for spoken texts.

,   short pause

.   sentence—final pause

...   longer pause

—   interruption (at end of speaker's turn); false start or sentence break

[ ]   editorial comment or clarification

The form of English speech has been preserved as accurately as possible to reflect its style and structure. The need to document several linguistic registers in interaction has led me to adopt the following conventions: in spoken and written discourse, English is in plain text. Words and phrases in Mandarin are romanized using the pinyin system. Both untranslated Mandarin words or phrases and discourse translated from spoken or written Mandarin are *italicized*. The local Dongbei dialect is also <u>underlined</u>. Unless otherwise indicated, all translations are my own.

THE FUTURE CONDITIONAL

INTRODUCTION

The English Modern

A common trope in political writings of China's socialist era was the notion that the people (*renmin*), united in common cause, were not simply building machinery or ships or railways but socialism itself. "Led by the working class and the Communist Party," wrote Mao Zedong (1977, 384), "our 600 million people, united as one, are engaged in the great task of building socialism. The unification of our country, the unity of our people and the unity of our various nationalities—these are the basic guarantees for the sure triumph of our cause." This mobilization of people and production, under the leadership of the Communist Party, was felt to be so strong, so unstoppable, that China would surely supersede the so-called developed countries in a matter of years, constituting nothing less than the rebuilding of the very foundations of Chinese society.

Whether the society that emerged under Mao's leadership or the one that has taken off following forty years of economic reforms fulfilled this triumphalist vision is a matter of some debate. This book, however, turns our attention to another great undertaking, one more recent but no less ambitious in its scope and revolutionary potential. While Mao saw the people's task as one of building socialism, the current transformation seeks to radically reconfigure the relationships between self and society, between citizen and the state, and between China and the world. Its goal too is the reinvention of Chinese society, but through the creation of a modern rather than a socialist future, while the means to achieving this end are premised on a range of linguistic and cultural practices. As many people asked me throughout my research, What if everyone in China could speak English?

1

At the end of the 1970s, as China was emerging from the political maelstrom of the Cultural Revolution, English was spoken by only a relative handful of academics, foreigners, translators, and interpreters. Despite a long history born of colonialism and missionization, the language had been nearly eradicated as a communicative resource due to its association with bourgeois values (Adamson 2004; Ji 2004). English became a required subject when university entrance examinations were reinstated in 1978, and foreign language education began to take off again in the early 1980s at the beginning of the "reform and opening up" (*gaige kaifang*) period (Pan 2015a), a time when the socialist ethos of state, economy, and society was gradually dismantled in favor of a model of explosive economic growth and private individualism. The two projects seemed to go hand in hand, as both foreign language education and market reforms oriented the nation away from its insular posture and bridged the divide between China and the West.[1] State educational policies have a habit of falling flat unless they speak to broader social movements and transformations, and, in this case, official support for English was intertwined with an acute desire by Chinese parents, students, and citizens to inculcate this global language as well. Today, by our best estimates, 300 million to 400 million people in China can speak or write English with some manner of fluency (R. Wei and Su 2012). In both size and scope, this transformation represents, quite simply, the largest, most ambitious language learning project in human history.

This is an ethnography of contemporary speech practices and English language learning in the northeastern Chinese city of Shenyang. It is based on sixteen months of research conducted over several trips from 2005 to 2013. Most of that time was spent in private English language training schools (*yingyu peixun xuexiao*) that complement language teaching in the public school system.[2] These have become ubiquitous in urban China in recent years, forming a core component of a multibillion-dollar foreign language teaching industry (G. Hu and McKay 2012; L. Wang 2004). As in other Asian countries, families spend a significant portion of their disposable income on private foreign language education for their children, including evening and weekend language classes at these schools found throughout the city.[3] I also visited a range of other schools, including senior, middle, and elementary schools, universities, and adult education centers. In all of these, I observed classes taught by multiple teachers at many different levels. I examined textbooks and other teaching materials, participated in pedagogical training, and recorded teacher-student interactions. I spent time with teachers in their offices as they worked with students, prepared for classes, or simply chatted among themselves. But my interests in foreign language in China also took me far beyond the classroom, into people's homes, public language performances, and local events like school promotions and teacher training seminars. I spoke with students about their motivations and desires for learning English as well as the language's place in Chinese society more generally. Between the curriculum and the lesson plan is a group of teachers discussing how to convey their ideas to a class. Between educational directives and the school is an administrator trying to appeal to parents to attract more attention and tuition. It is in these points of mediation, in other words, where we might ask how the desire for English is produced and, in turn, how that feeds back into state language policies.

Nearly everyone in the city encounters English on a more or less daily basis. Children learn it in public school from the third grade onward, and almost all students take classes in the private English schools I studied.[4] Young people need high scores on standardized national English tests to get into good schools, go to good universities, and eventually to get good jobs (L. Cheng 2008; Pan and Block 2011). Adults need English to succeed in professional careers, whether they be cops, lawyers, architects, bankers, or businesspeople. It is needed—or at least thought to be needed—to go abroad, to deal with foreigners, to participate in international events, or to take advantage of global opportunities (V. Fong 2011; Weihong Wang 2015). English words and phrases can be found on signs, menus, and consumer products throughout the city, spoken on radio and television by everyone from celebrities to street cleaners, and pop up in conversation among urban citizens on an everyday basis.[5] English is associated with wealth, civilized behavior, modernity, commerce, cosmopolitanism, and a future-oriented outlook on contemporary social events. This melding of temporal and spatial logistics with the practices of everyday speech is known as a chronotope and is a concept I will explore in more detail below. But given the importance of English in China today, it would be fair to consider English a quasi-official language with an extensive public mandate that runs throughout both the education system and society more broadly, affecting nearly every individual who dreams of a better future for themselves and their families.

And yet very few people, other than those educated abroad or in top domestic educational institutions, could be considered functionally fluent in English. Many people do work for international companies or regularly communicate with others outside China: academics write papers for international journals, entrepreneurs travel abroad, and interpreters translate for foreign tourists and businesspeople. But taken together, this handful of potential uses for English pales in comparison to the sheer number of students nationally and the all-encompassing inclusion of the language in structures of education, employment, and self-improvement. It is simply the case that most people in China will interact rarely, if at all, with a native speaker of English or use English as a lingua franca with non-Chinese in their lives. The vast majority of urban residents know English more as a utilitarian academic subject than as a vibrant spoken language, one that is tied to multiple-choice tests and educational credentials. Many people pepper their speech with English words and expressions, but these are often trendy and practiced tokens of global culture rather than spontaneous uses of natural fluency (see Q. Zhang 2012). Opportunities to actually use English conversationally outside of the highly charged testing environment of the education system are few and far between. For all of their growing sense of transnationalism, many Chinese I met in Shenyang remarked on how I was the first foreigner they had ever spoken to in person. Indeed, the most common venue where native-speaking English foreigners are encountered is the English language classroom itself.

This raises an important question related to the motivations and execution of this massive development project, but one also rarely considered by its architects, proponents, and agents: Why? Why teach an entire nation English? This question often unsettled my informants, friends, and teachers, who often countered by referring to ongoing economic and social transformations such as China joining the World Trade Organization or the 2008 Beijing Olympics. Their argument, in sum, was that the development of English in China is explained by global shifts in technology and capital, a growing integration of China within the transnational sphere where the lingua franca of business, trade, diplomacy, and science is English. China's place in the world is changing, I was repeatedly told, and people are changing with it. Just as Deng Xiaoping's proclamation that "to get rich is glorious" in the 1990s promised a new era of widespread wealth and prosperity, many people saw English as a key to unlocking their own, and the nation's, future potential.

Economic imperatives undoubtedly play a role in this phenomenon, but they also act as a cloak, a convenient ideological frame that obscures deeper, and more salient, cultural forces at work. The economic answer especially plays into a particular neoliberal logic of foreign languages as commodified products, with speakers motivated in their acquisition by choice, opportunity, and social fulfillment (Heller 2010; Holborow 2015; Shin and Park 2016). Following Lisa Hoffman's (2010) ethnography of discourses of human capital in China's employment markets, we can see how foreign languages have similarly become an attribute of the self-enterprising individuals she dubs "patriotic professionals." Alexandre Duchêne and Monica Heller see such processes as an inevitable consequence of late capitalism, writing that economic transformations on a global scale have encouraged us to "construct language as a technical skill, decoupled from authenticity" (2012, 10; see also Heller 2003; J. Park and Wee 2012; Rubdy and Tan 2008; Shin 2016). I will explore later in more detail how English has been integrated as a commodity within a growing marketplace for private language education, but my ethnography also underlines the ways in which English is both part of a larger national project and grounded in the particularities of Shenyang's sociocultural milieu. In particular, I highlight how uncertainties about the roles and positions of individuals within China's ongoing modernization drives both the consumers and purveyors of English language education. The massive uptake in English as an individualized skill has been accompanied by the public circulation of English as a token of a changing society, but one that is not equally available to all citizens. What many people termed the English fever (*yingyu re*) in Shenyang reflects a profound mixture of anxiety and yearning about skills and knowledge that Andrew Kipnis (2011) has dubbed "educational desire," and an almost universal acceptance of the language as a measure of current success and future potential in a globalized world. Those desires are all the more intense given the historical primacy of the one-child policy and a family structure that invests all aspirations in a single child (V. Fong 2004, 2011; F. Liu 2015).

This leads me to consider how individuals (language teachers, students, parents, administrators, and so forth) both understand and configure their positions within the educational system and society more generally. By way of its association with global domains of culture and modern forms of life and livelihood, speaking English has become a transformative process in the lives of many Chinese, often tied to the cultivation of a network of linked practices indexing global modernity including the display of particular commodities and brands, music tastes, media consumption, lifestyle pursuits, and so forth. English is one such key signifier: to speak English in China today is, in a very real sense, to be a different kind of person from those who do not. The logic of this equivalence motivates a vast array of pedagogical and communicative practices that range from the conventional to the bizarre—Li Yang's Crazy English program, for instance, obliges students to scream out their English lessons at the top of their lungs (J. Li 2009; Woodward 2008)—but all illustrate an overarching notion of what language means in this context. I therefore attribute the rationale for the mass adoption of English to what the linguist Braj Kachru (1986) termed the language's "alchemy," its power to cultivate the social value of individuals, reshape relations between differently situated actors and groups, and even propel the nation forward on its path to development.

The prominence of English in China today is the result of historical relations of colonialism and power that forged its global presence and the hierarchical ordering of linguistic inequality (Canagarajah 1999; Heller and McElhinny 2017). European languages have retained their dominance in many postcolonial societies, including India, the Philippines, the countries of Africa, and others, often to the detriment of minority languages in a process Robert Phillipson (1992, 2009) dubs linguistic imperialism. Christina Higgins (2009) argues that studies of global English have descended into a rigid dichotomization between creative and hegemonic perspectives on the language, with some praising its potential to liberate individuals from poverty or nationalism, while others decry its imposition by colonizers on their former subjects. The reality, she notes, is far more complex, involving a range of state policies, individual desires, and collective actions. Vicente Rafael reminds us, for instance, that imperial languages were never simply imposed from above by colonizers or language planners, but were in many ways embraced by revolutionaries, nationalists, and ordinary citizens. After independence, Filipino nationalists celebrated Castilian Spanish as a language that "would allow them to communicate at a distance, traversing differences in language, social rank, and territorial boundaries. It would translate the local into the national, which would simultaneously resonate with the languages of the larger modern world" (Rafael 2005, 13). The prominence of European languages in postcolonial nations reflects complicated desires and needs of individuals grappling with the contradictions of modernity and global capitalism.

To return to the contemporary Chinese context, I therefore argue that the nature of English language learning and the role the language plays in the contemporary educational, social, and political environments of Shenyang is a distinctly *Chinese* phenomenon, rooted in the concerns of people suddenly confronted with new forms of social, economic, and political stratification. The global apparatus of educational institutions, nongovernmental organizations, private corporations, and armies of transnational teachers and students has indeed shaped the nature of pedagogical practices, institutional forms, and even individual life courses on the ground in Shenyang. But similar to the ways in which socialism itself was a global project rooted specifically in the Chinese experience (Dirlik 2005), English in China is a nominally global language that is enacted and interpreted within an inherently local spatial framework. As Jan Blommaert (2010, 80) argues, "Languages and discourses move around, but they do so between spaces that are full of rules, norms, customs and conventions, and they get adapted to the rules, norms, customs and conventions of such places." In other words, as languages travel across the globe, their values are reterritorialized, imported into local systems of meaningfulness (Zentz 2015). To understand why English is so popular—why it is so intensely desired—therefore requires an ethnographic perspective that is grounded in the intimate, everyday goals and activities of ordinary Chinese citizens, not the machinations of global corporations or institutions.

This perspective is significant because we have entered an age of intensified language change and shift: even as many smaller languages have become endangered, global languages (and their geographic metropoles) have been transformed through a process often dubbed "superdiversity" (Vertovec 2007; see also Blommaert 2013; Silverstein 2015). New patterns of migration, new desires and intentions of those migrants, and the communicative technologies that link diasporic and transnational communities together have created complex interconnected webs of language and culture (Cho 2012; Goebel 2010; Ong 1999). Whereas conventional sociolinguistic analyses assumed a shared framework for the interpretation of speech events—that conversational participants could use familiar linguistic features to recognize certain types of discursive events such as a dispute, wager, or joke—in superdiverse communities these frameworks may be only partially shared or even stand in opposition to each other. For instance, Jasmine, one of the teachers I worked with quite extensively, called me one day to ask a question about American immigration policies. As I explained to her several technical details in English, I switched into Mandarin to add some clarification. There was silence on the other end of the line for a moment and then Jasmine queried, "Are you speaking Chinese to me because my English is not good?" What I viewed solely as an issue of communicative clarity, she viewed as one of metapragmatic evaluation, a critique of her own communicative resources and language capabilities. Likewise, Chinese students in English language classes frequently had trouble differentiating their foreign teachers' formal instruction from offhand comments or jokes. Foreign teachers often characterized their students as humorless automatons shaped by a strict educational system, but their jokes landed flat only because students had trouble keying sudden shifts into a casual stylistic tone. In superdiverse linguistic environments, therefore, the contextualization cues that allow participants to broadcast their intentions and interpret those of others may derive from multiple sources, leading to complex negotiations between speakers about the meaning of talk. Consequently, I do not focus solely on one particular group or demographic in Shenyang, but examine the rich interactions between Chinese-language students, teachers, foreign educated returnees, and expatriate native speakers who all inhabit this complex linguistic environment.

State educational policies that emphasize the acquisition of English for global competitiveness reflect a vision of languages as synchronic totalities. Much of the literature on English in China accepts, axiomatically, that a "thing" called English exists, coherent and well defined, residing in dictionaries and textbooks and the minds of native speakers. But speakers in superdiverse contexts may be confronted with multiple forms of an ostensibly standardized and coherent language. While the explicit goal of classroom pedagogies was the acquisition of an internationally recognized archetype of English, in practice there was frequent debate about what kind of English was the best, most useful, and, crucially, easiest to understand. British or American? Is a Scottish teacher better than a South African one? Should it be called a lorry or a truck? In addition, within the educational ecology of Shenyang there are multiple pedagogies and learning styles that translate into different patterns of speech. There is, for instance, the highly detailed technical knowledge of lexical form and morphosyntactic rules that forms the basis of success on discrete point tests critical to success in a highly competitive educational system. But there is also the looser, intuitive knowledge of English, often developed through private English language classes that focus on conversational English skills and are useful for developing communicative competence within a global setting.

There are so many of these forms and types of English language usage in China that cataloguing or attempting to systematize them into formal patterns strikes me as both a monumental and largely irrelevant task. Far more significant is exploring how these forms of English are mapped onto already established or emergent sociocultural personae and alignments. The answer to the question, "British or American English?," for instance, is crucially tied to evaluative frameworks and stereotypes of British and American speakers. Similarly, choosing which language to use in a given situation implies certain calculable sociocultural effects on how speakers are perceived, assessed, and have their actions interpreted by others. Although the model of a systematically coherent English exemplified by native speaker intuitions might exist as an idealized benchmark for the Chinese learners I worked with, the actual bases for appraising the legitimacy or illegitimacy of a particular instance of English usage can be fraught with questions unrelated to the form of the language itself—questions such as Where and how did this person study? Is she or he rural or urban? Local or outsider? A person in authority or someone with low social status?

If English, as a language, is destabilized in this environment, the boundaries between languages are also amorphous and indistinct. For instance, in one English class I observed, a foreign teacher asked her Chinese students how they had celebrated a recent holiday. In describing the food, one student—after consulting his dictionary—volunteered that he had eaten "sticky glutinous rice balls with black sesame filling." After some back-and-forth, the teacher declared this translation too oblique and encouraged the student to use the Mandarin word *tangyuan*. A different student pushed back, however: Shouldn't they be using English words in an English class? The teacher argued that it was all right because English speakers often use foreign food words such as pizza or sushi. But, came the question again, does that make them English? Language classes were frequent sites for discussion among teachers, students, and native English speakers about these types of uncertainties. What makes something English? How does one know whether it is correct or not? Who decides? Normally such questions could be posed as curious linguistic puzzles of little significance, but in the tense Chinese environment of foreign language education, they are pressing and important.

A consequence of this is that, for me as a native speaker, I even began to feel alienated from my own language. One is constantly confronted with speech that feels just a little atypical—slight changes in stress and pronunciation, words used just a little differently, sentence constructions that, although grammatical, felt unnatural. It was in China that I first heard the word "picayune" used in a sentence, and when I struggled to explain the difference between the possessives "have" and "have got." That feeling of being alienated from language—which leads Derrida (1998, 25) to remark, "I have only one language and it is not mine"—is a theme I will return to several times because it marked my informants' experience with language as well, and not just of learning English. It derives from the uncertainty around language boundaries I noted above. "Sociolinguistic systems are *not unified*," notes Blommaert (2013, 11). "A sociolinguistic system is always a 'system of systems,' characterized by different *scale levels*—the individual is a system, his/her peer group is one, his/her age category another and so on . . . Centers in a polycentric system typically occupy specific scale levels and operate as foci of *normativity*, that is, of ordered indexicalities." At higher scale levels—that is, at higher forms of collectivity such as nations—linguistic forms appear to be easily isolatable into coherent wholes as distinct languages. But as one zeroes in on smaller groupings, speech communities, and, finally, individual speakers, those boundaries dissolve in the course of everyday talk. They only remain as convenient—but in many ways contested—labels that speakers can deploy to characterize some type of speech as belonging to some type of category. Indeed, in rendering speech as text in this ethnography I have had no choice but to employ those categories to highlight how people perceive the nature of talk. But they are, nonetheless, *ideological artifacts* of a sociolinguistic system.

Rather than asking what English in China looks like and providing an extensive description of its form, my approach here is to ask what speaking English means. This question encompasses both a concern with meaning at the interactional level—how English may be used strategically by various conversational participants—and at larger scales, such as what English represents as a signifier in and of itself throughout Shenyang as a speech community. Jan Blommaert (2010, 5) makes a useful distinction between a traditional sociolinguistics of distribution "in which movement of language resources is seen as movement in a horizontal and stable space and in chronological time" and a new sociolinguistics of mobility that describes language-in-motion. In the sociolinguistics of mobility, conventional notions of languages—as bounded, countable, nationalized units—must give way to a view of language in use as sets of socioculturally mediated *practices* that are interpretable through *semiotic frameworks* (see also Agha 2007; Bucholtz and Hall 2005; Silverstein 2003a; Wortham 2006). We can therefore view the uses of English in everyday speech in China, whether in the classroom or in public greetings between friends, as articulating with its deployment in such diverse higher-scale fields as advertising, media, and entertainment. This requires us, though, to shift our focus away from the form of English—attributing the use of particular words to one or more linguistic categories as representing paradigmatic forms of dialect such as British, American, or Chinese English—to viewing English itself, and all its attendant indexical meanings, as the product of discursive practices.

Shenyang

The stage on which these discursive practices play out is Shenyang, the largest city in northeastern China, or Dongbei, an area that comprises the three provinces of Liaoning (of which it is the capital), Jilin, and Heilongjiang (figure I.1).

The city has a long and peculiar history. A small trading town until the seventeenth century, it became the capital of the Manchu Qing dynasty under the ruler Nuerhachi in 1625. After his successful campaign against the aging Ming state in

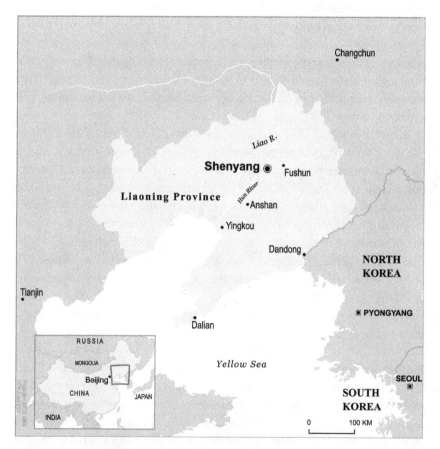

FIGURE I.1. Map of Liaoning Province, China

1644, Nuerhachi's son, Huang Taiji, moved the capital of the nascent empire from Shenyang to Beijing, but retained an extensive imperial residence in the city, still extant today as a tourist attraction. During the Qing dynasty, Shenyang was known as Shengjing in Chinese, or by its Manchu name, Mukden; it was not until the communist victory over the region in 1948 that the geographical nomenclature was finally standardized and Sinicized. After the 1911 Revolution that brought an end to imperial rule, Shenyang came under the control of various warlords, including Zhang Zuolin and, after his assassination by Japanese forces in the famous Mukden Incident of 1931, his son Zhang Xueliang. The Japanese invaded and established the puppet state of Manchukuo in 1932, with its capital in the city of Changchun, far to the north of Shenyang (Duara 2003). The Japanese recognized the industrial potential of Shenyang, situated as it is near extensive coal and iron deposits in the mountains to the east. During the Manchukuo regime, the Japanese encouraged the development of the steel industry of Shenyang, a feature that came to define it even after the Japanese defeat in the Second World War and the return of the region to Chinese control.

During the socialist era, Shenyang was an industrial powerhouse in heavy manufacturing and steel production. The population grew throughout the ups and downs of this highly politicized period, including the nationwide famine of the Great Leap Forward (1958–1962) and the chaos of the Cultural Revolution (1966–1976), when schools and universities were shuttered and almost all urban youth were dispersed to rural areas to engage in agriculture and learn socialism from the peasants. After the death of Mao Zedong in 1976 and the elevation of Deng Xiaoping to the role of paramount leader in 1978, China was steered toward a course of gradual economic reform and modernization. This reform period marked the rationalization of China's industrial strategy and the closure of many state-owned enterprises that were once the economic lifeblood of Shenyang, and the city has experienced a long period of economic stagnation and decline as the economy has shifted from heavy manufacturing (particularly steel, railroads, and petrochemical refining) to export-oriented production (P. Zhang 2003). Tens of thousands of workers were "stepped-down" (*xiagang*), the Chinese term for laid off, from factories all over the city in the 1990s (Giles, Park, and Cai 2006). This period has also seen a mass migration of rural citizens, who perceive few prospects or security in farming, into the cities. Together, they form a massive population of underemployed workers who eke out a marginal existence running bicycle repair stands, washing cars, cleaning offices, collecting recyclables, or operating small shops that sell newspapers, drinks, vegetables, or prepared foods.

At the same time, Shenyang has witnessed the same growing economic inequality that characterizes all of China in the twenty-first century. A man who shined shoes on the street near my apartment told me how he had once worked in a state-owned factory before being laid off. Summarizing a familiar sentiment, he concluded, "*Right now there are two distinct extremes in Chinese society. Those people who have things keep getting more things, and those people without just find themselves with less and less.*" Despite widespread increases in wealth and material goods since the beginning of the reform era for the lowest strata of Chinese society—the urban migrant poor and rural peasants—they have seen their relative standing in the national economy drop. Middle-class urban residents lead a lifestyle that was unimaginable thirty years ago—owning multiple apartments, driving cars, dining out in expensive restaurants—and still unreachable by a significant proportion of the populace.

According to the most recent national census in 2010 (National Bureau of Statistics 2012), the urban population of Shenyang was 8.1 million people, although these figures exclude a substantial number of people classified as the "floating population": those who migrate to the city but do not change their household registration. Shenyang is situated on the southeastern edge of the Manchurian plain. The city and most of the countryside surrounding it are flat for as far as the eye can see, which, because of the haze of pollution and dusty winds from the west, is frequently not very far. The slow-moving Hun River once marked the southern boundary of the city, with only a technology development zone and the city's airport located on the other side, but in the past decade new housing developments have been sprouting along the south shore along with a golf course and soccer stadium. The city is divided into nine major districts: Heping, Shenhe, Dadong, Huanggu, and Tiexi form the city's core, surrounded by the newer districts of Hunnan, Sanjiatun, Shenbei and Liaozhong. Each district has a somewhat distinct character: Tiexi, for instance, was long known as the industrial heart of Shenyang where most of the city's factories were located, while Huanggu is often called the "education district," and Heping features many government offices. Recently, the city government began closing down the remaining urban factories and moving others westward, to a development area called New Tiexi.

Some ongoing changes are gradually redefining the design and use of public and private space in contemporary Shenyang. Increasingly, the laneways between apartment buildings are being turned into parking lots for private cars. Car ownership has skyrocketed in recent years, leading to heavy traffic on the roads and a premium on parking spaces in complexes built before private cars became common. In some cases, cars spill out into the public streets outside the complexes themselves, causing confusion in the mornings as commuters try to thread their way through a maze of haphazardly parked vehicles. Traffic has increased to the point that a trip from one end of the city to the other that might have taken half an hour when I first arrived in Shenyang in 2001 now takes at least two hours during peak times. While major city roads are quite broad, encompassing between six and ten lanes of traffic, the previous lack of need for traffic planning has led to frequent bottlenecks and construction zones (where the city government is attempting to widen roads and improve access) that further impede traffic. All of these factors, including history, climate, economy, and modernization, affect the meaning of language learning and of individual languages in use in the city.

"I Am the Superstar": Language and the Multiplicity of Identity

At the home of a friend one night in Shenyang, I sat with several Chinese watching a television show called *Tiaozhan Zhuchiren*, also known by its English title, *Challenge to Be the Host*. Essentially a chance for aspiring television hosts and hostesses to display their skills, the show pitted contestants against each other in tests of oral performance, singing, wordplay, and joke-telling. On this occasion, one of the three female contestants was from Shenyang, and the presence of a local on the show evoked some interest from those in the room. After a collective song-and-dance performance, each contestant was invited to introduce herself. The Shenyanger addressed the television audience eloquently in perfect standard Mandarin, giving her name and hometown. She then shifted into English. "And my English name is Anne. I am hoping for your support."

The next component of the show assigned each contestant the role of an animal, and they had to defend why their animal was the best of the three using references to Chinese stories, sayings, slang, jokes, and anything else they could think of to present the animal's finest characteristics. Anne, given the role of a monkey, at several points used words and sayings from the local vernacular, Dongbeihua. Although Dongbeihua is comprehensible to other Mandarin speakers, it is marked by some unique lexical tokens and morphosyntactic features, and sounds heavily accented to outsiders. Finally, in an individual musical performance, Anne sang a popular Chinese song interspersed with English lyrics such as "I am the superstar." During the course of the contest, the thing that seemed to most impress the judges and audience, both televised and in the apartment with me, was Anne's ability to manipulate and invoke various types of language: English, Mandarin, and Dongbeihua. Her English made her sound stylish and sophisticated to my friends' ears, while her Dongbeihua added a common touch. Such nimble use of language, exclaimed one of my friends, was a clear demonstration of a clever mind.

Anne seems to have succeeded in a nearly impossible task, drawing on a range of speech registers and mixing them together to successfully present herself to the audience as an ideal television hostess. It is not altogether clear, however, how the mobile linguistic resources Anne deployed in her performance led the audience to view it favorably, how she staged, in Erving Goffman's (1959, 17) terms, an "impression of reality" that becomes a "real reality" and became someone with a clever mind. What linguistic and ideological processes are at work here? We may note, to begin, that Anne did not employ one singular voice but layered her performance with multiple contextually specific ones. The English she used to introduce herself to the audience was balanced by the standard accent in her Mandarin and the Dongbeihua in her voicings of particular animal characters. Had she, in contrast, introduced herself in Dongbeihua and voiced the animals in English, it would likely have sounded out of place because each of these voices also carries a distinct meaning for the audience, as particular forms of speech are viewed as extensions of particular types of social personhood. Anne, in other words, switched among both voices and identities as she variously positioned herself as a cosmopolitan actor comfortable on a global stage, a professional host for a national audience, and a warmly familiar local, enacting recognizable figures tied to distinct places and times.

Moreover, these voicings had to be convincing. I, for one, often tried to use Dongbeihua in speech with Shenyangers but could never pull off being mistaken for a local. Any discursive performance must satisfy a range of conditions to become, in the words of J. L. Austin (1962), "felicitous." That is, as Goffman (1983, 48) writes, our words must "be heard to draw appropriately on one array of presuppositions—that sustained by our hearers—and avoid being heard to make others—those which are not." For Shenyangers, there are many ways to convincingly portray these roles, including forms of dress, appearance, bodily habitus, and rapidity of speech. One of the most effective guarantees of linguistic authenticity, however, and thus a presupposition that speakers are who they represent themselves to be, is accent (Cavanaugh 2005; Sung 2013). To be taken seriously as a global or a local actor, you must sound like one.

Sounding local, for most Shenyangers, is not a problem. It comes naturally to people raised within the linguistic environment of the city and, because Dongbeihua is closely related to standard Mandarin, can be quickly acquired by those who have moved to the area. Indeed, the real issue for many people is the question of sounding too local, of not being able to abandon Dongbeihua when it is necessary to use either Mandarin or English. As with Anne's performance, the goal for most speakers is to be able to move fluidly between multiple speech styles according to the demands of the situation. The problem is that English and, to some extent, Mandarin require access to educational pathways that are not equally available to all citizens. Because of strong ideologies of linguistic homogeneity and uniformity, students who speak a regionally inflected variety of Mandarin are often treated as less sophisticated and intelligent than their metropolitan peers

(Blum 2004; Dong 2009; Kwong 2011). They are more likely to be discriminated against by teachers and denied opportunities for higher education. Similarly, an ability to use "good" English, free of vernacularized features and Chinese pronunciation, is thought necessary to be taken seriously as a modern citizen.

What is particularly interesting about this requirement, though, is the fact that, in most cases, the audiences evaluating speakers' claims to embody cosmopolitan forms of identity are engaged in similar forms of activity. Most of the people in the room with me watching Anne's performance on television were also, themselves, English students who tried, at times, to present themselves as globally situated actors too. Sabrina Billings (2013, 23), in her research on Tanzanian beauty pageant participants, echoes a similar dynamic, writing that "while *anyone* can adopt a cosmopolitan sensibility, some people, in any given context, are *more* cosmopolitan than others, at least in part due to unequal access to signs of cosmopolitanness." Tanzanian beauty queens, who favor English onstage in the projection of a modern, elite, and educated identity, gain audience approval by "speaking confidently," a complex metasemiotic scheme that includes prosody, use of standard pronunciations, lack of hesitations, and even a host of nonlinguistic factors such as hairstyle and dress design (Billings 2013, 96). When one or more elements of this sign system do not fit, what Agha (2007, 24) calls "indexical non-congruence," the audience may act to reject the speaker's identity claims and, in the case of the beauty queens, laugh them off the stage. Emulating a foreign, native English speaker's accent and style is therefore a key element of presenting oneself as a globally competent social actor.

So, while many scholars have become interested in the role of English in China, I contend that to fully understand English we need a clear picture of the speech environment as a whole, one that includes all of the language registers and practices that are prevalent in everyday interactions. Although English, Mandarin, and Dongbeihua appear nominally separate—or in the case of the latter two, dialects of the same underlying language—they are instead fundamental components of a comprehensive semiotic complex, a total social fact; the value of each is tied to the value of the others. In the next section, I explore this perspective in more detail, grounding it in the revolutionary work of the Russian linguist Mikhail Bakhtin.

Bakhtin in an Age of Globalization

The rediscovery via translation of the work of Mikhail Bakhtin, an early twentieth-century Russian literary theorist, was a revelation to linguists and anthropologists in the 1980s. I will focus here on two of the concepts he pioneered: heteroglossia and the chronotope. Heteroglossia comes from Bakhtin's realization, in his essay "Discourse in the Novel," that all speech is layered with multiple voices, genres, and styles. Our words are always predicated on the voices of others to whom we are responding, or referencing, or inciting, with their own unique traits and contours that are embedded in our own as we enter into dialogue with them. This leads him to proclaim that all languages, too, are internally stratified into numerous lects: dialects, sociolects, jargons, generational styles, and so forth (Bakhtin 1981, 262). The forces that draw these varieties together and unify them into a coherent language are, in fact, ideological in nature, but they are always found in opposition to "processes of decentralization and disunification" (Bakhtin 1981, 272) that spawn this prolific array of styles.

Although Bakhtin developed his concept of the chronotope in response to literary trends and novelistic practices, it too is rooted in the idea of discourse as a human activity. Whereas heteroglossia points to a social stratification of various styles, the chronotope places these styles in historical context. He begins with the realization that periods of literature have distinct relations to space-time. Ancient Greek romances, for instance, were ahistorical. "All of the action in a Greek romance, all the events and adventures that fill it, constitute time-sequences that are neither historical, quotidian, biographical, nor even biological and maturational . . . In this kind of time, nothing changes: the world remains as it was, the biographical life of the heroes does not change, their feelings do not change, people do not even age" (Bakhtin 1981, 91). In comparison, the modern novel is full of such biographical changes, often placing its characters in the course of very real and documented historical events such as wars or reigns or revolutions. Literary typologies—folklore, the chivalric romance, the Bildungsroman—are therefore not simply matters of style but inherently differentiated associations between space and time.

This is not to say, however, that chronotopes are confined to the pages of literary works themselves. They can only exist in literary analysis because novelistic chronotopes are in dialogue with the world outside them. Appreciating the organization of signs within a novel as deriving from a particular historical period—hearing, for instance, the pastness of works such as *Ivanhoe* or *Don Quixote*—is a fundamental quality of human perception that can equally be applied to everyday speech. "We always arrive," Bakhtin (1981, 252–253) writes, "in the final analysis, at the human voice, which is to say we come up against the human being." Perceiving a speaker's accent, for instance, allows the listener to localize the speaker's origin as coming from a particular place. But we also associate those places, and their inhabitants, with relationships to time. Bauman and Briggs (2003) dub this the poetics of Otherness in which outsiders to modern European societies—be they the poor, the rural, the savage, or the primitive with their oral traditions, folklore, and quaint ways of speaking—became representatives of a tradition predating those modern societies. Their voices come, as it were, out of the past, while others appear to beckon from the future. Speech thus always comes not only from *somewhere* but also from *somewhen*.

James Clifford was one of the first to adapt some of Bakhtin's concepts to the work of the ethnographer as part of the nascent postmodern critique of anthropology. An ethnographic text, he realized, was not simply the product of a single voice, that of the fieldworker bolstered by the assurance of scientific objectivity, but a polyphonic collection deriving from the intersubjective nature of ethnography itself. "It becomes necessary to conceive ethnography, not as the experience and interpretation of a circumscribed 'other' reality, but as a constructive negotiation involving at least two, and usually more, conscious, politically significant subjects" (Clifford 1983, 133). Clifford's adoption of Bakhtin is, however, bound to the modality of text, and in particular the ethnographic text as a novelistic analogue. Before long, however, linguistic anthropologists began to discover a rich vein of potential in Bakhtin's work. Barbara and Dennis Tedlock (1985) applied Bakhtin's dialogism to the intertextual relations between Quiché Maya texts and weaving, while Jane Hill (1985, 731) illustrated how, in the Malinche region of Mexico, Mexicano is layered with Spanish in classically heteroglossic fashion, arguing that everyday discourse is "a translinguistic battlefield, upon which two ways of speaking struggle for dominance."

It is the very instability of languages constituted as distinct wholes, and their presumed decoupling from other semiotic modalities such as gesture, text, or, as the Tedlocks show, weaving, that is of interest here. English in China is characterized by both an ideological unity (the language as personified in the body of the stereotypical native speaker) and a practical disunity (the proliferation of types, genres, styles, and sources of authority that structure everyday conversational practices). Anne's use of English in the television competition I described above, for instance, purports to reference a comprehensive, and comprehensible, language. But the exact phrasing of her usage ("And my English name is Anne") draws intertextually on one particular source of English, that is, discourse in the Chinese English classroom. "I am the superstar" is likewise drawn from the hybridized genre of modern Mandarin pop music that itself blends multiple linguistic traditions including Mandarin, English, Cantonese, Taiwanese, and other East Asian speech practices (Moskowitz 2010). English is therefore embedded in a range of other forms of local discourse and cultural practice through which people seek to differentiate themselves as particular types of social actors.

Drawing on both Bakhtin and the semiotics of Charles Peirce, scholars such as Michael Silverstein, Asif Agha and Jan Blommaert have constructed a robust analytical framework to describe such flexible forms of language use. Rather than attempting to categorize linguistic differences in grammatical terms, Agha develops the concept of "register" to describe "repertoires of performable signs," involving both discourse and its co-occurring nonlinguistic signs, "linked to stereotypic pragmatic effects" (Agha 2007, 80). Registers are reflexive models of language use sedimented over time through repeated iterations of metapragmatic discourse—talk about talk, such as the audience evaluations of Anne's voicings above—that serve to regiment and organize speech into socioculturally defined patterns that are, in turn, tied to identifiable personae (Bucholtz and Hall 2005; Goebel 2008; Woolard 2008; Wortham 2006). The "pragmatic effects" Agha refers to are the connections we make between particular registers and their associated stereotypic speakers that influence how hearers interpret and react to encounters with those registers, a process called "enregisterment." The result is a kind of social cartography wherein speakers can employ different registers to associate themselves with certain times, places, personalities, and attitudes.

The units of meaning at work here are indexicals, sign elements that indicate or point to other sign elements in a relatively indirect manner, such as the way that particular words or speech styles are heard as feminine or masculine (Ochs 1992; Peirce 1974, 227–308; see also Eckert 2008; Hanks 1999; Nunberg 1993). Indexicality enables speakers to reference complex webs of signifiers indirectly, merely by employing elements of a register such as an accent, intonation, or choice of word. In Shenyang, for example, mixing English words into one's speech positions the speaker as embodying values of modernity and cosmopolitanism. Because they are constituted through their ideological coherence, what Silverstein (2003a) refers to as "indexical order," registers can also always undergo a process of entextualization: they can be detached from their contextual surroundings and transplanted into new discourse environments, allowing endless chains of reference and citation by speakers back to previous contexts, thus reinvoking, perhaps in slightly altered form, the original's pragmatic effects (Bauman and Briggs 1990; Nakassis 2012; Silverstein and Urban 1996; Urciuoli 2010). Anne did this, for instance, in her English introduction by transplanting familiar forms of classroom discourse into her televised performance. By associating discourse at one point in time with discourse at another point in time, we can also effectively borrow its spatiotemporal characteristics and establish the two as "co-eval" chronotopic moments (Silverstein 2005).

The ability to take advantage of these indexical processes and secure positive audience responses to one's speech is not equally available to all. While language education—especially under the logic of neoliberalism—posits a kind of meritocratic potential for all students, linguistic authority in fact rests on prior relations of social inequality (Bucholtz and Hall 2005; Heller 2001; Woolard 1985; see also van Leeuwen 2007). As Pierre Bourdieu (1991, 69) writes, "The relations of power that obtain in the linguistic market . . . are manifested and realized in the fact that certain agents are incapable of applying to the linguistic products offered, either by themselves or others, the criteria that are most favorable to their products." In other words, a speaker's legitimacy—as an authorized user of a particular register—does not depend solely on educational credentials, but on their ability to manipulate and control indexical patterns of language use and social identity. I have already mentioned accent as one modality of legitimacy—a way of ratifying the speaker as someone who "knows English"—but others include rapidity of speech, use of advanced vocabulary, and knowledge of current slang as well as exhibiting familiarity with globalized brands, media, and culture. One further and often underappreciated source of authority in the Chinese linguistic marketplace is racial identity, which I explore in more detail later in this book. These modalities are not simply individual attributes or achievements but socially dependent variables requiring privileged access by means of social class, mobility, wealth, and so forth. A Shenyanger who has studied abroad will always have their English afforded more social capital than a domestic student, no matter their actual abilities. The indexical order of speech is always a reflection of the social order and relations of inequality that stratify it.

Chronotopes and Chinese Landscapes

Heteroglossia and the chronotope have rightfully had a significant impact on recent sociolinguistic and linguistic anthropological work on discourse, meaning, and identity.[6] There has been a tendency, however, to favor the time-character of language over its spatial character—in other words, to view the *chronos* as primary and the *topos* as secondary—and to map these discursive relationships onto relatively macro-level scalar distinctions: past and present, tradition and modernity, metropole and periphery, and so forth. Speech can represent a variety of historicities, modernities, or futures, but the role of the environment, and in particular the built environment, in creating and sustaining these linguistic differences is relatively underappreciated. The exceptions to this trend (e.g., Cavanaugh 2012) remind us of how much language in use is tied to the social space in which it becomes manifest.

"(Social) space," wrote Henri Lefebvre, "is a (social) product" (1991, 26; see also Certeau 1984; Corsín Jiménez 2003; Feuchtwang 2004; Ingold 2000). Space is not simply the background to human activity, an emptiness waiting to be filled; it is the creative result of those activities and the embodiment of social relations. Lefebvre argued that the meaning of space is the product of the work of both bourgeois professionals—urban planners, government officials, architects—who devise the organization of spatial form, and the ordinary citizens who inhabit that space on a daily basis. "Every space is already in place before the appearance in it of actors; these actors are collective as well as individual subjects inasmuch as the individuals are always members of groups or classes seeking to appropriate the space in question" (Lefebvre 1991, 57). Their actions therefore may not always create the physical form of the landscape they inhabit, but people do continuously shape how it is interpreted, as when what was once a sacred tomb (built by an architect to embody some kind of social value) later becomes a kitschy tourist site or a national monument.

In his later works, Bakhtin stressed that chronotopes are always complex and layered dimensions, not only tied to particular times but rooted in particular socioculturally defined places. Temporal signs may be interpreted differently in separate locations, or may be wholly uninterpretable outside the spatial contexts of their production. Bakhtin (1986, 29) cites, for instance, Goethe's autobiographical accounts of his travels through Italy, where he marveled that weather may look timeless at the base of a mountain, but is seen quite differently by an observer at the top watching the emergence of clouds, wind, and rain. When Goethe witnessed a neat row of trees in a small town, he did not see in them the timeless cycle of growth but the action of a conscientious magistrate thirty years in the past who must have arranged for their planting. Landscapes are not static representations of particular time periods but exhibit a range of temporal relationships in juxtaposition. "The simple spatial contiguity (*nebeneinander*) of phenomena was profoundly alien to Goethe, so he saturated and imbued it with *time*, revealed emergence and development in it, and he distributed that which was contiguous in *space* in various *temporal* stages, epochs of becoming. For him contemporaneity— both in nature and in human life—is revealed as an essential multitemporality: as remnants or relics of various stages and formations of the past and as rudiments of stages in the more or less distant future" (Bakhtin 1986, 28). Space is therefore layered with time, each moment of its historical development to be found integrated into its contemporary shape and future potential.

The social landscape of China, I will argue, lends itself particularly well to this perspective. This is partly due to a common tendency to discuss spatial differences in temporal terms, but also to an underlying logic of spatial form in China I call *recursive enclosure*. In the first instance, spatial divides in China between rich and poor areas, or between urban and rural areas, are often experienced as temporally discontinuous (Solinger 2013; Z. Zhang 2000; L. Zhang 2006). The countryside is labeled as *luohou*, which can be translated as a state of backwardness, of falling behind. Urban residents who travel to the countryside or are confronted with rural migrants perceive them as a return from the past: their language, their food, their clothes, their houses, all are what "we" had twenty years ago. From the urban perspective, this can be experienced as a form of nostalgia, as when urban residents travel back to the village to enjoy traditional meals and entertainments, such as dancing or wordplay, and several restaurants in Shenyang specialized in "coarse grains" (*culiao*) such as millet and barley instead of rice, indexing both village cuisine and the privations of the Maoist period. For rural residents, the temporal discontinuity acts as a less permeable physical barrier, separating them from the agency and presumed boundlessness of urban life. Being *luohou* therefore entails a sense of isolation, a feeling that one is not connected to dynamic or powerful areas within the imagined space of the Chinese nation, while leaving *luohou* behind and ascending the spatial hierarchy—by, for instance, moving to Beijing or going abroad—allows one to transcend those limitations and access spatiotemporal locations associated with the future.

Furthermore, China's urban space has become notoriously fragmented given the rapid pace of teardown and construction. The physical transformations of Chinese urban space have been a topic of frequent study and debate as some forms of China's material history—the winding *hutong* alleyways of Beijing, for instance—are demolished, and others—palaces, temples, and other tokens of imperial power—are preserved (see for instance Campanella 2008; Gaubatz 1995; L. Ma and Wu 2004; Q. Yang 2015). But underlying these physical discontinuities is a spatial practice that creates and reinforces forms of spatial difference. Landscapes in China tend to be clearly delineated and marked with material barriers between one space and another, stereotypically in the form of walls that form inward-focused enclosures. Each enclosure is itself enclosed within higher-order spatial formations—walls built within walls—creating an ordered sense of progression as people move from outside to inside, from global to local, and from stranger to intimate in navigating their surroundings. Walls and other boundary-marking mechanisms are the product of spatial practice, but also lay the groundwork for the multilayered, heteroglossic linguistic practices of contemporary Shenyang. Landscapes, timescapes, and soundscapes come together in the modern Chinese city in complex and important ways.

To illustrate these ideas, let me turn to a visit I had with Mr. Zhou, a local handyman and former colleague of my mother-in-law who came to my apartment after an electrical outlet blew out. As we waited for a replacement to be delivered, Mr. Zhou sat down at the kitchen table, set out with nuts and sunflower seeds, and looked around the relatively new residence I was living in. He was impressed with how it contrasted with his own home, which he said had only concrete floors instead of hardwood, and was duller and dirtier. I offered Mr. Zhou a cigarette, but he refused, saying that it would make the apartment smell bad. To make conversation, I asked Mr. Zhou what he thought of Shenyang. He responded as follows:

It's alright now. It's changing a lot. Before, Beijing and Shenyang were the same—everywhere was poor. I know, I've been to Beijing many times and I saw how it was before. Everyone lived in tiny homes. Beijing and Shenyang were the same. But Beijing has many advantages. It's the capital city, right? So it developed faster. Everything is new, there are tall buildings everywhere. But now, Shenyang is changing too. In five years, we'll be where they are now. The countryside, well, that's the poorest place. There's just no way for the common people. They are twenty years behind us. If you look at Shenyang, Shenyang used to be all one-storey apartments. Everywhere! That's how it was when I was young. This area, right here, used to be court-yard houses. Only over there [pointing north] in Beihang, in Beishichang [both nearby market areas] were big buildings, big apartments. Now it's that way everywhere. The last of those one-floor apartments has been torn down. We all live in big buildings now.

Mr. Zhou's description of the urban and rural landscapes is a fascinating medita-tion on spatial and temporal contrasts within China's emergent modernity. Note how his discussion of the physical transformation of space, its specifically local-ized points of renewal indexed through building height, brackets the formulation of a temporal yardstick: some places are a certain number of years ahead, some a certain number of years behind. Each place is in a state of constant flux and change, but all share a developmental teleology, with progress in each geographic location—countryside, Shenyang, Beijing—calibrated to a different velocity rel-ative to the others and at different critical points along that trajectory. These spa-tiotemporal comparisons are not static but relative to a particular here and now and to different spatial scales—neighborhood, city, nation—of comparison. The dynamic of modernity is therefore narrated by Mr. Zhou through the differenti-ated timescales of otherwise geographically contiguous spaces, that is, the various neighborhoods, cities, and regions he cites. We see the past through the image of the humble, one-storey courtyard home, contrasted with a present of "big build-ings" (in which "we" all live now) and, by extension, a projection of each particu-lar space into a template of the future represented by even taller buildings (ruptured and separated from the past by the demolition of those old homes).

Language is ordered and understood within a similarly material framework. Certain kinds of language are expected in certain kinds of spaces, but certain kinds of language can also shape or alter the perception of spaces as well, affecting how we act and understand what is going on around us. Where we are plays a role in determining how we talk and how we evaluate the ways that other people talk. In short, language is always embedded within socially produced space, space that has been given a particular moral valence, a political economy of ongoing relationships and interactions constituted by the ways people move around, within and between locations (McElhinny 2006; J. Park 2014; Raffles 1999; Urciuoli 1991). As we shall see, discourse provides a *spatiotemporal texture* to the landscape, a distinct, phenomenologically rich, lived experience that transcends maps, diagrams, blueprints, or other common representations of spatial form (Lefebvre 1991, 57).

Keith Basso's (1996) long-standing work with the Western Apache in Arizona highlights, for instance, the ways in which particular topographical features are socialized within a discursive medium of stories and narratives highlighting both historical events and the lessons that people can draw from them and apply to contemporary actions. Apache place-names are often linked to stories that invest the landscape with a moral dimension—places where ancestors fought, mistreated each other, or did not share. These places (and their stories) admonish those wandering through the landscape to behave as they should rather than as they might selfishly wish to. "For the place-maker's main objective is to speak the past into being, to summon it with words and give it dramatic form, to *produce* experience by forging ancestral worlds in which others can participate and readily lose themselves" (Basso 1996, 32). The effect of this narrative theater is the collapse of normal temporal distinctions made between past and present, on the one hand—the foundation of Western historiographies that prioritize the *when* of events—and a Cartesian presocial space, on the other hand, to, instead, imagine a discursive frame in which ancestral voices, not disembodied but speaking through the place-maker, use the landscape to provide moral instruction on current events and dilemmas. "Knowledge of places is therefore closely linked to knowledge of the self, to grasping one's position in the larger scheme of things, including one's own community, and to securing a confident sense of who one is as a person" (Basso 1996, 34). If language thus inhabits a landscape (Gorter 2006; Hélot 2012), it can do so in a way that entangles both complex temporal reconfigurations and an encompassing moral calculus (Blommaert 2013).

Shenyang's landscape is an apt case study of how language is embedded in both space and time. As Mr. Zhou describes, the countryside, characterized by a distinct agricultural relationship to the land and to the memory of socialism, occupies a position antecedent to that of urban space. That is where people expect to hear vernacularized Dongbeihua. In the city, on the one hand, urban residents style their chronotopic modernity through standardized (and perfectly enunciated) Mandarin, or push certain spatial structures into the future through the presence of globalized languages like English. Luxury apartment complexes, for instance, usually employ English in their advertising to highlight their cosmopolitan aesthetic and associate themselves—and their residents—with globalized spaces and transnational mobility. On the other hand, protesters or beggars can use

Dongbeihua to evince their authenticity—sometimes also drawing on the visual and discursive signs of socialism—to add legitimacy to their message (see Henry 2009). Even an international entrepreneur might entertain customers in a small restaurant and speak in Dongbeihua to mark her ties to the local setting, one who knows the terrain and can navigate it profitably. Dongbeihua, Mandarin, and English can therefore be regarded as asynchronous linguistic practices tied to particular geographic spaces within this highly segmented physical landscape.

The Discourse of Modernity

Past, present, and future do not act here as straightforward temporal reference points set to the tick-tock of passing time. We can infer from the multiplicity of temporalities described by Mr. Zhou and the fact that they all cohabit a single moment (that of my fieldwork) that time here has a certain imagined quality. Past, present, and future are not given but fashioned in the act of discourse, layered onto and laminated with the spatial practices I described above. Rather than pastness, for instance, referencing a moment simply antecedent to the current one, it is an experiential category, a sensation of one place or one person being desynchronized from another. This sense of temporal dislocation is the interpretive product of signifiers known as qualia, a category of indexes manifested in sensuous, experiential, and abstract qualities such as texture, smell, taste, and so forth (Peirce 1974, 374–377; see also Chumley and Harkness 2013; Gal 2013; Harkness 2015). As I will show, the temporal experience of pastness is a semiotic product (a qualisign) of a web of experiential qualia such as loudness, chaos, dirtiness, and darkness, while futurity is linked to quiet, order, cleanliness, and lightness, connections that are enacted and reinforced through everyday forms of talk. This perspective implicates modernity as an analytical category and how it has informed scholarship on Chinese society, foreign languages, and globalization more generally.

When Shenyang opened its metro system in 2010, flat screens in the stations looped a series of videos educating the city's citizens on how "civilized" (*wenming*) people ride the subway. The vignettes showed passengers making way for those disembarking and allowing a wheelchair-bound person to board first, and a woman playfully swatting her boyfriend for trying to eat a messy snack during their journey. Similar civilizing educational campaigns were launched before the 2008 Olympics in Beijing and the 2010 World Expo in Shanghai. Such mediatized representations of moral behavior highlight a prevailing and ongoing transformation in contemporary China. In the eyes of most urbanites I spoke to, traditional forms of sociality, interaction, and livelihood are giving way to ones that are considered global and modern. Many of my conversations with people about social change contained several iterations of the common phrase "China is developing now" as a way of explaining the source of these transformations, but the exact nature of that development on a national scale was relatively opaque. Instead, people turned to accessible signifiers of that change: tall buildings, coffee shops, global brands, car ownership, and so forth.

There is nothing particularly new about this feeling in China. Not only has "modernity" been a topic of interest to historians of China's late imperial and republican periods; it has also excited and motivated Chinese citizens for the past hundred years at least (see Dikötter 2006; Dong and Goldstein 2006; P. He 2002; L. Lee 1999; Yeh 2000; Zarrow 2006). Writing in 1926, the American-educated Chinese philosopher Hu Shih wrote, "A new age has dawned. We have realised at last that certain things must be given up if China is to live" (S. Hu 1926, 271). China, he argued, was in the process of abandoning its traditional culture in favor of the hallmarks of Westernized modernity, including language, science, the "emancipation of women, the extension of the franchise, the protection of the laborer, and all that social legislation which is centred upon the idea of extending the greatest happiness to the greatest number" (275). Doing so would unlock, he maintained, both the spiritual and material prosperity of the West for Chinese citizens. The sentiment Hu expressed nearly a century ago can still be heard in Shenyang today, meaning that for all the passage of time and the sense of progress—through liberation, revolution, and economic reform—most of the people I spoke to still described China as being on the cusp of a transformation, one nearly within reach even if constantly deferred.

Modernity has often been configured as a particular political economic relationship between rational citizens and the nation state (Giddens 1990). James Ferguson (2006) explains that modernization, especially in its late twentieth-century developmentalist guise, is a package of related elements that combine economic and technological growth with sociopolitical reforms. The logic of many development projects in the Third World, as well as the source of the vocabulary of modernization, was an understanding that modeling the mechanics of the First World industrialized nations would lead developing nations along the same path, eventually unlocking all of the presumed benefits of Westernized living standards: smaller nuclear families, rationalized markets, strong democratic institutions, and secular individualism. "The effect of this powerful narrative was to transform a *spatialized* global hierarchy into a *temporalized* (putative) historical sequence. Poor countries (and by implication, the poor people who lived in them) were not simply at the bottom, they were at the beginning" (Ferguson 2006, 178). Modernity is, in other words, a chronotopic experience rooted in particular sociocultural practices that have been imbued with future-oriented values. These values are the product, as Ferguson notes, of narratives that circulate through social networks and the media as explanatory frameworks for why some nations or groups are modern and others are not (see also B. Lee and LiPuma 2002).

When I spoke to Shenyangers about the future, the terms of their own modernization narratives were consistent and clearly expressed. *Xiandai* (modern) is one of a series of related terms that describe and refer to the teleological end point of China's progress; others are *fada* (developed), *xifang de* (Westernized), *shishang* (fashionable), *guoji* (international), and *guowai* (foreign). These terms were frequently implicated in discussions of how Shenyang is developing (*fazhan*) or modernizing and followed a surprisingly consistent template. There were four common themes I will outline here. First, people were in agreement that English would continue to grow in popularity, leading to a time when everyone (or at least everyone urban) will speak it as a second language. Second, people extrapolated the relative prosperity of the reform era as continuing indefinitely into the future. As China becomes a more powerful nation, they argued, incomes will increase, and people will have more money to spend on consumables and luxuries. Third was an increasing sense of mobility, as Chinese citizens will have greater freedom to study and travel abroad, often targeting tourist destinations in Europe and the United States as particularly desirable. Finally, everyone envisioned that the inhabitants of this idealized future will exhibit more civilized forms of behavior, embodied in the term *suzhi*.

As described by Hairong Yan (2008, 113), *suzhi* "refers to the somewhat ephemeral qualities of civility, self-discipline, and modernity. Suzhi marks a sense and sensibility of the self's value in the market economy. As such, it is often used in the negative by the post-Mao state and educational elites to point to the lack of quality of the Chinese laboring masses." *Suzhi* entails a combination of thought and action that indexes superior citizens. This includes everything from higher education to wealth, manners, and adherence to certain linguistic norms of politeness and self-control (e.g., not swearing, speaking without exuberant emotion). *Suzhi* is not simply the domain of social elites, however, and proper *suzhi* is discussed and expected of citizens from every social stratum. *Suzhi* is often cited as a factor in the experience of unpleasant events caused by others. For instance, one morning I exited my apartment to find a large dog turd in the stairwell just outside the doorway to my apartment. As I moved to step around it, one of the community cleaners came running up the steps, out of breath and apologizing effusively. "*Sorry, sorry. It's just those people upstairs with their dog. Why don't they take it outside? They just walk it in here and it shits in here.*" I responded that people in Canada are responsible for cleaning up after their dogs, and the cleaner nodded. "*Yes, that's what they should do. Even here, that's what they should do. But their quality* [*suzhi*] *isn't good.*" Discourses of quality are therefore metacommentaries on social development and the proper place of various citizens within the economic and political fabric of the nation-state (see Anagnost 2004; V. Fong 2007; Jacka 2009; Kipnis 2006, 2007; Tomba 2009).

Schools, which in China have often taken a primary role in moral education (Stafford 1995), have proven to be an important site for the cultivation of high-quality citizens. Woronov (2008, 2009) describes in great detail the implementation of "education for quality" programs in Beijing primary schools that encourage a child's intellectual, moral, and physical development. Children are a particularly important target for disciplinary practices meant to raise the overall quality of the Chinese population, because "not only do they represent the future, but their bodies are the site upon which the terms of the national future are being worked out" (Woronov 2009, 571). These initiatives are often targeted at rural or ethnic youth who, from the state's perspective, represent the groups most in need of such disciplinary intervention as a way of bringing impoverished areas, and their residents, in line with new urban values (Hansen 1999; Kipnis 2011; Murphy 2004). The overall goal, however, is to make schooling a process not only of educating national subjects but of stimulating the processes of modernization and development that accrue to citizens who manifest those ideals.

It is therefore unsurprising that English education has become so deeply embedded within the modern Chinese educational project. "*You know, if you don't speak English,*" one father said while discussing his child's studies, "*it's like being half illiterate . . . English is going to become more and more popular. It is a big language now.*" The use of "illiterate" here is a clear reference to both individual quality and its negation in the form of the uneducated rural villager. To be modern, one must speak English. I described above the video playing in the Shenyang metro educating people on how to ride the subway in a civilized manner; it is also important to note the prominence of English (and the complete absence of Dongbeihua) in that space. Directions to landmarks and exits were given in both Mandarin and English text, while announcements of stops or reminders to passengers were broadcast bilingually. While these accommodations may assist the occasional monolingual foreign visitor at finding the correct stop, the more important function is to encode the space of the metro as a modern one where English is heard and, importantly, where riders can be expected to understand it. Learning a foreign language is therefore but one of many cultivating processes that neoliberal subjects have adopted to position themselves within this rapidly changing chronotopic landscape.

In Shenyang, modernity is an attribute of people, or more precisely, certain types of people. They become modern by doing certain types of things with certain types of others. They live in certain types of buildings, eat certain types of food, drive certain types of cars. They act in ways that are modern: they drink coffee instead of tea, play golf instead of mah-jong, do yoga instead of tai chi. This is really what modernity means to Shenyangers, a personal attribute developed through everyday forms of being and acting and talking differently from those who are not modern and are being left behind. In the chapters that follow, I pay attention to how people narrate and make sense of the assemblages of places and practices that define modern urban space, such as homes, communities, and markets, treating them not as spatially adjacent structures but as temporally discontinuous topologies. The luxury apartment is juxtaposed to the village house, the street market to the designer boutique, as displacements of both time and space. In this progression along the trajectory from past to future, with its attendant moral judgments of increasing civility and personal quality, language practices are implicated as both diagnostic—determining what kind of space it is—and symptomatic—exemplifying what is either wrong or right about that space. Individuals are understood to be part of this flowing tide, embedded within and traveling right alongside the gradually modernizing landscape, albeit from radically differing points of origin and with diverse current positions. Life histories are thus not simply narratives of changing material circumstances but also changing moral constitutions and speech practices.

DIRTY TALK

Hybrid Registers of Chinese and English

One day, outside a branch of Hong Ri, one of the larger English schools in Shenyang, I saw Petra talking with an older couple. I waved to her. She looked surprised and a little self-conscious, but when I approached she introduced me to her parents, who had come to drop off an umbrella for her. I asked them how they were, and we spoke a few words to each other, but over the course of our short conversation Petra became visibly upset. Within seconds she interrupted and began to berate them. *"Fine, fine, fine, don't talk anymore. How can you be like this? Your speech is just too dirty [tu]. Just don't talk anymore. Go, go, go,"* she said, pushing them back toward home. As they left and we entered the school together, I asked Petra if she was okay. She just shook her head and told me her parents could not speak well because they were from a rural village (*nongcun*). I had noticed they spoke with a relatively thick accent but had managed our brief conversation without any major difficulties. Petra, however, seemed deeply embarrassed that they had spoken in Dongbeihua.

What was striking to me about this incident was both Petra's reaction, particularly given the value placed in China on filiality and the presumed deference children are supposed to show their parents, and the fact that Petra, despite usually speaking unaccented Mandarin in class, would sometimes use Dongbeihua words, phrases, and pronunciations herself when joking with her coworkers. Why did she chastise her parents for speaking in a way similar to her own? One clue to answering this question can be found in her use of the descriptor "dirty" for their talk. *Tu* means, literally, dirt or soil but can be extended metaphorically to represent rusticity, simplicity, and anything associated with the countryside. The Chinese anthropologist Fei Xiaotong argued long ago that, in a historically rural society, *tu* represents not only the agricultural character of Chinese village life but the stable link between groups of peasants and the lands to which they are bound. "This immobility, this enduring attachment to the soil, points to a relationship between people and space. Being fixed in space, people live in solitude and isolation. But the unit of isolation is not the individual but the group" (Fei 1992, 40). That positive connection of the Chinese, as a whole, to the land has changed in the modern era, especially as rural populations have migrated to urban areas. In Shenyang, *tu* is almost always used negatively as a descriptor for things that evoke tradition, poverty, and rurality. It can label anything, such as clothing, food, hairstyles, physical appearance, names, mind-set, and, most especially, language.

"Dirty talk" is therefore language tinged with rurality and locality, the very opposite of English. In Shenyang, it almost always refers to the local dialect. People who speak it are called peasants (*nongmin*) or workers (*gongmin*) rather than urban citizens (*shimin*). Dongbeihua itself is often derided as backward (*luohou*), which lends the register its chronotopic association with pastness. There are proscriptions, sometimes explicit and sometimes implicit, in using Dongbeihua in formal contexts such as schooling or media. Shenyangers were nearly universal in their agreement that speaking Dongbeihua in a formal job interview would be disastrous, while speaking it in professional workplaces could lead to dismissal. This is particularly true of English schools, which, as representatives of China's nascent modernity, cultivate an image of globalized authenticity. A teacher's use of Mandarin was carefully monitored in the classroom, often more so than her English; those who employed Dongbeihua could be fined by management or even fired. City-born teachers sometimes made fun of coworkers who came from the countryside and were perceived to use Dongbeihua excessively. At one English school, the owner's rural accent was only thinly disguised, a source of great amusement to the teachers, who tirelessly parodied his speech patterns in the teachers' office when he was not around.

Nevertheless, there are times and places where Dongbeihua is acceptable, even desirable. Use of the register among close friends connotes intimacy and locality. Older generations, particularly those from the laboring classes with minimal levels of formal education, speak it almost exclusively; it therefore has a strong association with family and the casual atmosphere of domestic space. Dongbeihua is heard in local street markets when people negotiate prices, or in small eateries when they order a meal, but rarely in luxury malls or upscale restaurants. A popular trope holds that business negotiations take place in Mandarin, but both parties celebrate afterward at a restaurant or karaoke bar while speaking Dongbeihua with each other. Finally, Dongbeihua is often associated with comedic performances such as *xiangsheng* [crosstalk], a type of verbal duel that was often performed by local theater troupes in the past but has now found its way onto television, radio, and the internet.

Mandarin, Dongbeihua, and English: these three different types of language are used in the city, each with its own values and indexical associations.[1] In this chapter I explore how these different registers are constituted and enacted in everyday forms of discourse but also how they interact in linguistically complex ways. Despite their presumably separate status as unique linguistic codes, they frequently manifest themselves in the voice of a single speaker, although at differing times and in differing contexts. My aim will be to show how their coherence as separate codes is not given beforehand but a product of metapragmatic discourse—comments like Petra's that, either directly or indirectly, make social valuations of linguistic registers transparent—that regiments and organizes speech ideologically into different orders of indexicality. Various types of speech (English, Mandarin, Dongbeihua, and all of the attendant variation within them) are tied to distinctions and categories in the sociocultural field, enregistering equivalences between hierarchically ranked linguistic categories and stratified social categories. The devaluation by Petra, for instance, of her parents' speech is naturalized within the broader sociocultural context through repeated interactional episodes where that speech, Dongbeihua, is linked to stigmatized social categories and social types (e.g., the backward peasant or the uneducated laborer). It is therefore the comparability between linguistic codes and the ways they point to contrasting stances and social roles that is of interest here.

The shape of this semiotic complex is a product not only of how contemporary speech practices are enregistered with social value but of the social dynamics that have been shaping Chinese society over the past half century or so. The pastness of Dongbeihua and its association with rural society reflects the profound social and economic transformations that have shifted wealth and power to urban centers. This was perhaps most salient for my informants who were born as singletons after the introduction of the one-child policy, instituted as a population control measure in 1979. Now in their thirties, they grew up in the midst of the reform era. They were also typically exposed to Dongbeihua in the home as children. As concern with social mobility and status has come to affect Chinese middle-class households, language practices have shifted accordingly, and middle-class parents now overwhelmingly speak Mandarin to their children. This was a conscious decision for most, and it was combined with intensive efforts to erase or control the presence of Dongbeihua in their own speech. Theirs is also the first generation in China for whom English-language acquisition became universally desirable, and who now strive to have their children acquire it as well. The patterns for evaluating and understanding the type (and therefore social entailments) of different varieties of Chinese therefore act as templates for understanding the type (and therefore social entailments) of different varieties of English. Learning English, in an important sense, extends and furthers the transformations that people associated with shifting to Mandarin, transformations that allow individuals to enmesh themselves in higher orders of social, economic, business, and political relations. Much like the Melanesian kula traders described by Nancy Munn (1986, 15), adopting highly scaled language practices constitutes an "extension of self" in sociocultural space-time through which "actors produce their own value." Shenyangers build on their experiences with Dongbeihua and Mandarin, including the social types these registers evoke, and recursively extend them to thinking about the meaning and value of English and its varying forms.

Let me return to Petra and the spat with her parents in front of Hong Ri. As I said, on the one hand, Petra was agitated by her parents' use of Dongbeihua with me, despite the fact that she frequently used it herself in informal settings. Her parents, on the other hand, spoke in a way inescapably marked as Dongbeihua by their accents. And in this case, they were using it not only in public but in front of an esteemed foreign visitor (an inescapable part of my own social positioning). Speaking this way reflected badly not only on themselves but on their family, and Petra was acting to save face; she was, in other words, protecting her parents from their own potential embarrassment. I frequently encountered such attitudes toward the use of Dongbeihua in my presence: my university Chinese instructors refused to teach it to me, while people who did speak Dongbeihua almost invariably praised my own use of standard Mandarin, which, to their ears, was the mark of a progressive and modern individual. When I tried, on occasion, to use Dongbeihua myself, the response was nervous and hesitant laughter.

Petra's response to her parents' language usage was therefore a product not just of their talk but of the relationships between speakers and addressee and the dynamic interactional patterns that defined our different personae within the broader Shenyang speech environment. Had their addressee been different (if they had been talking to a neighbor, for instance) or their own identities (crosstalk performers) or the setting (perhaps in their home), or if they had deliberately been able to *choose* to address me in Dongbeihua rather than forced to by the limitations of their speech repertoire, Petra's response would likely have been different. The contextual nature of indexical order points to a more complex understanding of register value than simply positive or negative; after all, sometimes speaking Dongbeihua is a good thing. Different registers operate at different spatiotemporal scales, with, in this case, Dongbeihua evoking a sense of locality and English a level of translocality. Dongbeihua represents the scale of the region, Mandarin the nation, and English the world. English's place at the apex of this chronotopic scale, indexing modernity, futurity, and expansive movement through globalized space, and its ability to redefine the time, place, and position of those speaking it, are inversions of Dongbeihua's geographically delimiting and isolating character. In this chapter I therefore address the interrelationship of these three registers and map out the sociocultural terrain within which their values are embedded.

A City in Three Registers

The main language of everyday discourse in Shenyang is standard Mandarin Chinese (called *hanyu* and, for spoken language, *putonghua*), the predominant language of mainland China. For ease of reference I will use the term "Mandarin" for spoken Putonghua here, as it refers explicitly to the Beijing speech variety that is considered standard throughout the country. Mandarin is the largest member of the Sino-Tibetan language family that also includes Burmese and Tibetan. There are about nine hundred million native speakers worldwide, with the vast majority living in the People's Republic of China (Wiedenhof 2015, 1). Aside from foreigners resident in the city, Mandarin is the primary language of all urban Shenyang residents, and is used in almost all daily social interactions. It is the language of media, education, government, and business. Moreover, Mandarin carries with it clear ideological assumptions about ethnolinguistic homogeneity and cultural nationalism; it is presumed to be the medium through which Chineseness is experienced at a national, and increasingly transnational, level (Dong 2009, 2010; Spolsky 2014; Q. Zhang 2006).

The second, Dongbeihua, is a regional dialect of Mandarin characterized by certain unique phonetic, lexical, and syntactic features that differentiate it from the standard language. Dongbeihua is not incomprehensible to Mandarin speakers, but the accent and forms of expression can confound clear understanding for those not familiar with it. Intelligibility is also related to the speaker's accent, and when it is strong, Shenyangers describe it metaphorically as thickly flavored (*weir nong*). Accent varies with geography, education, and age, leading to clear indexical associations between speech and social categories: rural origins, seniority, and lower levels of education are associated with the use of Dongbeihua, while urban residence, youth, and higher education are all implicated by the use of Mandarin.

The third language is English. Nearly everyone under the age of forty has received at least some English-language education in school. According to the national curriculum, English instruction begins in the third grade of elementary school with at least eighty minutes of instruction per week, rising to four hours of instruction per week in the fifth grade and continuing through to the end of compulsory education (A. Feng 2009). Despite its presumed universality, however, the national English-language curriculum has been implemented unevenly across China (G. Hu 2005; Y. Hu 2007, 2008). Rural schools are often unable to adequately comply with the regulations due to a serious lack of skilled teachers, while students in urban schools often exceed the instructional time stipulated in the curriculum. In the public schools I visited in Shenyang, English-language teachers might not be fluent but were nearly always competent and capable of instructing their students in the language.

Beyond the classroom, English is pervasive in written communication and oral speech. English words and phrases are frequently incorporated into advertising and retail signage (even for domestic brands), commercial billboards, tourist sites, and even government promotional posters (Pan 2010, 2015b). Major restaurant chains usually provide English translations on menus. Hospitals, schools, hotels, private companies, markets, and even many government offices prominently display Mandarin-English bilingual signage. In everyday conversation, English words and phrases regularly slip in and out of people's speech. Technologies, software, foreign brands, foreign foods, and many other things are referred to using English terms rather than their Chinese equivalents (Q. Zhang 2012). Even people with minimal foreign-language education recognize and use a small stock of English words that circulate widely throughout the urban speech community. The conventional Mandarin greeting *nihao* and parting *zaijian* are often replaced, especially by younger speakers, with "hi" and "bye-bye," while the China Telecom error message, heard when calling a mobile phone customer already on the line, plays in both Mandarin and English. In other words, English is a high-prestige sociolect that references a speaker's sophistication, education, and social capital. Use of English, especially forms of standard English associated with foreigners, is highly valued and the mark of a cosmopolitan, modern, and highly educated global citizen.

One might therefore posit, then, that the linguistic situation in Shenyang is an example of triglossia, with several competing language codes organized into an ascending hierarchy. The problem with that view of the situation, however, is that the languages do not compete in the conventional sense of the term; in practice, they shade and blend into each other. Their distinctness as separate "codes" within the speech environment of Shenyang is merely an ideological product of the different values attached to them as semiotic registers (Makoni and Pennycook 2007). Certainly we can describe the typological form of Dongbeihua and its distinctness from Mandarin—and I do so below—as well as provide a complete grammatical description of English. But as Asif Agha (2007, 84) argues, what we often describe as linguistic structure—the words and morphosyntactic rules of a language—are not just linguistic categories but also sociological ones. At the heart of Bakhtin's (1981, 270) notion of heteroglossia is the idea that, as he says, a unitary language is "not something given [*dan*] but is always in essence posited [*zadan*]." Dongbeihua, Mandarin, and English are convenient labels for speech practices that remain ideologically distinct only because they index different social values and conversational stances. In the course of interaction, however, speakers draw on a multiplicity of languages, genres, and registers, often combined in creative and novel ways.

Dongbeihua and Mandarin

Dongbeihua has been the subject of extensive linguistic description and analysis by both Chinese and Western scholars (M. Han 2007; Y. Li 2008; Simmons 2016). Because the term covers a vast dialect region comprising China's three northeastern provinces (Liaoning, Jilin, and Heilongjiang), numerous subdialects and classificatory schemas have been proposed. Some aspects of Dongbeihua, while distinct from Mandarin, are shared with other northern Chinese language varieties such as the Beijing and Shandong regional dialects, although these features may occur in Dongbeihua with more frequency. Although many Chinese scholars attribute the contemporary form of Dongbeihua to the influence of Manchu (Y. Li 2008, 96), it is more likely the product of the mixing of various Mandarin dialects during the intense period of immigration to northeastern China in the late nineteenth and early twentieth centuries (Simmons 2016, 64).

The most widely recognized elements of Dongbeihua are lexical. Some notable examples include the nonstandard contractions of the words *shenme* (what) and *zenme* (how), which in Shenyang are often pronounced *sha* and *zha* (see table 1.1, and also S. Ma and Jiang 2005).

Other notable words are *moji*, meaning "slow or laggardly," *maitai*, meaning "dirty," and *huyou*, meaning "to trick or con someone." Dongbeihua also includes

TABLE 1.1 Comparison of terms in standard Mandarin and Dongbeihua

ENGLISH	STANDARD MANDARIN	DONGBEIHUA
what	*shenme* (什么)	*sha* (啥)
how	*zenme* (怎么)	*zha* (咋)
thing	*dongxi* (东西)	*wanryi* (玩儿意)
brother (metaphorical)	*gemenr* (哥们儿)	*yemenr* (爷们儿)
cheat/hoodwink	*pian* (骗)	*huyou* (忽悠)
knee	*xigai* (膝盖)	*boluogair* (波罗盖儿)
slow/lethargic	*man* (慢)	*moji* (磨叽)
dirty	*zang* (脏)	*maitai* (埋汰)
strong/robust	*lihai* (厉害)	*gang gang* (刚刚)

some Mandarin words that incorporate a wider semantic range. The word *zheng* in Mandarin means "whole," "complete," and "in order." In Dongbeihua, however, it takes on a range of other meanings including "speak," "drink," "put," "install," and "deal with"; the exact denotation is generally inferred from context.

Phonetically, Dongbeihua is prominently marked by the merger of standard Mandarin's alveolar and retroflex consonants. In the Shenyang subdialect, these two classes of sounds are all usually realized as alveolars (M. Han 2007, 78; Simmons 2016, 69).[2] Thus, in pinyin, *sh* and *ch* are often pronounced in Shenyang as *s* and *c*, respectively, to the extent that a shibboleth of Dongbeihua is pronouncing the city's name as _Senyang_ instead of Shenyang. Certain Mandarin alveolars—and this is associated with particularly "thick" accents—become retroflex in Dongbeihua, such that the word for wipe or rub (*ca*) is pronounced _cha_ (this is also true of the word _zha_, noted above). Although Dongbeihua shares Mandarin's four tones, the pitch contours are slightly different. The cadence and prosody of Dongbeihua are difficult to accurately describe but convey by analogy an impression of minor inebriation. Comedic portrayals of Dongbeihua frequently include scenes of drinking, thus cementing the association between intoxication and Dongbeihua.

A final category of difference between Dongbeihua and Mandarin is morphosyntactic. Rhotacization, meaning the addition of a retroflex r-suffix on many words, is much stronger than in other northern Mandarin dialects and is applied in more cases, including words like "flavor" (_weir_) and "wife" (_xifur_) (Simmons 2016, 73–74). Dongbeihua word formation relies on a host of novel suffixes not found in Mandarin, such as *-batou*, *-le guangji*, and *-hu*. For instance, the word _shibatou_ means "a realist," and _shanhu_ means "to exaggerate." Idioms in Dongbeihua, an essential element of Chinese pragmatics, usually follow Mandarin Chinese patterns, but are also more likely to have parallel or repeating structures, such as *qiangmao qiangci*, meaning "tousled and slovenly" (C. Feng 2008).

Dongbeihua has recently achieved a significant level of fame in China through the efforts of the local entertainer Zhao Benshan, who, beginning in 1990, regularly scripted and acted in comedic skits for China Central Television's (CCTV) annual New Year's Gala (Mu 2004; J. Gao and Pugsley 2008). Stooped, grizzled, and invariably clothed in a wrinkled old Mao suit, Zhao often appears onstage as the consummate backward villager playing his part against another perennial character, the educated, sophisticated, and cosmopolitan urban citizen (frequently played by Zhao's longtime collaborator Fan Debiao). Zhao embodies the local dialect, while his other, the urbanite, speaks standard Mandarin. This gala, watched by hundreds of millions every year, spread both Zhao's brand of comedy—including conflicts between urban and rural Chinese, wordplay, and slapstick—and knowledge of Dongbeihua throughout the country. Zhao has also written, directed, and starred in a series of "village romance" television dramas that were similarly broadcast on CCTV to a national audience. He has nurtured the careers of many local comedians and actors—often referred to as his disciples (*tudi*)—who have gone on to similar success. All of this is to say that Dongbeihua is often easily recognized by Mandarin speakers across China even as it retains a sense of localized difference. Because of the subject matter of Zhao's comedy and other popular depictions, Dongbeihua is tied to a particularly rural, poor, and uneducated social identity (Simmons 2016, 66).

Voice and Localization

A key point to be made here is that, while it is possible to outline a linguistic description of Dongbeihua, Shenyangers do not typically make judgments about what counts as Dongbeihua in such terms. As Bonnie Urciuoli (1985, 363) realized some time ago, "What actually comes into contact are not codes per se, but speakers whose linguistic practices and identities vary." In other words, the identification of what is being spoken in any given setting (as Dongbeihua or Mandarin) is tied to the social identity of the speakers and then negotiation of that identity in the process of interaction. The act of detecting linguistic differences and enregistering them with social value becomes a self-reinforcing phenomenon as speakers understand the nature of their differences or similarities with each other as deriving from structured differences or similarities of language. The coherence of indexical order in linguistic variation is an artifact of the ideological formation of social difference rather than its cause. As Miyako Inoue argues, the recognition of particular registers is predicated on a politics of hearing: "Although hearing someone's voice on the street might seem natural and obvious, perception (whether auditory or visual) is never a natural or unmediated phenomenon but is always already a social practice" (Inoue 2006, 38; see also J. Dong 2017). Shenyangers are "heard" as speaking Dongbeihua as a consequence of acts of identity formation.

Dongbeihua is classified as a *fangyan* in China, a term often translated into English as "dialect" but that literally means "place-language." As Victor Mair (1991) has noted, the term *fangyan* dates back to the Han dynasty scholar Yang Xiong. It was the title of Yang's monumental work on Chinese language classification, which consisted of lists of regional synonyms for various words. Such a project promoted the idea of a central, standardized, and stable language—the one used at the imperial court—surrounded by a host of regional varieties, providing a model for linguistic analysis that was consistent throughout the imperial era and indeed persists today in popular Chinese ideas about language. In both Yang's classical work and modern use, *fangyan* makes no claims to familial or structural relationships among language varieties but instead to a vertical and hierarchical relationship between a standard, state-sanctioned code and its surrounding regional vernaculars (J. Dong 2009; C. Li 2004; Tam 2017). Indeed, as Mair (1991, 4) points out, imperial lexicographers classified not only various Chinese languages as *fangyan* of Mandarin but also Mongolian, Korean, Japanese, and even European languages.

In practical terms, the analysis of language variation therefore proceeds from very different premises in China, namely, that variation is not the product of the parallel evolution of two separate linguistic systems from an ancestral one but of geographically specific variation from a nationally centralized standard. Dialect implies a mutual intelligibility between speakers despite systematic and regularized linguistic differences. *Fangyan* implies, conversely, a sense of language variation rooted in particular regions. Geography, rather than linguistic form, is the basis for linguistic analysis, leading Mair to propose topolect as a more accurate translation than dialect. In other words, the key metric for identifying Dongbeihua is not establishing a linguistic typology that allows the linguist to sort words or phrases into particular categories but simply asking, How do people from Dongbei—those sharing a regionally delimited social identity—speak?

And people in Dongbei employ multiple stylistic elements that identify themselves as being *from* Dongbei and thus not from elsewhere, including lexical choice, rhotacization, idiom construction, word formation, and so forth that I outlined above. One might more beneficially think of Dongbeihua as a group of linguistic features that indexically mark that person as coming from the Dongbei region and, within that region, from a certain social and educational stratum. Moreover, the number, frequency, and intensity of these forms in a person's speech (its "thickness") allow a range of gradations between unmarked Mandarin and marked Dongbeihua; some utterances, and the associated speaker, can be considered more Dongbei than others. Examples of this can be found in table 1.2 where, for instance, the Mandarin Chinese utterance *ni gan shenme*, "What are you doing?," is unmarked in relation to the two forms to its right, both of which are identified as Dongbeihua. However, while *ni gan sha ne* is inflected with the Dongbei accent and lexical choice, *ni ga ha ya* varies even more from the standard and is therefore experienced as "thicker" by listeners. In the second example, the Dongbeihua word *erhu* ("being foolish"—the infixed *le* indicates the perfective aspect) replaces the standard *sha*, but even more marked is the transposition of the pronoun to the end of the sentence. The other examples show the progressive localization of words through increasingly dialectal pronunciations.

The boundary between Mandarin and Dongbeihua is therefore as much ideological as it is a structured pattern of regularized linguistic differences. Realizing the practical ambiguity of what are often conceptualized as clear linguistic code distinctions is part of a recent turn toward recognizing the ideological bases of

TABLE 1.2 Gradations between unmarked and marked forms of Mandarin/Dongbeihua

UNMARKED (WEAK)		→			MARKED (THICK)
WHAT ARE YOU DOING?					
Ni gan shenme?	→	*Ni gan <u>sha</u> ne?*		→	*Ni <u>ga ha ya</u>?*
DON'T BE SO FOOLISH.					
Ni bie zheme sha.	→	*Ni bie <u>er le hu</u>.*		→	*Bie <u>er le hu ni</u>.*
PERSON					
ren	→	*renr*		→	*<u>yinr</u>*
HOW					
zenme	→	*<u>za</u>*		→	*<u>zha</u>*

ethnolinguistic belonging and identity. For instance, in Jillian Cavanaugh's (2012) description of Bergamasco, a local variety of Italian, she notes the challenges her local informants had with describing the dialect and identifying instances of it in her transcripts. The transcription consultants she worked with, all of whom identified themselves as locals, often found themselves at odds in categorizing various types of speech and interpreting their meanings in context. "In many ways, these discussions became investigations into what it was that made speakers sound 'Bergamasco' to the transcribers, progressing from a transcriber's judgment that an utterance or a word 'sounded Bergamasco' or 'wasn't good Italian' to a closer look at exactly what it was that produced this perception" (Cavanaugh 2012, xv). Not only was the attribution of a word or accent to a particular linguistic category often ambiguous, but the categories themselves could be subject to intense metalinguistic discussion and revision; the identity of a nonstandard Italian word could be linked to region, social class, or a host of other sociological categories.

Similarly, Sasha Newell's (2012) description of *nouchi* in Côte d'Ivoire, an urban speech register combining elements of French, English, and Dioula while drawing heavily on American pop culture, suggests that *nouchi* is first and foremost a way that certain types of people speak: the urban gangster, the bandit, the *bluffeur*. These identities are ambivalent, as they connote both criminality and a sense of toughness, cunning, and living by one's wits. *Nouchi* is not a clearly delineated language code so much as it is a stylistic posture associated with particular figures who speak and act in a patterned way, who perform particular styles of dances, consume particular brands and products, and share a worldview and mode of comportment when engaging with that world. What counts as *nouchi* is a product of the identity and attitude of its speakers (Newell 2012, 37). Voicing contrasts between weaker and thicker Dongbeihua, or between Dongbeihua and Mandarin, are similarly experienced as entextualized forms of social personhood.

Enregistering Dongbeihua

In her grammatical description of Dongbeihua, the Chinese linguist Feng Chan-grong adds the following note about the dialect's "colloquial and lively nature":

> Unlike the solemn, serious and deadpan Mandarin, [Dongbeihua] is plain, straightforward and not suited to polite discourse. It can freely express one's thoughts and readily reveal one's emotions. It is the most convenient form of communication, the most common form of colloquial expression. At the same time, Dongbeihua's dynamic combination of syllables and tones, modification of tonal and stress patterns, as well as its use of neutral tone and rhotacization, constitute its distinctive tonal rhythm, giving Dongbeihua its naturalness, pristine cadence and beautiful musicality. Therefore, Dongbeihua is the most concise, most spirited, and most lyrical of any means of oral communication. (C. Feng 2008, 76)

Most Shenyangers would agree with Feng's contention that use of Dongbeihua is more natural, warm, and comforting and less pretentious than Mandarin. They recognize its lack of status in the linguistic marketplace but praise its sincerity and simplicity. Professor Sun, who opened a stall at the local antiques market after retiring, told me that Dongbeihua was like a pair of jeans with a hole in them. The jeans themselves are ugly, but when a beautiful woman puts them on, they become beautiful too. "*In aesthetics this is called turning ugliness into beauty [hua'e weimei]. Now, the Shenyang dialect is very dirty [tu], people sneer at it, but art can turn it into something beautiful . . . It's like Picasso's or Van Gogh's art: it looks like it is just chaos, but the level of artistry is actually quite high.*" Such a characterization of Dongbeihua's innate beauty and authenticity was echoed by many of the people who used it in everyday social interactions. Yet, those same people could become anxious, reticent, and at times even angry when Dongbeihua was used in places where it did not belong or with audiences who might judge it negatively.

Because of the lower status of Dongbeihua, many people, especially those younger and more professionally minded, made great efforts to eliminate any trace of it from their speech patterns. Sophie, a teacher who worked for several different schools throughout my fieldwork, told me that during her final year of high school she wanted to standardize her speech. She took a dictionary and made a list of all the words that were affected by her accent, and then went through the list, practicing ten words a day, every day for an hour, saying each word again and again until she was satisfied that her pronunciation was sufficiently standardized. Working in this way, she claimed to have lost her local accent within a year. Tanya, a local graduate student pursuing a degree in English, had also expended a great deal of effort to "erase" her Dongbei accent and force herself to speak standard Mandarin. Nevertheless, Dongbeihua occasionally sneaked back into her speech. Once, Tanya's professor forced her to stand in front of her classmates after she accidentally spoke with a Dongbeihua accent in class. The professor corrected her and then had her repeat his own standard pronunciation back several times before he was satisfied.

These practices are informed by an understanding of Dongbeihua's indexical value, the range of types, emotions, characteristics, and practices with which speaking a given code is semiotically linked. As Tanya summarized the incident with her professor, "Sometimes, even with my teacher, I make that kind of mistake. I will say *sehui* [society], but it should be *shehui*. I feel very, I think, awkward when my language . . . can I say, it betrays me?" What is betrayed here is not only personal information, such as hometown or socioeconomic status. Rather, the intrusion of the vernacular into inappropriate social contexts acts as a betrayal of the individual speaker's chronotopic performance of modernity, and a revelation to the listener that the speaker belongs to the unsophisticated class of peasants and laborers rather than to an elite and educated minority. Not only students but professors, too, can be subjected to this type of critical linguistic gaze. Members of the Chinese language department at one of the local universities underwent annual training seminars with "experts" from Beijing who taught standard pronunciation and corrected any dialectal elements in their speech.

Dongbeihua does have its place in social interaction. As I said, when teaching their classes or meeting with parents, the English teachers I worked with maintained a strict adherence to standard Mandarin. But afterward, as they joked with others in the teachers' office or ate lunch together at a nearby restaurant, the words and accent of Dongbeihua might slip into their speech. Some older people who were particularly proud of Dongbeihua talked about it spreading throughout China based on the power of Zhao Benshan's comedic performances. Professor Sun frequently talked about a "*Dongbeihua renaissance*" that derived from the language's infectious qualities. He liked to brag that on a recent trip to Beijing he had found a school for teaching Dongbeihua to businessmen, who learned it so that they could establish the same feelings of trust and sociality that Dongbei people feel for each other. Dongbeihua is therefore understood as both an expression of local authenticity and an extension of traits and qualities embodied by its speakers (X. Li, Ju, and van den Berg 2016). It is spoken in informal settings and spaces such as parks and apartment courtyards, places where the risks of being labeled uneducated are far lower than the risks of being labeled an outsider. People recognize its use as fun, humorous, and lighthearted. And importantly, it ties speakers to a sense of localized social belonging, insiders to a geographically delimited speech community of like-minded others who share the same aspirations and frustrations.

The complex nature of Dongbeihua's value framework, ranging from affection to shame, is key to understanding its place within the linguistic marketplace of northeastern China. Darren perhaps explained this to me best. He came from a family with extensive business interests in the city. His parents enrolled him in specialized English classes, but he described himself as a lazy and unmotivated student. After high school he traveled with a friend to Xiamen in southern China and found work in a hotel. Because he could speak English fairly well, he found himself doing favors for foreign guests: running errands, buying drugs, finding escorts. In his early thirties at the time of my fieldwork, he owned a bar in the downtown district that catered to foreigners and Shenyangers who styled themselves as modern. During the day, he also worked for a variety of English schools and foreign companies as a kind of fixer, utilizing a vast network of contacts to help businesses negotiate with government offices, attract foreign investors, or set up joint ventures.

As we discussed Dongbeihua one night over drinks in his bar, Darren mapped the meaning of the dialect onto the regional politics of the Chinese nation, with the north divided culturally from the south. He traced this historically to the thirteenth-century divide between the Jin (northern) and Song (southern) dynasties:

> The traditional thinking is different between northern and southern China. You know, ancient time, only the south is China, the north is Jin, like another dynasty. The people are different, even in that time. Song people are kind of cowards, right? They live in a rich, warm place. Easy to make money. The north, you got to fight over land, fight over food, you need friends. South people only trust themselves. North people make friends more easy, you know, buy someone food, drink, get drunk together. In Dongbei we speak the same language, a little like Mandarin but different, so we're the same people, have the same kind of idea.

Darren mixes both geographical and linguistic determinisms into his understanding of local culture. History, environment, and language conspire together to create strong local bonds between people united against outsiders. Northeastern Chinese are characterized here by their sociality in contrast to southern individualism, a sense of community developed through generosity of food and drink and through the use of a common language.

As Darren continued, however, he explained how these local forms of identity hindered new forms of global engagement:

> You want to have a modern, developed company, you want people can speak that language. It's not prejudiced, it's just . . . it's just a matter of education. People are more educated in the city. You're from a small town? What can you teach me? People from the small town come here,

they want to correct their accent, learn the nowadays fashion and go back home and show people the new way.

My accent isn't local. Sometimes I sound like I'm from south, or from Beijing. When I came back Shenyang for good, I got off the train station and I'm outside look[ing] for a taxi. And I say, "Take me this or that street in Tiexi," and he just say "Okay, fifty yuan." What's that, man? It's like five miles away. So I'm shouting and we push each other and I'm hitting and the people around us just looking. Then the other taxi drivers, they like want to help their friend, so they start punching on me. And nobody helping! And I say it in the local accent, I scream, "Hey, help me you bastards!" And then they stop the fight.

Localized forms of identity are perceived as ill-suited to global modernity, and so Darren argues that "modern" endeavors require new kinds of social actors, ones who are educated and proficient in a particular language. But note how his story ends on a kind of resolution of these two orientations. With his accent that can come from multiple places, Darren is able to navigate multiple affiliations. He can be both local and global by effortlessly switching among different registers. English facilitates engagements with foreigners and global corporations, Mandarin with representatives of governance and the nation-state, while Dongbeihua can be used whenever one needs to draw on local sentiment. Dongbeihua is crucial wherever the promotion of regional solidarity is important, but its appropriate use is restricted to those particular times and places.

In 2001, a local musician named Xue Cun uploaded a video to a popular Chinese website with the title *Dongbeiren dou shi huo Lei Feng* (Northeasterners Are All Living Lei Fengs). During the socialist era, Lei Feng, from the nearby city of Fushun, was hailed by Mao Zedong as the model soldier, an embodiment of communist ideals of self-sacrifice and generosity. Today he remains a revered local hero, even if the values he extolled are, ironically, detached from the contemporary political and social context. The video went viral and quickly became a shorthand for the qualities and traits that exemplify the regional identity of Dongbei. Accompanied by a cartoon depicting the events described, the song is as follows:

> *Lao Zhang drove his car to Dongbei—Wham* [a car accident]!
> *The other driver acted like a scoundrel—he ran away!*
> *Luckily a Dongbei person came along*
> *Sent him to the hospital for five stitches—he's okay!*
> *Lao Zhang treated him to a meal*
> *And could not drink only a little.*
>
> *He said:*

All of us here are Dongbei people
All of us here grow quality ginseng
All of us here eat pork stew with noodles
All of us here are living Lei Fengs
We don't have that kind of person
After an accident, how could he not help that person?
All of us here have mushrooms on the mountain
That one, he was not a Dongbei person

Cui Hua! Bring out the pickled cabbage.

This song quickly moved from the internet to radio, where it still receives frequent airtime, and later became the theme song for a locally produced sitcom called *A Dongbei Family* (*Dongbei yi jia ren*). Xue Cun articulates a local Dongbei identity through several elements: products like ginseng and mushrooms and common foods like pork stew with noodles and pickled cabbage. Locals help people, like the Dongbei person who takes Lao Zhang to the hospital after his accident, as opposed to individualistic outsiders—"scoundrels"—who run away. When Lao Zhang is placed in another's debt, he repays him in the locally appropriate manner: through food and, most especially, through mutual consumption of alcohol. Finally, they call out to the waitress Cui Hua, a name bearing distinct rural overtones. Through all of this, the lyrics themselves are locally inflected with the Dongbeihua accent and marked forms such as the use of *anmen nagar* rather than Mandarin's *zanmen zheli* for "all of us here" and Dongbeihua's pronunciation of "person" as *yinr* rather than Mandarin's *ren*.[3]

What is most ironic about the popularity of *Dongbeiren dou shi huo Lei Feng* is that those who enjoyed it the most—the technologically savvy listeners who spread it across the internet—are also the very people who devote the most effort to not speaking Dongbeihua themselves in public. In numerous parody videos, these urbanites reenact the local identity through language and dress, wearing the padded village girl's coat or green jacket and fur hats of revolutionary soldiers, while singing out the lyrics together. The local exists in these cases as spatial frame, in both the lived space of Shenyang and the virtual space of the internet video. But the local is immediately reconstituted as something to be transcended. Recall that Sophie and Tanya made extreme efforts to eliminate Dongbeihua from their speech aimed at placing or positioning themselves within a new urban configuration of social action—that is, one in which people are oriented outward and conceive of themselves traveling to, and engaging with, larger geographies and structural processes. Yet, it seems that the goal was not to eliminate Dongbeihua altogether but to control it, to invoke it at will in particular circumstances and at strategic times. To avoid being betrayed by Dongbeihua, as Tanya phrased it, the vernacular must move from the latent to the active part of one's speech repertoire. Doing so ensures that it only slips in where it is wanted or needed, as in Darren's example of the fight with his taxi driver. At the same time, self-control over Dongbeihua is balanced by a parallel fantasy structure in which outsiders were seen to be desiring the register's indexical values, as in the case of the Beijing businessmen ostensibly desiring to speak Dongbeihua. Ideally expunged from the speech of young speakers, Dongbeihua returns as a spectral image of itself, enjoyed and treasured once again, but always at a distance in the safe idiom of humor and play.

An Excess of Englishes

English was first heard spoken in China in the seventeenth century as British adventurers, traders, and privateers began to challenge the Portuguese monopoly on trade through the port of Macau (Adamson 2004; Bolton 2003). Imperial China heavily restricted trade with Europeans, isolating it to certain coastal ports, regulating who they could interact with, and forbidding the learning of Chinese languages by outsiders. Several contact languages sprang up during this period, including a variety called Pidgin English that blended English vocabulary and Chinese grammatical structures in a way that allowed Chinese business agents to facilitate trade with the British (S. Evans 2006, 46–49). By the late nineteenth century, English was being taught in China through missionary schools and the Tongwen Guan, an imperial language school for Chinese diplomats (Biggerstaff 1961), but most students only ever developed limited fluency, and its utility was limited to areas such as trade, Christian proselytization, and foreign affairs. In Shenyang, the first English-speaking resident was the Scottish medical missionary Reverend Dugald Christie, who lived there for thirty years beginning in 1883. He taught English informally to several of his Chinese assistants, but his instruction was not systematic, and most left his employ after a short period (Christie 1914).

The Chinese Revolution of 1911, which overthrew the imperial state and ushered in a Republican government, also changed the scope and scale of foreign-language education. The former treaty ports of Shanghai and Hong Kong became cosmopolitan centers where European and Chinese cultures blended together (H. Lu 1999), and the study of English in Chinese schools became more common in these urban areas (Henry 2013b). However, the political and military situations in China became increasingly unstable in the 1930s, and many foreign missionaries and teachers left the country in response to the growing war with Japan. In the aftermath of the Second World War and the Communist Party's victory, some English teachers and educators did remain in China (Brady 2003), but the vast majority were expelled. English may have remained on the curriculum, but it was not until the reform era of the 1980s and 1990s that English education again took off in response to popular demand (Ross 1993).

When it comes to English in Shenyang today, the values of Dongbeihua are inverted. English comes from outside; it is global, foreign, and unfamiliar. While Dongbeihua is subject to a kind of alienation—a distancing of the language from the self only to be recaptured as a flexible signifier—the educational desire for English is premised on a growing sense of control, familiarity, and mastery of the language. It is a medium through which speakers can extend their influence, their capacity to affect and participate in wider spatiotemporal frameworks. Successful acquisition and use of English marks a person as engaging with translocal social contexts and engendering potentiality for the future. Nevertheless, there are multiple avenues to achieving this control, the exact pedagogies and strategies of which are subject to frequent debate among students and teachers.

There has been a shift in the past several decades in research on language and globalization from talking about the spread of English (e.g., Crystal 1997; Garcia and Otheguy 1989; Kachru 1992) to talking about the proliferation of Englishes (Canagarajah 2013; Kachru, Kachru and Nelson 2006; Kirkpatrick 2010; Tupas 2015). This focus on the plurality of Englishes maps onto growing postmodern and postcolonial critiques of the idea of English as a single coherent linguistic system belonging to the West, and Western speakers, at the expense of non-Westerners who have, nevertheless, grown up speaking the language as their own. Despite this interest in variation, however, much of the scholarly effort is dedicated toward describing and cataloguing the multitude of Englishes and thus, in a sense, standardizing them as well. By comparison, a semiotic view of English in China leads us to understand the language itself as inherently unstable and fragmented. In contrast to scholars who contend that there is a distinctive Chinese variety of English (e.g., C. Cheng 1992; D. He and Li 2009; Wei Li 2016; Xu and Deterding 2017), just one of many in the world, here I will argue that there are multiple forms of English in China tied not to region or native language of the speaker but to the context of their production. Again, these are semiotic registers that derive their coherence not from any grammatical typology but from their place within the overarching order of indexicality that describes their use in context.

Oral English and Examination English

Liu Boshan was in his final year of high school when I interviewed him in the midst of preparing for one of the biggest events of his life: writing the National College Entrance Examination (NCEE, usually referred to in Chinese as *gaokao*). When I asked if he enjoyed learning English, he immediately made a distinction between two different types of the language: oral English, which he learned at Hong Ri, and "*mute English*" (*yaba yingyu*), which he learned in school. Oral English, he said, is fun. "*Sure, you still have to memorize words, but you don't have to learn phonetics. You study it because—how can I put this—because you are interested in it. And the* stickers," he said, referring to the rewards teachers hand out to students, "*they give you that kind of stuff.*" The purpose of oral English is mainly, he argued, to cultivate a feeling for the language and a deeper level of understanding.

In contrast, "mute English" is English learned for examinations like the one he would soon take. It is mute because students rarely speak it out loud—perhaps in recitation from the text or in practiced dialogues in class but never conversationally or spontaneously. All of it is based on studying out of books. The only purpose is to answer questions correctly on the tests students take throughout their lives. "*Because China has that kind examination culture in education, even if you don't have an interest* [in English] *you have to study. You like it, you have to study. You don't like it, you still have to study.*" Liu had done remarkably well on the English portion of his high school entrance examination, and achieved high grades in his English classes, but he hated studying this way because the knowledge of examination English did not transfer into any practical skills. The knowledge itself was useless, he told me, outside of the examination.

The incongruity between the two forms of English Liu identified (oral and mute) is not simply one of pedagogy. These are, in fact, very different types of English. Liu and others I interviewed talked about oral English as freewheeling and inventive. Because it is developed through dialogic practice (that is, in conversation with others), oral English is responsive to context, playing off of the perspectives, motivations, and ideas of one's interlocutors. The following dialogue, for instance, is from an oral English class at a private language school between Winston, a Chinese English teacher, and his student.

> WINSTON: Do you think it's important for student to develop singing ability? To practice singing?
> STUDENT: Yeah, of course.
> W: Of course . . . *She sounds very confident.* Why?
> S: Because . . . I'm—
> W: Because I'm interested? . . .
> S: Because I'm being—Because everyone goes to the karaoke.
> W: Really? Everyone? I don't—Am I not everyone?
> S: With your friends, one of the best ways to, you—to get together again is sing—
> W: Sing!
> S: Sing all together.

W: And that shows? . . . And that shows?
S: Your people skill.

This exchange lasted about twenty-five seconds from start to finish. Winston begins with a question and solicits an answer from the student. Note how he immediately challenges the student to expand on her answer. There are also two interruptions to the student that prompt her to reformulate how she constructs her answer. In other words, in a typical oral English class, students are not simply responding to questions but often constantly reacting to inputs from their teacher in terms of how to answer; the teacher in turn reacts to the composition of the student's answer both topically and grammatically.

The resulting conversation is inherently dialogic in the sense that the student's answer is the product of co-constructed discourse between herself and her teacher. For Bakhtin (1981, 279–280), dialogism is "the natural orientation of any living discourse," which he describes as language that is "oriented toward a future answer-word: it provokes an answer, anticipates it and structures itself in the answer's direction." In contrast, examination English is largely monologic. There is no opportunity for teacher or student to challenge or influence the other because they are not in dialogue. The exam asks a question, and the student answers, either correctly or incorrectly. Examination questions are also divorced from any kind of situational context; they are addressed to a mass audience who encounter these decontextualized questions on an examination paper with no background or information on the speakers, setting, previous dialogue, or ensuing dialogue. Consequently, examination English is a higher-order scalar view of language that emphasizes coherence, unity, and objectivity (Blommaert 2015a). Knowledge of examination English is technical and exacting, deeply tied to standardizing ideologies of correctness. These varying contexts of production between oral and examination English lead to very different experiences of the respective languages in use.

English examinations in China are dominated by multiple-choice questions. For instance, the 2017 NCEE English test was two hours long and divided into four sections: listening (thirty points), reading (forty points), practical language knowledge (forty-five points), and writing (thirty-five points) (see L. Cheng and Qi 2006). This examination is written by Chinese educators in consultation with national curriculum and testing committees and accounts for 20 percent of a student's final score when determining their options for higher education.[4] For listening, students answer questions about conversations played for them, while reading involves answering questions about a series of provided texts. Practical language knowledge asks students to select the correct word (or word form) to insert into blanks in a given text. Writing consists of two parts: correcting errors in a text and writing a one-hundred-word composition. Of the 150 points available, 100 come from answering multiple-choice questions.

Tests are not simply methods of evaluation but, as Elana Shohamy (2001) asserts, disciplinary tools. The term "washback" in language testing describes how the nature and design of a test shape the pedagogical strategies of teaching, imposing certain behaviors on test takers by defining what they need to know and how they need to learn it.[5] It can also encompass the effects of testing on sociocultural practices and beliefs. For instance, English schools and public schools regularly post their students' high scores on banners near their entrances, along with the names of the universities those students have been accepted into. Bookstores in China are chock-full of guides, practice exams, specialized dictionaries, and other materials intended to help students prepare for the NCEE. There are tremendous institutional and family pressures on students to study hard and perform well on this examination. All of these practices constrain the type of English that is taught in public school and how students come to understand the language: not as a communicative system but as a collection of complex lexemes and rules.[6]

Most of the questions students encounter are straightforward and unremarkable, but a significant number involve, from a native speaker's perspective, ambiguities in terms of syntax, lexical choice, or pragmatic effect. Let me cite just two of the thousands of practice test questions students encountered, both from the published guidebooks I consulted and in the classroom.[7] One question, from a 2014 NCEE preparation test, asks:

> There is no _____ in persuading him to give up computer games.
> A. doubt   B. wonder   C. point   D. value

Which is the correct answer? The answer guide provided with the test lists C, the word "point." However, the sentence "There is no value in persuading him to give up computer games" is a perfectly legitimate English syntactic construction and even seems pragmatically appropriate to the situation laid out in the question. But given that there can only be one correct answer, the guide notes that "according to the context, the answer is evidently C." The use of "context" is layered here because it appears to refer both to the grammatical context of the sentence and to the larger educational context of the examination itself. In other words, the examination questions test knowledge that students have acquired in their English-language classrooms, and that knowledge alone, rather than its practical application in actual conversational settings, is what matters on the test. This constitutes a separate register of English from that of the native speaker's intuition. Approaching the exam from a native speaker's perspective biases outsiders toward viewing this as a naturalistic interactional episode, when, in fact, it is deeply rooted within Chinese pedagogical discourses.

The other question illustrates some of the lexical depth students are asked to demonstrate. During a graduate student English preparation course, Sophie projected the following up on a screen for her students:

The bear _____ the hunter from behind.
A. grabbed   B. grasped   C. clutched   D. clasped

After some guesses from the students, Sophie turned to me, the only native speaker in the room, to ask for the right answer. I sat silently for a few seconds, if memory serves, squinting at the screen with my mouth open in confusion. Finally, I hastily explained I was not sure which answer was correct and that perhaps, in some way, all of them could be used in the sentence. There was an awkward moment before Sophie smiled broadly, gave a little laugh, and then explained to the class that the correct answer was in fact "clasped." All of the other words, she informed us, require the use of opposable thumbs, an anatomical feature that bears do not possess. In deference to my inability to answer, she concluded, *"Sometimes English is very complicated, but I hope all of you will study hard."*

What should we make, then, of examination English and its disjuncture from oral English? Examination English implies a kind of ideological violence as it strips dialogue down to its most isolating, monologic, context-free form. There is no specific bear or specific hunter, only generic semantic categories defined by, in this case, the arrangement of their digits. It denies the inherent ambiguity of most discourse in place of denotative specificity—the notion that there are clear right and wrong answers related to clearly identifiable real-world objects and actions like "persuasion" and "clutching." The examination therefore shifts linguistic expertise from native-speaker norms to Chinese experts (i.e., test designers and teachers) who can compose, judge, and teach the content of the English produced for the examination and in the students' answers. Examination English and oral English are therefore not just different pedagogies or acquisitional strategies; they constitute two different registers of the same language. In practice, students with strong backgrounds in either one of these educational methods will produce very different types of speech. Students with examination backgrounds may choose more complex vocabulary when speaking, while those with oral proficiency speak as quickly as possible.[8]

Cool English

At the Happy Family Shopping Mall in Shenyang, a billboard outside the main retail office displays the names and pictures of a *"group of heroes,"* the company's top employees. A text box explains that the heroes are chosen competitively from across all corporate divisions on the basis of their service ability, professional knowledge, and personal quality. Over six months, in what the company described as a "PK *competition*" (PK *bisai*), the selection of heroes was whittled down from divisions, to teams, to groups of twelve employees, to six, three, and then, finally, the winner. Under the winner's carefully posed picture was the caption "PK *king*." Most Shenyangers identified "PK" as an English word and often used it with the assumption that I, as a native speaker, would understand its meaning. I did not. The origins of the phrase only became clear to me when I joined Dylan, a university English teacher who aspired to open his own school, and his friends at a downtown internet bar. As we played a first-person shooting game over our networked computers, Dylan turned to me just as I had been killed on the computer screen and taunted me with "*wo* PK *ni le*" (I PKed you). He then pointed out to me the message flashing on his screen: Player Kill. The phrase was popularized by the televised singing competition *Super Girl* (*Chaoji Nusheng*), which seeks to annually crown China's top female vocal talent and has been broadcast on and off since 2006. Each week, the two bottom-ranked contestants PK, meaning they compete head-to-head, after which the audience selects the contestant who will leave the show. The phrase now appears with striking regularity in Chinese media and popular culture, such as the list of heroes at the Happy Family Shopping Mall, and describes any competition where a group of contenders are gradually narrowed down to a winner.

PK thus began its life as internet slang, derived from an English phrase, for the act of killing another player in competition and eventually came to mean the act of competition itself. In the process, the English was transformed and resignified to the extent that a native English-speaker could not recognize it. Other examples of English pervading everyday communication include the way students raise their hands when they need to use the washroom—they shape their fingers to form a *W* and a *C*, to represent the British phrase "water closet"—and the use of popular catchwords from Western media such as "Bazinga!," which is commonly uttered by the character Sheldon on the American television show *The Big Bang Theory*.

PK, WC, and Bazinga are not simple examples of code-switching in the conventional sense that speakers shift between "semantically, grammatically, and phonologically permissible alternates" in conversation (Blom and Gumperz 1972, 409). Rather, these are multivalent signifiers deployed within complex webs of meaning that do not sort clearly into one or another language. The linguist Suresh Canagarajah (2013) calls such hybridized modes of communication "translingual practice," arguing that globalization has increased the meshing of once disparate codes together in conversational practice. PK is not English, and yet it is *emblematically* English in the sense that it represents the language, along with all of its indexical entailments, to the Chinese listener or viewer. These types of hybridized signifiers are part of a register type Jan Blommaert (2015b, 17) refers to as "lookalike language," the "outcome of a very complex form of indexical appropriation and semiotic recoding, resulting in a rather unexpected form of intense 'cool' meaningfulness." English phrases on T-shirts, pencil cases, wedding photographs, advertisements, fashion accessories, and thousands of other examples that can be found in Shenyang can therefore be gathered under the label of "cool English."

Cool English is produced for very different purposes and takes very different forms than the oral and examination Englishes I outlined above. Cool English purports to have an unmediated foreign origin—although, as we can see with PK, this may not actually be the case—directly acquired from foreign friends, study abroad, or consumption of Western pop culture. It also exhibits very different indexical entailments when deployed in conversation. The lexical depth and exacting grammar of examination English highlight a speaker's association with success in the Chinese educational system, while oral English situates a speaker within a global speech community. Cool English, however, accomplishes an implied assimilation by the speaker of Western cultural values and outlooks—such as the value of individual competition (the PK)—which many thought "foreign" to Chinese culture but have become common aspects of social practice in the neoliberal economy. The emphasis in cool English is not on communicative clarity, a clear denotational message, but on directly associating the speaker with English's indexical values.

Tiger was a manager at Washington English, one of the more expensive private English schools in Shenyang, He was in his late thirties when I met him, stocky, dressed in Western name-brand clothing, hair fashionably tousled, and sporting a goatee. He had attended a university in Australia and frequently reminded me and the Washington English students and teachers of this fact. One evening, he was scheduled to give a lecture at the school titled "How to Learn English Effectively." Tiger began by telling the assembled students that learning English requires not just hard work but a set of goals such as being able to dominate a conversation, being able to quarrel in English, or making an impromptu speech on a topic. The next step is to conquer one's fears. Speaking rapidly, he outlined for students the major barrier to English fluency for Chinese students. "*Do you know what the key problem is for Chinese people studying English? One word*: face. I can't lose my face. I can lose my blood but not my face. But you always be so modest, you can't improve your language. So feel free to make a lot of mistakes in the beginning. Feel free to lose your face. Nobody will laugh at you. Learning English is like many times losing small faces, you just need to be confident." For Tiger, the barrier to English fluency is face (*lian*), a fundamental cultural value governing Chinese social interaction (Kipnis 1995; Oxfeld 2010, 25–26).

He implicitly asserts that his language acquisition has been successful because he has been able to discard this obsession with face. The key to mastering English is, by extension, to become like an English speaker, to discard this element of Chinese subjectivity and embrace a Western-style individualism (of someone who, dismissing the evaluations of others, is unafraid to make mistakes)—in other words, to become foreign oneself (cf. X. Liu 2002).

When I asked Fanny, the head Chinese teacher at Washington English—who also had a degree from a British university—what she thought of Tiger's lecture afterward, she scoffed. No one in the room could understand him, she complained, because he spoke too fast and the words he used were too advanced. This was becoming a popular teaching style at some English schools in Shenyang, she claimed, because it made the speaker look like he or she knew the language, but in effect it was just an act. Tiger's lecture, and cool English in general, are primarily aimed at this kind of performance, but it is more than simply an act in the dismissive sense Fanny intended. Rather, it is a performance aimed at invoking certain indexical values that come to be associated with the performer as a particular kind of person. The performer, as Erving Goffman noted, "exerts a moral demand upon the others, obliging them to value and treat him in the manner that persons of his kind have a right to expect" (Goffman 1959, 13). Cool English makes a demand that its performer be treated as one who has transcended local forms of sociality and attachment, one who embodies presumably Western values and exercises them as part of an English-centered linguistic persona.

Once, after I had just finished interviewing an English teacher at a public middle school, a student arrived for a tutorial. The teacher introduced me to her student and encouraged her to say something to me in English. The student waved her hand at me in embarrassment and refused, saying "*No, no, I can only speak that kind of Dongbei English.*" In this chapter, I have described how the constitution of different registers is a semiotic effect of their mapping onto dynamic sociocultural ideologies and characterological types. The meaning of the phrase "Dongbei English" can, I argue, only make sense within the specific contours of the complex heteroglossic value frameworks of Shenyang that I outlined above. The student was not referring to any new dialect of English but positing, I believe, a convenient analogy among the multiple scalar levels of indexical order to express her lack of confidence. In other words, she refused to speak English to me because it would be heard as "too local" due to her nonnative accent and potential syntactic errors; in effect, it would make her "too local" as well. The ambivalence over language and its sociocultural effects—what indexical associations listeners make when they hear Dongbeihua in particular contexts—is the ambivalence over locality itself and Shenyang's place in the broader spatial framework of the Chinese nation and the world more generally.

We can see here how such ambivalence is reflected within other cultural discourses such as the concept of face and how it constitutes people as morally situated individuals in relation to the broader sociocultural field. Petra's parents risked a loss—or what Munn (1986, 13) would term a spatiotemporal "contraction"— of face because of their inability to exercise control over their language choices. This would not have been a concern for speakers who could appropriately model standard Mandarin speech practices in public interactions. Tiger, in contrast, performatively enacted a social type that had, by embodying foreign values, transcended the concern with face altogether. My description of speech practices in this chapter has therefore, by necessity, been interwoven with descriptions of educational, geographical, and technological ideologies and practices—in other words, they are entangled with China's cultural and social transformations.

China is in a state of both social and linguistic upheaval as new forms of wealth, social legitimacy, and language practice come to the fore. Whereas the Maoist state once engineered a vision of the nation united by a single set of spoken practices (Putonghua translates literally as "common speech"), the speech environment in Shenyang is now deeply stratified by a range of different registers, including Dongbeihua, Mandarin, and English.[9] In navigating diverse types of social encounters, Shenyangers aim to deploy these multiple registers in ways that best reflect their strategic goals—to position themselves, for instance, as set-upon locals in need of help in a fight, or cosmopolitan outsiders able to market their linguistic expertise to aspiring students. In each case, it is the ability to flexibly exploit different registers, and thus embody contextually appropriate social types, that accrues the highest social capital. In the process of acquiring these linguistic skills, individuals effect their own movement along a path of greater spatiotemporal control, moving from local arenas of social action to global ones. In contrast, individuals like Petra's parents, who are unable to wield any semiotic register other than the locally situated Dongbeihua, find their social capacity, their potential to manipulate networks of relations with other actors, most delimited.

THE MORAL ECONOMY OF WALLS

Recursive Enclosure and Linguistic Space

Professor Deng once taught comparative literature at Liaoning University, but had also studied in Hong Kong, England, Switzerland, and Germany. The frontispiece of one of his books, a monograph examining the influence of "primitive" art and religion on Chinese literature, is a picture taken of him in front of a Chinese restaurant in Geneva in 1986: tall, softly smiling, graying hair slicked back, dressed in dark sunglasses and a handsome suit. Intelligent, genial, and soft-spoken, he was still a formidable person to talk to. When I met him, he was a widower and had been retired for several years. He lived with his daughter, also a professor, in a moderately sized apartment near the university. His daughter ran an English school out of their living room, teaching classes to the children of her neighbors. On the weekends, furniture was pushed aside and a few rough wooden desks set up in front of a whiteboard for students to read and recite their lessons. Professor Deng, with his elegant British diction, sometimes taught quick conversational lessons to the students, but spent most of the noisy classroom time in his room reading. Whenever I visited to watch the class in action he would invite me into this small room, narrow and crowded with books and papers, him sitting upright on the single bed against the wall, me on one of the plastic blue stools borrowed from the classroom.

Professor Deng took a deeply philosophical approach to language. Waving his arm to his daughter's class beyond his door, he asked me if I understood why English was so difficult for Chinese students. "It's not a question of languages," he answered himself, "it is a question of nations. Language is only the surface. Under that is the depth of human experience: history, culture, religion, all stacked up like this." He illustrated this by moving his hands one on top of the other. The differences between China and the West are deep, he continued, deeper than most people can appreciate. One reason is that China does not try to make its culture approachable. "We Chinese, the trend is always towards isolation. When Chinese are defeated, the doors close." Professor Deng held his arms in front of him and swung them shut like gates. "And when there is victory, well, then the doors also close. All of us behind our walls. Do you know Robert Frost? 'Good fences make good neighbors?' Well that is China. We love our walls, and China is like the Great Wall. If you want to know Chinese, just learn about walls." I mused at this point that one of the latest gambits in American immigration policy was to create a wall across its southern border with Mexico. He chuckled and shook a finger at me. "Ah, you see, this is very good. The Americans are becoming more Chinese every day!"

Recursive Enclosure

Despite the joke, there is a very real sense in which the Chinese landscape is defined by its walls and, consequently, by an architecture of enclosure (Knapp 2000; D. Lu 2006; Y. Xu 2000; Zhu 2004). Many different kinds of everyday lived space in China, in both the historical and contemporary periods, are physically demarcated by framing or bordering motifs such as walls, fences, roads, ditches, lines of trees, and so on. In China, the paradigmatic form of the wall is not one-dimensional (running in a straight line) but two-dimensional (forming a square), and therefore also enclosing and signifying the space inside as separate and distinct from that outside. Buildings tend to face inward rather than outward, emphasizing seclusion, privacy, and, most importantly, difference from the outside world. These enclosed spaces are themselves enclosed within higher-order spatial patterns (cities, regions, and the nation) that form vertical hierarchies as well as horizontal equivalencies among similarly ranked spaces, a dynamic first recognized in the 1960s in a series of articles by G. William Skinner (collected in Skinner 2001) that has become the foundation for Chinese cultural geography. Such spatial dynamics are, of course, by no means unique to China, but they are significant there in terms of both their ubiquity and their symbolic intensity.

Historically, the most visible of these walls was the city wall, both a defensive and a symbolic construct, so essential to cosmological notions of authority and order that "an unwalled urban centre was almost as inconceivable as a house without a roof" (D. Lu 2006, 128; see also Y. Xu 2000, 86–88). Within the city walls, further walls divided wards, ethnic districts, market areas, temples, gardens, and administrative buildings. Although these structures were often cannibalized during the socialist era to provide bricks and other construction materials, walls remained important markers of work units, factories, schools, and offices under Mao (Gaubatz 1995). During China's recent period of rapid modernization and urbanization, walled architecture has been reappropriated to signify a distinct Chinese cultural heritage. Private construction replicates the logic of earlier times with residential districts and office complexes contained within walled compounds. Whether in the face of marauding armies in ancient times or rural migrants today, the rationale for walls revolves around the desire to keep out the forces of chaos and protect those within (D. Lu 2006, 124–142).

Clearly demarcated walled spaces, each one nested inside another, provide order as they structure and arrange the landscape into conceptual units of social space. This pattern of recursive enclosure makes the chronotope a powerful analytical tool, as these spaces are symbolically infused with time values that shape a range of social practices, including language. If we examine, for instance, the spatial and architectural aesthetics of China's premodern period, the symbolic order manifested an ideology of synchronicity among all of the various components of the imperial system, from the lowest-level bureaucratic office to the imperial palace itself. This order fragmented during the revolutionary movements of the early twentieth century, only to be reconstituted (at least in idealized form) in the Maoist period. But it is the powerful symbolic apparatus of the asynchronous urban landscape today that engenders China's chronotopic modernity as a new form of lived experience.

Traditional Architecture: Recursive Enclosure from House to Palace

Traditional forms of architecture in China—under which I include here buildings of the imperial period as well as explicitly premodern buildings such as peasant dwellings built in a traditional style—were laid out on the basis of multiply recursive forms of enclosure. Buildings were inward-focused, abutting the margins of the property and surrounding an open courtyard. Palaces, temples, and even private homes during the imperial period were constructed in this fashion, with a high exterior wall delimiting inside from outside and only a few gates or doorways as points of entry and exit (Xiao Hu 2008). Within this centrally enclosed space there were almost always further walls and gateways separating the public outside from the private inside, leading to a progression, as one entered a building, into increasingly embedded and proscribed spaces.[1] Even simple structures like rural homes were typically posed at the head of a courtyard opposite a gate, and in cases where these homes were expanded the tendency was to create a pattern of enclosure rather than expand in a straight line. These elements can be traced back to the Western Zhou period three thousand years ago and are considered distinctive features of the Chinese architectural style (Knapp 2000, 21–70; Sicheng Liang 1984).

Liu Xin's description of a rural Chinese home in Shaanxi is a prime example of this architectural aesthetic in the rural countryside (X. Liu 2000, 39–51). A person enters the household first of all through a gate into a walled courtyard, which consists of structures for storing food, shelter for animals, and the family toilet. At the rear of the courtyard is the entrance to the household head's residence. Through the door of the house, one first encounters the public space where family members receive guests, with women sitting on the bed (itself enclosed by a wall) and men sitting at a table with a view out the entrance toward the public space outside. Important guests or close relatives are invited further into the house to sit at the kitchen table and share food. The inner third of the house, blocked from public view by a curtain, is a dark, private space for storing food, used only by members of the household. In his analysis of the architectural configuration of the rural household, Liu argues that social and cultural values are embedded within its design, particularly in how the symbolic dimensions of inside and outside correspond to the identification of family and guests: kinship is defined as much by who is admitted into the innermost spaces of the home as it is by genealogy (X. Liu 2000, 50; see also Knapp 2000, 33–34; Y. Yan 2005). The graduated series of enclosures progress from outer to inner, public to private, and are associated with a similarly graduated scale of emotional values ranging from outsider to insider, distant to intimate, and suspicion to trust. These symbolic values are materialized in the form of walls, gates, doorways, and curtains, to indicate just where such public and private spaces begin and end.

At the opposite end of the spectrum, and on the grandest scale, the Imperial City in Beijing, with the Forbidden City at its center, exhibits much the same spatial logic (Barmé 2008, 25–46; Meyer 1991; Zhu 2004). The heart of imperial power for over five hundred years from the late Ming through the Qing dynasties, the imposing form of the Forbidden City (or rather, the city within a city within a city) is itself divided into two halves: the southern outer courtyard once used for formal audiences and affairs of state, and the northern inner courtyard that served as a private residence for the imperial family. The outer courtyard contains three audience halls, and the inner courtyard three residential palaces. Entrants proceeded from the southern gate northward into an inner courtyard with an elevated audience hall at the north end. Here were hosted grand processions and imperial audiences, where decrees were issued and meetings with ministers held. To each side of the audience hall were gateways proceeding northward through a series of smaller but more intimate (and therefore more important) audience spaces. After transiting to the inner courtyard, the journey northward played in reverse fashion, with the emperor's private residence followed by a hall of seals and finally the empress's residence, near the relatively small northern gate. The inner courtyard was accessed only by the emperor's most trusted ministers, eunuchs and officials.[2] Like the rural house, the palace displays a spatial logic in which the journey from outsider to intimate is marked by a series of discrete, recursively contained spaces within the building's outer walls, a pattern also replicated in the design of such diverse urban structures as private residences and temples.

But the imperial palace is not even the highest-order representation of this logic, as one has only to look at a classical map of Beijing to recognize (see figure 2.1). From above, the walls encircling the Forbidden City (the small rectangular complex at the center) and the Imperial City (the larger rectangle surrounding it) are themselves enclosed within the walls encircling Beijing itself. And beyond that,

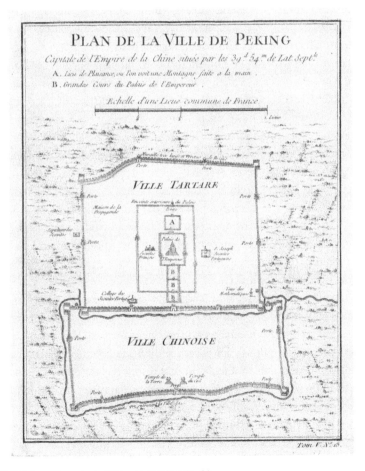

FIGURE 2.1.   Plan de la Ville de Peking (n.d.)

Image courtesy of the Division of Rare and Manuscript Collections, Cornell University Library.

thirty miles to the north, the Great Wall, in theory, encircled the empire just as borders now encircle the nation. As Zhu Jianfei notes, "From inside out, the Palace, Imperial, Capital and Outer Cities, and an open rural space further away, formed one sequence of descending order in social status and spatial positioning" (Zhu 2004, 46). This pattern can be found repeated in the form of other imperial Chinese cities, all of which shared a marked similarity of form (Chang 1977; Y. Xu 2000). The social value of enclosure derives not from any one wall or structure, but from how each represents one instantiation of a more universal cosmology. In this sense, the peasant's home and the emperor's palace are structures of a fundamentally similar kind, separated in space but linked as representatives of an overarching symbolic logic. Proceeding down the chain, we move smoothly from nation to city to home to individual in a series of interlocking steps, identifying each as part of a common whole. In the imperial Chinese imagination, recursive enclosure served as nothing less than the structural glue binding people together as members of a common social and cosmological order.

That order was maintained not simply by the physical barriers separating the different types of social space but by the activities carried out by individuals within them. Ritual practice (encompassing the Confucian notion of *li* as "ritual" or "propriety," the power of human activity to hold chaos in abeyance) formed part of the rationale for spatial form in Chinese cities, with urban space both directing and reflecting the flow of symbolic activities such as sacrifice, religious processions, ceremonies, and even everyday social interactions conducted in accord with metaphysical principles of imperial unity. Angela Zito (1997) has shown how Beijing was laid out with the metaphysics of the annual imperial Grand Sacrifice in mind. The emperor, sitting on his throne facing south, defined an axial center mediating the asymmetrical forces of *yin* and *yang*. Located around the city in cardinal relation to the imperial throne were the various altars (to the Sun, the Moon, the Ancestors, Soil and Grain, and Heaven) according to their place within the ritual pattern of sacrifice, culminating in the Grand Sacrifice to Heaven that encompassed all the others (Zito 1997, 121–152). During the climax of the Grand Sacrifice, the emperor reversed direction and faced north to Heaven, much as the son faces north to the south-facing parent or the ancestral tablet in household sacrificial rituals. This spatial and metaphysical reversal by the emperor echoed the continuity of the filial Chinese male's biographical trajectory (from son to father to ancestor in turn) and established an important resonance with the greater social order mediated by shared ritual practice (see also Ebrey 1991; Sangren 2000; Watson 1993). Imperial sacrificial practice was, like the imperial palace itself, simply the fundamental spatial and social arrangement of the Chinese household writ large, with the emperor standing in as son to Heaven and father to the people. The strength of these linkages was due to the relative cultural homogeneity of the

Confucian scholar-gentry class, mediated by a common linguistic and literary tradition. Recursive enclosure in the imperial period thus established a chronotope of universal synchronicity in spatial form and ritual action, where each sacrifice (whether by a patriarch to his ancestors or by the emperor to Heaven) or ritual utterance reconstituted the empire as an enduring, unchanging, and permanent feature of the cosmos.

Revolution and Synchronic Fragmentation

Synchronicity, which for so long provided stability and unity to imperial rule, fractured in the late nineteenth and early twentieth centuries in response to European incursions. Cosmopolitan cities such as Shanghai and other extraterritorial Treaty Ports established by foreign powers brought "traditional" China and the "modern" West into close contact, along with a new consciousness of time prompted by these strange cultural juxtapositions of old and new (Esherick 2000; H. Lu 1999; Yeh 2000). As Leo Ou-fan Lee writes (partially quoting himself), "In this new temporal scheme, present (*jin*) and past (*gu*) became polarized as contrasting values, and a new emphasis was placed on the present moment 'as the pivotal point marking a rupture with the past and forming a progressive continuum toward a glorious future'" (L. Lee 1999, 43–44). China's repeated military defeats and perceived technological handicap with respect to the West forced Chinese intellectuals to call the static space-time of the imperial order into question, searching for a way to salvage a distinctive Chinese identity from the perils of the disruptive modern world beyond its borders (Samuel Liang 2010; Qian 2011). The chronotope of early twentieth-century China was thus revolutionary in both literal and metaphorical senses—conventional notions of stability, centralized rule, patriarchal authority, and social class were being upended at the same time as the political system itself was engulfed in disorder.

By the time of Liberation in 1949, communist leaders perceived the disparities between urban and rural, rich and poor to be detriments to national unity and proposed a new justification for socialist nation-building: the country restored to a singular utopian space-time uniting all peoples and classes. This was the predominant theme, for instance, of Mao's "On the Correct Handling of Contradictions among the People," where he argued that despite the success of the revolution and the changes brought about by the Communist Party, small pockets of dissent continued to exist. He termed the varying visions of national development "contradictions" and advised their elimination through a strategy of "unity-criticism-unity": "starting from the desire for unity, resolving contradictions through criticism or struggle, and arriving at a new unity on a new basis" (Mao 1977, 389–390). Unity within the Communist Party had allowed it to triumph in

China's civil war, and unity among the people would allow them to "devote themselves to peaceful labor and make China a socialist country with modern industry, modern agriculture, and modern science and culture" (387). In other words, Mao's grand view of socialism, its very purpose, was to resynchronize the nation around a new universal chronotope, one oriented toward the future rather than the timeless present.

Mao's socialist utopia imploded during the maelstrom of the Cultural Revolution in the late 1960s and early 1970s. After Deng Xiaoping pushed an agenda of gradually opening up to capitalism and the West in 1978, the familiar asynchronicity of the Republican period returned, but this time on a national scale. Deng's famous dictum "To get rich is glorious" and the proviso that "some will get rich before others" highlighted both the modernizing transformation of Chinese society and its fragmentary application. The architecture of enclosure (and its multiple recursions) has created a landscape today of varying spatiotemporal values, and an experience of moving through both time and space as citizens cross boundaries from one type of enclosed space to another. The forward momentum of development is ultimately realized in the form of the modernist fantasy space, physical monuments to the potential of an affluent future, such as five-star hotels, shopping malls, metro stations, and new apartment complexes. Walls thus work to create a spatial consciousness in China, confining and enclosing, and thus signifying, different types of environment.

Modern Structures: Lived Space in Shenyang

The aesthetic of enclosure remains an important component of lived space in contemporary China. When walking down a street in Shenyang, the pedestrian is usually not passing by a series of discrete buildings or structures, but rather navigating past the outside boundaries of enclosed spaces, punctuated from time to time by gates of one sort or another. The spatial arrangement is characteristic of nearly every type of building: schools, hospitals, government or corporate offices, and, most prominently, residential complexes are all demarcated and enclosed by walls, with a single large gateway for motorized access and perhaps a few others for pedestrians and bicycles. The access these gateways provide is also not fluid, as most main gates feature imposing metal gates or retractable traffic barriers. Pedestrian gates now often have locks or keycard access. Until recently, even public parks were surrounded by high walls and could only be accessed through small gates.[3] These barriers are as much symbolic as they are practical, reinforcing the division between inside and outside.

The most expansive examples of such walled structures are the factories for heavy manufacturing in Tiexi district in the western end of the city (although many of these have been relocated to rural areas to provide room for urban expansion and to control pollution). Other than one or two gates, each side of the square-enclosed factory space is lined by a wall half a mile long. Even relatively modest residential areas today are at least two hundred yards on each side. The overall impression of the pedestrian wandering the urban landscape is of crisscrossing streets of loud, heavy traffic with outward-facing public commercial space that encloses private spaces (domestic, institutional, or corporate) of relative peace and quiet. The transition between these two types of space is still marked; buildings and walls act as barriers between the interior areas and the outside world, with gates that both physically and symbolically segregate while providing points of access.

Most people in Shenyang today live in residential apartment complexes. Although some particularly wealthy housing developments are geared toward individualized townhouses, the predominant model is a group of apartment buildings ranging from five storeys to twenty or thirty at the highest (with often a mix of heights in any given complex), arranged in such a way that the continuous outer boundary of apartments encloses several stand-alone or attached buildings as well.

Figure 2.2 shows, for instance, the apartment complex I lived in during my initial fieldwork in 2005. The complex is bounded by paved streets on three sides and a concrete wall to the east, on the other side of which is another apartment complex. There is, as with most complexes, a single main entry gate. Despite the potential convenience of the main road to the north, this gate is, like those of traditional structures, oriented south. These gates are large enough to accommodate two lanes of traffic, but in newer complexes (those built since the early 2000s) they can be considerably larger and are typically embellished with decorative touches such as gold paint or curved metal bars. Smaller gates, in this case the four openings on the west side, provide other points of entry to the complex for pedestrians and bicycles. In more recently constructed complexes, a back gate is often available for private vehicles to enter and exit, along with access to parking. Within the enclosed space itself are an interconnected set of paved laneways providing vehicular access to each row of apartments. The apartment buildings themselves are divided into a series of contiguous vertical sections, served by a single stairwell with ground floor access (and in taller buildings an elevator). Each floor of the section may then have two to four apartments accessed through individual doorways. An apartment's address within the complex therefore consists of three numbers: section, floor, and unit.

The final bastion of privacy in this graduated series of enclosed spaces is the family apartment itself. Despite high levels of private security and relatively low crime (especially in new residential communities), individual apartments are always fronted by heavy steel security doors, often with more than one locking mechanism. Although all of these doors have peepholes or metal grates for residents

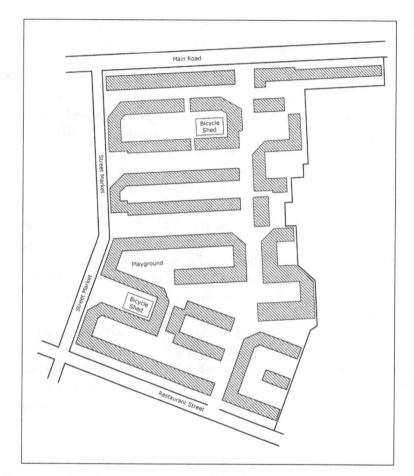

FIGURE 2.2. A Shenyang residential apartment complex

to examine the exterior, people almost always rely on sound to identify who might be outside. A knock at an apartment door typically leads to a tonally rising "*Shei a?*" (Who is it?) inquiry from within, and if the knocker is welcome, the door is opened. Again, the door acts as both a symbolic and physical bulwark, where its very impenetrability marks the differing textures of indoor and outdoor space in the context of the family residence.

As the most interior of this nested hierarchy of space that moves from public to private, the apartment also represents the most intimate sphere of daily social and linguistic interaction. I was repeatedly struck by the relaxed nature of sociality in the residential sphere, often to the point of personal embarrassment, as when, for instance, my wife's friends would strip down to their long underwear before joining us for dinner around our table. Whereas linguistic interactions outside the home frequently involve a high degree of ongoing reflection on word choice, topic appropriateness, and pronunciation, private residential speech is remarkably unguarded. Politeness formulae are abandoned—indeed, their use is often read as an effort at social distancing accompanied by the rhetorical query "*Zanmen shi sha guanxi?*" (What's our relationship?). Arguments start easily and are resolved quickly, and people tend to speak their minds. People feel free to talk about politics, complain about the government, or directly criticize others in ways they would feel reluctant to do in public. Code choice is also governed by informality, and I heard English used by only a handful of individuals at home, and in those cases it was almost always directed only at me. Once, as we ate barbecued pork around a small gas stove in his kitchen, I asked Charles, one of my key informants, if he was teaching his six-year-old son English. "*No,*" he said simply, "*but I have a tutor for him.*" I suggested that since both he and his wife were quite fluent they could use English more often in the home. Charles screwed up his face and clucked his tongue. "*It's not that easy,*" he replied, "*Actually, I don't think we could do it, it would just feel strange.*" Charles did not elaborate further, but the sense of unease about English in the home, a foreign language in this most intimate of domestic spaces, was a common sentiment. Fanny argued that her son (eighteen months old at the time) would be too confused by English in the home, since the words for things are longer. And although Professor Deng's daughter, whose school I described earlier, taught English out of her home, the implements of teaching—the whiteboard, desks, and chairs brought out during class—enacted a symbolic transformation of the space from home to classroom.

Outside the walls of the apartment, between the exterior paved laneways, are leisure spaces marked by greenery, public exercise equipment, and, in wealthier complexes, decorative ponds or pavilions. As private real estate markets heated up in the 1990s, new residential developments sought to differentiate themselves from the more modest socialist-era construction by creating larger and more elaborate green spaces, what Fraser (2000) terms the "oasification" of residential urban design in China (see also Pow 2009; Wu 2010; L. Zhang 2010). Older residents often spend several hours each day spinning large exercise wheels with their arms or striding on stationary walkers. They stroll around with grandchildren or just talk to each other under the trees, propped on small folding stools. Men gather to play cards, mah-jong, or Chinese chess. Inside the complex, the atmosphere is therefore typically friendly, relaxed, and, for the most part, quiet. Occasionally a car will drive past, someone will shout their arrival at the ground-floor security door rather than buzzing up, or a refuse collector or gas seller may wheel through on a bicycle cart banging a small cymbal to announce their services. Birds chirp and dogs bark, people talk quietly in small groups, but very little disturbs the soundscape inside the complex. Outside, however, the busy sounds of the streets—

the car horns, traffic, construction, loudspeaker announcements of various businesses or hawkers, and animated conversation—suffuse public space in a ceaseless jangle. The dynamics of private inner space are therefore shaped by the character of its occupants and the relatively relaxed nature of social interactions, often indexed through speech with a heavy flavor of Dongbeihua. As distinct from outside public areas, I never saw anyone self-conscious about the use of a local accent, and even most young people, who tended to otherwise prefer standard speech, would slip into the dialect with friends and neighbors after passing the gate into the interior.

The interior space of the apartment complex also features only relatively informal commerce, by which I mean transactions between neighbors. Financial transactions are for the most part limited to occasional first-floor residents who convert part of their living space into a small shop selling soft drinks, ice cream, beer, snacks, and other convenience items. Other small storefronts might offer therapeutic massage services, video rentals, or hairstyling. It is only when one moves outside the enclosed space of the apartment complex that proper commerce occurs. The first three floors of exterior-facing buildings marking the outer boundary of the complex are retail spaces rented to restaurants, convenience stores, cigarette and alcohol sellers, shoe repair shops, clothing outlets, and any of a host of other small businesses. Language schools located within the apartment complex are small, either part of the teacher's personal residence or converted from a single two- to three-bedroom apartment. These, like the school owned by Professor Deng's daughter, cater mostly to residents within the complex. The larger English schools are located in the exterior faces of the complex, and therefore feature larger and more numerous classrooms as well as a clientele drawn from the larger district

If recursive enclosure during China's imperial period created a sense of synchronicity, my description of contemporary lived space in Shenyang makes clear that at some level these spaces are now temporally discontinuous. Whereas in the past simultaneity was produced through the enactment of similar ritual practices at different levels of the hierarchy—sacrifice at the level of household and empire—the experience of lived space inside the modern residential complex is radically different from that outside, and is mediated by new types of "ritual" practice such as commodity consumption, work, leisure, and other types of modernist social praxis. These spaces shape distinct forms of habitus, with gates serving as transition points, symbolic barriers between types of human social activity. But rather than being merely different types of space, inside and outside in contemporary China correspond to the differential experience of time as well. Some spaces contain a chronotopic qualia of "pastness," while others have one of "futurity," spanned by a spectrum of gradations between the two poles.

Where to Live? A Material History of Residential Communities

One of the most important decisions for a Chinese urban household is where to live. Aside from mundane considerations such as cost and location, potential homeowners must consider the identification of any potential purchase with a particular cultural and class formation. As Zhang Li writes of the southern Chinese city of Kunming, housing "provides the physical and social ground on which the making of the new middle classes becomes possible" (L. Zhang 2010, 3; see also Pow 2009). To live in an apartment in a given community is to claim membership in a particular class-based habitus, formed through lifestyle and patterns of consumption, that is identified with particular temporal stages of social and economic development. Upper- and middle-class communities are now constructed, for instance, on the assumption that residents will own a car and an array of consumer goods, while lower-income communities make no such provisions. Indeed, most Shenyang residents judged class membership not on income—since true wealth was often derived from what my informants called "flexible money" (*linghuo qian*), that is, money earned indirectly as a consequence of one's status and position, such as the money teachers earned by tutoring students at home—but on residence.

Within a landscape of constant renovation and innovation, the production year of a residence contains great import. Only a few residential areas within Shenyang that predate the socialist era remain. Most *hutong*, neighborhoods of meandering earthen streets and one-storey residences, were finally demolished in the early 2000s.[4] These were residences for the poorest of the poor: rural migrants, failed petty entrepreneurs, destitute retirees. Very few of my Chinese contacts (none of whom lived in such an area) were willing to wander through them, as *hutong* were associated with poverty, disease, criminal elements, and urban decay. "*Too dirty, too disorganized*" was a typical negative evaluation. Only slightly less distasteful are the socialist-era communities (usually called *xiaoqu*, literally, "little district") built in the 1960s and 1970s. These gray poured-concrete buildings have minimal living spaces and amenities. Their relative age and shoddy construction mean that they are generally in poor condition—cracked windows and walls, drafty, dusty, infested with cockroaches and other pests. Before they moved, my in-laws inhabited such a building, built in 1955 and assigned through my father-in-law's work unit. The first time I visited, my mother-in-law met us at the downstairs entrance with a flashlight; the stairway windows were so caked with grime and obstructed by bicycles, boxes, and other detritus that no sunshine could illuminate the stairs. Inside, there was a single room for my wife and her parents, a small kitchen, and a squat toilet. They were overjoyed when they received word that the government would demolish the building to make way for a new apartment complex, even if most of their savings had to be spent on buying a new home.

The reform period of the 1980s saw the first emergence of private homes, separate from the assigned residential quarters of work units. With a booming real estate market, new apartment complexes in China—now designated "flower gardens" (*huayuan*) or other fanciful terms—have sought ways to differentiate themselves through amenities, aesthetics, and ostentatious design (L. Zhang 2010). They sport large decorative gates, striking colors, and signs of wealth such as fountains and lakes (see figures 2.3 and 2.4).

Recently, several new complexes have attempted to appropriate signifiers of "foreignness" such as Western architectural motifs and idealized foreign names (Giroir 2006; Wu 2010). Communities in Shenyang such as Appreciate Europe (Xinshang Ouzhou), Holland Village (Helan Cun), and Cambridge Garden (Kangqiao Huayuan), through their names and advertising images of horseback riding and famous composers, associate themselves explicitly with an imagined Western/modern lifestyle. Another new Shenyang residential complex, named simply Club, encouraged potential buyers to examine their "foreign apartments and elite lifestyle habits" while taking as its logo an English bowler hat. In these examples and others from the literature (e.g., Fraser 2000; L. Zhang 2010), we see explicit associations between foreignness and luxury, modernity, and wealth.

FIGURE 2.3. A modest apartment complex in Shenyang called National Olympic Modern City, with south-facing main entrance

FIGURE 2.4. The opulent entrance to Sky Dragon Homeland

Appreciate Europe in particular billed itself as a "bilingual community" in which all residents would be fluent in English—although how this fluency would be determined and monitored was left unspecified during my trip to their marketing showroom. Real estate advertising sells not only the product itself but the symbolic dimensions of residential belonging, of membership in a particular group of people with a particular spatial and temporal orientation; and in the case of these new residential communities, the orientation is outward to the cosmopolitan milieu of the global citizen and forward to the future.

The enclosed space of the apartment complex thus creates a distinct spatiotemporal texture within its interior, keyed to its moment of production and, increasingly, by efforts at branding that space as modern, global, and cosmopolitan. Membership within a community, established through the act of purchasing an apartment but also living within it and furnishing it in a symbolically appropriate manner—in accord with one's status and class position—confers belonging to the chronotopic identity of the space itself. One becomes modern by way of the everyday rituals of social praxis: living in a wealthy apartment, dressing like a modern individual, driving an expensive car, and speaking in a modern fashion. The spatiotemporal texture of the space is mimetically reproduced as the texture of the individual. And to be modern means to not simply occupy a future-oriented space but also to transcend the boundaries of lower-level spaces, just as the world traveler transcends the boundaries of the neighborhood and nation; to be able to, in other words, move with relative ease between the relative pastness of the countryside to the presentness of the street and the futurity of the foreign restaurant or English school with great regularity.

The Landscape of Shopping

One more example of chronotopic modernity will, I hope, establish the ubiquity of this kind of spatial logic in Shenyang. On a summer afternoon I met Sophie and some of the other Hong Ri teachers at the food court of a large shopping mall. Stores can be found along every major street, but "shopping" usually involves travel to dense retail environments that allow for an entire day of walking and browsing. This highly gendered activity, called *guangjie* (literally, "to wander the street"), is a common pastime for women in China. Although men sometimes accompany their girlfriends or spouses—indeed, I was often told that the measure of a man's commitment was his willingness to spend an entire day shopping with his girlfriend and purchasing anything that she desired—the far more common sight is small groups of women, often arm in arm, striding from mall to shopping center to department store.

At the food court, the women were energetically discussing fashions, the small purchases they had made, and their plans for the remainder of the afternoon. I bought a bowl of noodles and asked a few questions about what they had seen that day, and learned that they had visited a range of different types of shops. When I asked them to tell me about the differences between shops and malls, Sophie grabbed my notebook and started writing down the different types of shopping venues available in the city. "The first one happened, that was when I'm a young person, the street market. There the seller just put the clothes on the blanket, or hang them from the fence. They take the train Beijing, and buy the clothes there, like the really fashion clothes, and bring them back Shenyang for us to buy. That was like 1980s."

As she continued her list, Sophie and the other women began to detail a chronological development of shopping in the city and, with it, shifting practices of buying and selling. But while some have declined in popularity, and a few, such as government-operated department stores, have disappeared altogether, almost all of the options are still valid destinations for *guangjie* practice. In other words, like residential choices, Sophie and the others envisioned shopping as a series of hierarchically linked conceptual spaces that developed genealogically and exemplify the social practices of the eras in which they emerged, but are also contem-

poraneously present today. Each space has its own linguistic and cultural characteristics, its own chronotopic identity, and these in turn derive from associations
with emerging notions of consumption and social class. Shopping is not simply
a wandering through space, as one travels from one retail option to the next, but
traveling through time as well, moving from the street markets of the 1980s to
the luxury malls of tomorrow.

As the economy began to open up in the 1980s, households shifted from rely-
ing on their work units to private markets for food and consumer goods (Croll
2006; Veeck 2000). The first such markets to emerge were street markets and night
markets where farmers or vendors could sell their products directly to consumers, including everything from farm produce and prepared foods to clothing and
electronics. By the late 1980s, larger and more permanent markets became common, including vendor markets (*tanwei shichang*) where vendors rent stalls in
large indoor spaces selling all manner of consumer goods, and specialized markets gathering together vendors of similar products (such as seafood markets or
fruit markets). All of these types of market still exist today. Customers in both
the street markets and vendor markets typically haggle over prices, and much conversation consists of back-and-forth quoting of prices, justifications for the
quoted prices, and attempts to convince the other party to raise or lower theirs.
Government-owned department stores (*baihuo shangdian*) were also popular during the 1980s and 1990s because they offered a range of consumer goods for sale,
but all have now either closed or been privatized.

In the mid-1990s, three new types of retail space were built: large privately
owned shopping malls (*baihuo shangchang*) with many different stores and brands,
department stores (*gouwu zhongxin*) featuring a common retail space for a range
of consumer products, and full-scale supermarkets (*chaoshi*) that combine food
with other household goods, electronics, hardware, and so on. Many multistorey
supermarkets also host private retail spaces (including clothing brands or fast-
food outlets) on their entry levels. Prices are always posted on the shelves and are
nonnegotiable. Over time the size of these retail outlets and the number of foreign brands they offer have both increased.

The final and most recent retail category is the luxury mall, which began to
appear in the 2000s. These tend not to identify themselves by terms like "shopping center" or "mall," but indirectly by using unique names such as New World
(Xin Shijie) or Joy City (Dayue Cheng). New World opened in the early 2000s in
a busy downtown retail area, and promoted itself as a retail destination for foreign designer brands. In design, it closely resembles a department store, with a
single retail space partitioned into areas with various types of goods and brands
(jewelry, sportswear, footwear, etc.), but with foreign rather than domestic products. In contrast, Joy City, which opened in 2009, is much like a modern American

shopping mall—a series of branded outlets housed in a single building. Most of Joy City's stores are international outlets, and a large portion of these are luxury or designer labels.

As these shopping options emerged at different times over the past thirty years or so, they became linked to, and exemplify, shifting behavioral and linguistic norms. As one moves up the chain of different retail spaces, prices increase and become nonnegotiable, interactions between seller and buyer become more formal and routinized, and alphabetic letters gradually supplement, and then replace, Chinese characters in visual text such as brand names and promotional advertising (Pan 2010, 77–80). Street markets and vendor markets, for instance, rarely employ any language other than Chinese in their signage and advertising. Spoken language by both vendors and local customers tends to be heavily flavored with the local accent. Due to the merger of alveolar and retroflex consonants in Dongbeihua, these markets were the only shopping venues where I could be confused as to whether I was being quoted a price of four (*si*) or ten (*shi*) yuan; vendors often clarify the issue with common hand signs signifying numbers one through ten. In shopping malls, however, merchants usually incorporate an English brand or store name along with a Chinese one, and both staff and customers tend to speak standard Mandarin. Signage in luxury malls is predominantly in English, and employees frequently use English with anyone who appears to be foreign or returned from abroad. The types of free-flowing conversations with vendors over the price of goods give way to staccato formulaic speeches in department stores naming products and listing promotions. Employees using Dongbeihua here can have their pay cut or even be dismissed.

In terms of food, vendor markets typically have simple food courts or wandering food-sellers with a few different offerings such as noodles and rice bowls. Shopping malls more commonly have extensive food courts covering a single floor and offering a range of foods, including regional specialties from around China and local delicacies. Luxury malls usually have several floors of chain or high-end restaurants offering noodles, hotpot, Korean-style barbecue, and international foods like pizza.[5] Other perceptual differences are important in the experience of these different retail spaces. Vendor markets tend to be dark, busy, loud, and a bit run-down. Luxury malls are bright, quiet, and gleaming in their newness, but with fewer shoppers. Other venues exist somewhere in between these two extremes.

Although shoppers in luxury malls tend to be younger and wealthier, most of the people I visited these spaces with shopped at a range of different retail locations. On a warm summer day, a group of shoppers like Sophie and her Hong Ri colleagues might start at the Palace 66 luxury mall, visit the Happy Family shopping mall for lunch, browse the stalls at Shenyang Spring vendor market, and finally pick up groceries at a supermarket. The result is that individual speech practices shift in accordance with the retail space; haggling at a vendor market takes place in the local dialect, while asking to try on clothing in a shopping mall occurs in standard Mandarin, and exchanges of greetings in a luxury mall occur in English. While it might seem strange that young urbanites, the ones most likely to reject the legitimacy of Dongbeihua, use it in street markets and vendor markets, it helped establish them as locals, and thus mitigated the chances of them being cheated or quoted unfair prices. The success of haggling interactions, according to both shoppers and vendors I interviewed, was heavily dependent on use of Dongbeihua.

Like residential complexes, different shopping venues therefore exist in different relative space-times tied to the moment of their emergence within Shenyang's retail landscape. Both the genealogy and the aesthetic of these different retail options was well known to most people, who could shift their linguistic and behavioral practices with ease as they moved from one type of store to another (some of these are summarized in table 2.1). The exceptions of course are those people who, like rural villagers, find themselves excluded from higher-order spaces due to various forms of marginalization; they have neither the money nor the time to shop in more expensive retail venues. When I accompanied one acquaintance, an unmarried middle school teacher still living in a very small apartment with her parents, into the nearby luxury mall for the first time, she gazed around the brightly lit space in wonder. "*It's just like a dream*," she exclaimed to me, highlighting a perceived disconnect between her own spatiotemporal belonging and the modernist fantasy space of the luxury mall. The dream only becomes

TABLE 2.1 Chronotopic qualia in Chinese spatial practice

	PAST	PRESENT	FUTURE
Housing	Rural village Socialist era *xiaoqu*	Modern *xiaoqu*	Luxury *huayuan*
Shopping	Night market Street market Vendor market	Shopping malls/center Supermarket	Luxury mall
Language practices	Dongbeihua	Mandarin Chinese	English
Aesthetic qualities	Dark	→	Light
	Chaotic	→	Ordered/organized
	Loud	→	Quiet
	Dirty	→	Clean
	Local	→	Global
	Cheap	→	Expensive

reality for those with the financial, linguistic, and cultural resources to transcend local space-time.

Urban space in China is organized around a temporal logic that distinguishes between old, backward areas (old neighborhoods, old markets, old public parks) and modern, future-oriented ones (high-rise apartments, shopping malls, and technologically sophisticated public squares with laser light shows and massive video broadcast screens). Once, while I was out with a friend, he pointed to the Torch Building, a landmark office tower at the north end of Government Square. *"For a long time, that was the tallest building in Shenyang. Everybody knew it and you could see it from far away. But now look at it, it's so small!"* Indeed, the Torch Building is puny next to its more modern neighbors, which rise up to cast their own shadows over it. Its blue glass exterior, now stained and dull, also appears outmoded next to the gleaming white facades of nearby buildings.

Shenyang is always in a constant state of renewal, the landscape littered with monoliths enrobed in the green mesh that signals a building under construction. But as the mesh comes down and the bright newness of the building emerges, nearby areas begin their own transformations, marking this building that was once "new" as now "past." Thus the physical project of modernity in China is the continuous transformation of old spaces into new ones. Old buildings should be torn down, old neighborhoods and subdivisions swept away, and gleaming new apartment complexes and office towers should be built in their place. Disordered (and disorderly) space will be replaced with order; old neighborhoods described as chaotic and dirty will be transformed into clean and organized spaces, preferably enclosed by luxurious signifiers of the residents' status, such as opulent gates and gardens. In time, though, the bright colors will be slowly subdued by the constant dust that blankets the city. The sense of novelty will wane as other constructions arise that supersede each given style.

The logic of architectural enclosure in China, deriving from an imperial heritage that deployed it as a ritual technology for developing timeless synchronicity among the empire's far-flung territories, now marks the city as a vast landscape of temporally discontinuous spaces. Through everyday practices, choices, and interactions, urban residents define and ascribe membership in these spaces, and thus tie people to a spatiotemporal identity, a sense of where they belong within China's imagined geography. Lower-order membership is associated with both backwardness and a sense of limited social horizons, a confinement to the boundaries of the village or small city. Higher-order membership is perceived as both future-oriented and transcendent, in the sense that people understand themselves as belonging to a class of globally mobile and brand-savvy consumers who can move freely up and down the hierarchy of temporally defined spaces, a state that Aihwa Ong (1999) refers to as "flexible citizenship" (see also V. Fong 2011; X. Liu 1997).

But it is the way in which space, time, and language interact within the discursive formation of Chinese modernity that is of particular interest here. Language inhabits a spatiotemporal geography in Shenyang, with words and accents indexing each person's location within this environment both physically (where they are from) and temporally (how they are oriented in terms of being "ahead" or "behind" others). Modern languages belong in modern spaces, while antiquated ones belong in antiquated spaces. Thus, Dongbeihua is properly thought to be a language spoken in the countryside, or by the poor and elderly residents of Shenyang's older neighborhoods. For those who can speak standard Mandarin, Dongbeihua belongs in private domestic spaces, signifying close social relations among family. English, in contrast, is a language expressed, both verbally and graphically, in popular shopping districts and corporate enterprises. One of the ways of transcending limitations of time and space, the feeling of being stuck or left behind in the continual march of technological progress and economic development, is to transform oneself linguistically—after all, if one's identity as a rural peasant is indexed by one's accent and words, the way to move beyond that is to speak like an urban resident. And likewise, if one wants to transcend the limitations of Chinese urban space and become a global social actor, free to move about the world, one needs to be able to speak the languages that inhabit those spaces. In the next chapter, I show how personal stories often narrate self-transformation as both linguistic development and geographical movement from lower-order social spaces to higher-order ones.

BETTER TO DIE ABROAD THAN TO LIVE IN CHINA
Narratives of Life and Learning

Late in my fieldwork, Sophie left her job at Hong Ri and found work as an English instructor for a school preparing students to take the foreign-based Graduate Management Admission Test (GMAT) for study abroad. She invited me to meet the headmaster, her new boss, and visit the school, which was housed in a rented conference hall at a public library. I arrived to find about fifty desks arranged in front of a projection screen. Large red banners adorned the walls with inspiring slogans written in gold Chinese characters: "*Knowledge changes destiny, learning creates the future.*" "*Make half a year of hard work the last struggle of youth, in exchange will come a great turning point in your life.*" The students watched recorded video lessons by a professor from Beijing's Qinghua University, and then spent an hour with Sophie reviewing test questions.

After the class, we relaxed in the empty hall, eating tea eggs and talking about her new job. Sophie told me that all of the students were taking the GMAT in hopes of studying abroad, but she was not optimistic about their chances; very few of them were well prepared. I asked Sophie if she planned to study abroad, but she sighed and said it was too late for her. She then offered the following explanation:

> Before, China is like have no water. We're walking in the desert, and there's no water. But, look, over there. There's a pool of water. It's cold. We want to drink it. We walk there to go to the pool. *That was my parents' generation.* Now [*xianzai*], we can see the pool, and we are still walking, but we can't get there. We can smell the—the sweet perfume, but it

will take several years for us to get there and to drink it. Then, it will be our children's turn. They are the ones who can drink the water and play in the water.

Sophie's description of China's modernization as analogous to wandering through the desert in search of water mixes a complex interplay between broad social and economic forces (the "sweet perfume" that marks China's ascent as a developing country) and self-reflection on her own role in relation to them (the delayed satisfaction of her "thirst"). If Chinese citizens are really, at this moment, striving in the desert, they are also asking themselves if the direction they are taking with their lives is the best one, whether they are being "left behind" in the race to this fabled oasis, and what meaning their journey should take if only their child will be able to take advantage of it.

Although the desire for English in China is often assumed to derive from overwhelmingly economic imperatives, the stories people tell about their acquisition of the language and how it is entangled in their lives, struggles, and aspirations complicates this picture. English is more commonly situated within social discourses of "modernity" or "development" that integrate individual and nation, the personal with the political (Gu 2009). Foreign language acquisition is understood within an encompassing social, moral, civilizational, and even libidinal approach to future temporalities. A middle-schooler named Alice once approached me during a class break and shyly handed over a two-page letter in handwritten English (which I reproduce here including her layout, corrections, and spelling):

Mr. Henry,

How time flies! Half a month has ~~pasted~~ passed already, we ~~have~~ had a good collaboration, didn't it? Thanks to the god to give us such a wonderful chance to know each other! During these days, I have realized much argument and learned much knowledge! From you, I know that: Life should be filled with happiness and cheerness we should treasure time what we own, treasure everything around us.

A celebrity has ever said: "In fact, the world doesn't lack beauty, but lacks the eyes, which ~~we~~ seek beauty" . . . A problem has puzzled me for many years:—What's the purpose of living in the world?—position?—fame and wealth?—close relatives?—sincere friends?—apprance?—knowledge—ability? I think, you can't lack any of them, but you can't really have whole of them: Maybe I have missed many things I should grasp but, time can't return I should have self-confidence to stand in a new starting line.

An idle youth. A needy age. I will study sturdily ~~in~~. After all, better late than never → Beat down the hardness! (Act over the difficulties).

Do you love the pop-star I found in his ~~do~~ body there is energy can't be used ~~over~~ up. I believe that is contribution; devote oneself ~~for~~ to the whole world, for human! . . .

Alice's letter interests me on several levels: It highlights many of the stylistic conventions of Chinese written English in that it draws on a broad and occasionally idiosyncratic range of lexical resources in its expression. It shows an extensive level of care and revision, both in the flowing cursive handwriting and in multiple edits. And it very carefully positions Alice as an individual social actor within the overall framework of China's development. Note for instance the narrative configuration of her own epistemological stances and transformations in relation to society at large. Alice poses a question that has troubled her "for many years," namely, her purpose in the world. She lists a number of possibilities but concludes that one can neither fulfill all of them nor lack any of them. In the meantime, the world has passed her by ("Maybe I have missed many things I should grasp"), but she commits to standing "in a new starting line." Alice juxtaposes her past ("an idle youth") with the demands of the present and effectively commits herself to working within existing social structures to achieve her success ("I will study sturdily"). That these narrative insights were delivered by a fourteen-year-old girl also highlights their widespread embedding in the discourses of education and development in China.

Stories matter, and two things should become clear from those presented here by Sophie and Alice. First, overarching social transformations are neither monolithic nor divorced from human agency. They are instead representations of events that circulate throughout speech communities in accord with a broader political economy favoring some interpretations over others. As the Chinese cultural theorist Sun Wanning notes, commonsense understandings of inequality in China "require a consistent process of naturalization, whereby certain kinds of statements about 'poverty,' 'income disparities' and 'disadvantaged communities' are repeatedly and regularly made in the guise of depoliticized speech" (Sun 2013, 31). We may note here that both Sophie and Alice, no matter their reservations about the ultimate efficacy or immediacy of modernity, are still, as ethnically Han middle-class urban residents, situated as privileged social actors. Rural citizens or ethnic minorities typically find themselves barred from such participation. Second, individuals stand in relation to these stories not as coherent selves or unitary subjects merely observing events as they occur; rather, the events themselves are the chronotopic anchors on which selves are produced (Ochs and Capps 2001; Waldram 2012; Wortham 2000). As the historian He Ping (2002, 3) writes in the context of an early wave of modernizing discourses among Chinese intellectuals in the 1980s, "Modernity in a certain sense was a story that people told themselves about themselves in relation to others." Similarly, the stories people tell themselves today, stories about who they are, where they come from, and where they are headed, are shaped by understandings of contemporary social forces such as modernity, capitalism, development, and the temporal discontinuities they evoke.

As I interviewed more and more English students, teachers, and professionals, their descriptions of learning the language and what it meant to them seemed to form a kind of narrative template. This is not to say that each story was identical, or even that each story followed the template in its entirety. Taken together, though, the stories reveal a common plot structure beginning with descriptions of the self in childhood as naïve and lacking in comprehension, followed by a growing awareness, openness, and sense of personal growth and transformation only fully realized when the teller had traveled abroad. Cheryl Mattingly (1994) argues that the need to make sense of disparate and random events leads to the imposition of a plot structure on lived experience that can be shared and discussed with others. This plot structure of English acquisition was framed against the backdrop of Shenyang as a chronotope, the temporally backward and spatially isolated city, which can be transcended through successful language acquisition. In this sense such narratives are similar to what Nancy Abelmann describes as "social mobility stories" in South Korea. "Unlike life histories, usually considered to be chronological accounts of people's lives, social mobility stories take up the particular problem of social origins and destinations . . . These social mobility stories are also examples of reflections—both of a private and a more public nature on the social fates of individuals—that are widespread during eras of rapid social transformation" (Abelmann 1997, 786–787). Indeed, similar narrative plots that entangle individuals with broader social transformations have been recounted in ethnographies from throughout Asia (H. Evans 2008; Hsu 2007; Nakano 2000; Osella and Osella 2006; Rofel 1999).

Chronotopic narratives rely on forms of deixis, words or phrases where the precise reference depends on context. Sometimes deixis is expressed in terms of space—"here" and "over there," for instance, in Davidson's (2007) analysis of East German terms for the former East and West territories of a now-united Germany—but more often in terms of time and the temporal indexing of verbal or adverbial tense (Perrino 2011). Sophie's parable is structured around a series of demonstrative adverbs, beginning with "before," followed by "now" and "then." These adverbs not only establish a temporal sequence to the narrative, deictically indexing past, present, and future, but also imply a chain of logical causality. Actions in the past have led to consequences in the present and conditions for the future. Entailments from previous actions are accompanied by a growing sense of awareness, confidence, agency, power, wisdom, wealth, and/or mobility. But just as temporally discontinuous spaces may be geographically contiguous, the narrative logic does not simply mark the passage of linear time. The narrative space is shared with other non–English speakers who have failed to effect these transformations—they are still mired in the past despite inhabiting the same temporal present. Depending on the nature of these autobiographical trajectories, sometimes the narratives culminate in the realization of transnational personae capable of transcending the limitations of the local social context; in others, though, a variety of obstacles such as age, class, gender, or lack of social connections halt narrative self-development in its tracks, leaving only failed potential or the determination to provide a better grounding for one's children to succeed in the same path.

The Folly of Youth and the Discovery of English

The nature of childhood has changed significantly in China's postsocialist era. The relative freedom and autonomy of previous generations of children have been replaced, under the one-child policy, by a stringently managed educational pathway intended to provide material success and security in the future (V. Fong 2004; F. Liu 2015). This has resulted in tremendous pressures on children in terms of schoolwork and testing, along with significant parental investment in all aspects of a child's life. Children today are often characterized as constrained, overworked, and enervated. The physical deprivations of the socialist past have given way to the mental deprivations of today, as children are corralled inside to study intensely and bear the full weight of familial responsibilities in the future. When I accompanied Jasmine to the park once with her family on Children's Day, a national holiday in China, we watched her four-year-old daughter run around chasing birds, with a popsicle in one hand. Jasmine admitted that there are not enough opportunities for such play. She characterized the lives of children today as pitiful (*kelian*) and bitter (*ku*). Later, she recounted the following for me in a brief period between classes:

> I remember when I was young, ahhhhh [satisfied sigh] I could finish my homework just in half an hour then I could go outside and played with my classmates. But now? In some primary schools, students have to do their homework until ten o'clock. Then, they need to wash up and go to bed quickly, and for the next morning they have to get up very early. And for some middle school students they usually go to bed at half past eleven, every day like that. They don't have the weekends, because on weekends they need to come here! In fact, sometimes I really think they are so poor.

But I can't persuade their parents. And something more important is, if I persuade them "don't come here" then I will lose my job!

Still, Jasmine made her daughter attend English classes at her school. Every teacher I met complained about the educational demands placed on young children, but none were willing to lessen the pressure on their own child. One of the rationales I repeatedly heard for moving abroad was, in fact, that children had less pressure in Western educational systems.

Discourses of childhood are as constitutive as any other of chronotopic modernity, shown by the juxtaposition between previous generations of children experiencing an essentially "timeless" childhood and today's hyper-accelerated educational barrage. What interested me in many of these discussions, though, is how English speakers positioned their own childhood, tending to highlight their inability to comprehend the weight of their own actions and responsibilities. As one woman put it, "*I didn't have any feeling because at that time I am very young, I am acting very naïve.*" When it came to making decisions about their study or their futures, they talked about themselves as not understanding (*bu dong*) and foolish (*sha*). Several parents I talked to attributed a similar sense of bewilderment to their own children, who, they said, did not understand how important education is and treated English more as a hobby than a serious subject of study. Children, both in memories of the past and in discourses of today, cannot comprehend the significance and importance of the decisions they face, which must instead be entrusted to parents. For those who can now speak English, childhood was a time before they started to learn the language and open their eyes to the outside world.

Ding Lu was a teacher at Hong Ri in her late twenties. Unmarried at the time, she was dating a much older divorced man who was relatively wealthy. Lu was not a highly proficient English speaker, but she was a talented writer and worked hard to cultivate an educated Mandarin accent, setting her apart from other teachers who sounded more local. When I asked her about how she first started learning English, she responded:

> When we were small, the conditions were not really ideal, so I didn't even encounter English until grade six. Our elementary school teachers didn't have any English, they just knew Chinese and math and a few other fields . . . but no English. So I really only started learning English from junior high school onwards. I remember very clearly, at the time our age—our age was younger than most, but in the first English lesson we only learned four words. And by the end of class, I didn't remember anything.

Not remembering the lesson frustrated Lu greatly because her parents and teachers all considered her a very bright child. But she discovered that none of her classmates could remember the lesson either; none had studied English before, and all were befuddled by the idea of a new language.

Lu described in great detail her first English teacher, a woman whom she characterized as patient yet also strict and demanding. It was because of her discipline that, by the end of junior high school, all of the students could recite any textbook lesson from memory. *"She could call a name, 'Lu!' and I would stand up and recite that short dialogue. If it was a two-person dialogue, my deskmate and I would cooperate together. Because of that requirement, the foundation of our English was very good even if we had started late."* At first, her teacher gave the students tests every week, and then later every day. Sometimes she tested their oral English, sometimes their written English. When Lu's class participated in an English competition, a third of them made it to the citywide finals.

After junior high school, however, Lu's family could only afford to send her to an average high school. She began to struggle with English, as the teachers knew very little and were unable to explain the complex grammatical rules. Her other grades suffered too, and Lu had to settle for a second-tier city university. She majored in foreign trade, but explained to me that it was not her decision. *"My father made me choose this major . . . He told me that if I only study a language, the scope of its practicality is very small. There is more opportunity in economics."* Although she hated economics and math, the program also had a significant English component at which she excelled. At this point in the narrative, Lu returned to her junior high school English teacher and the lessons she had learned from her.

> *When I just started studying English, when I recall that first lesson, it was very hard. Four words that I couldn't remember . . . Maybe everyone needs a little time for fresh experiences to be understood. But I think this English environment [yingyu huanjing] is very important. At that time, my teacher didn't inspire a lot of interest, she didn't play games or anything like that in class . . . but I felt compelled to work hard. At first I felt compelled, but later I gradually got closer to that teacher's point of view.*

These types of teacher-centered narratives were quite common. Through them, English speakers in China tended to highlight their own lack of control over their early study; learning English was something forced on them by their teachers and their parents. They did not understand why it was valuable or important, why it was necessary to their future. Such stories were also frequently rife with complaints about teachers who were too strict, who forced their students to complete staggering amounts of homework or embarrassed them for being unable to answer in class. But as Lu's narrative shows, this is often matched with a gradually increasing respect for the lessons being taught, not only about English itself and its value as a communicative resource but also about socially desirable character attributes and moral stances.

More examples of this particular genre of narrative can be found in the stories told to me by others. Winston, a charismatic university English teacher who was in the process of branching out into private instruction, told me that as a child he was very shy. Winston's father, a businessman, would bring him to meetings and introduce him to foreign clients, pushing him to speak English with them. "My first teacher," he added, "made me be the representative for the English class. So every morning I had to stand in the front and lead everybody to read. I think that really did something for my early confidence, you know?" When Winston started attending English competitions, prompted again by his parents' encouragement, he felt nervous every time he was on stage, but gradually began to find success. "I would go, and every time I finished the contest, I grew, like, a whole lot. And then my name got around, and people started to invite me to share experience and everything."

Jasmine also had a story about her own developing confidence in English:

> I remember one day, our teacher told us a story . . . it's about a policeman. Someone was killed, and our teacher wanted us to guess how that person was killed. I was curious about that, and I was interested in that kind of things, that is detective story. So I tried to think about, and suddenly I know the answer but the teacher only want us to say that in English, so I forced myself to say that, okay, in English. When we had the break time, I said that to my classmates in English, 'cause their English is better than mine. And they encouraged me, they said, "Okay Jasmine, later you can just tell teacher like this, it's very great." And after that, my teacher said, "Wow, you are so great, your answer is correct. Right, the person was killed like that." So after that, I just had confidence, step-by-step, then I could speak more. If I can practice more, of course, my English will be better and better.

Implicit in these narratives then is a sense in which the world of children is delimited by attributes such as foolishness, shyness, and naïveté. It is the introduction of particular teachers or the guiding hand of parents that steer children toward English and its developmental potential. At the beginning they may be forced to learn, but discover through it personal lessons of diligence and perseverance. Their personalities become more open (*kaifang*), their demeanor more confident (*you zixin*). English begins to engender possibility.

Constructing Viable Transnational Personae

Lao Kong English was a relatively new entrant into an already crowded language teaching marketplace, but brought with it a new approach to marketing their classes. They had no foreign teachers, and their advertising stressed instead that foreigners came to them for the educational expertise they offered. The school publishes a weekly newspaper featuring articles on their teachers lecturing in foreign countries, accompanied by stories of students living abroad, biographies of famous Western athletes, suggestions of food to order in French restaurants, and so forth. In the school's lobby were several displays showing photographs of life abroad, mixed with application checklists for various foreign worker visas. Dominating one poster was a picture of two of Lao Kong's teachers living in the United States, a man and woman posing in front of their large two-storey home. Under the title "*Lao Kong will send you to America as a teacher!*," the poster explained that the two teachers had completed their English coursework at Lao Kong and were now working abroad as agents of the school. Another panel included Chinese translations of American newspaper articles discussing teacher shortages. In effect, Lao Kong was promoting its school not on the premise of teaching language to students but on providing a pathway for students to travel and live abroad through language education. Many people I talked to understood their language study in a similar vein. If childhood stories of learning English recapitulated a sense of personal growth and expanding confidence, further language acquisition served to inculcate new transnational personae in comparison to less fortunate monolingual others.

The sense that English can create new forms of individual potential and self-transformation was illustrated for me by a discussion at a public English Corner—an unofficial and loosely organized public space dedicated to people wishing to speak English—one night in downtown Shenyang.[1] I was questioned by several Chinese about my goals in life. When I told them I mainly wanted to live comfortably, one woman compared me to the Daoist philosopher Laozi. A man then stepped forward, wearing a neat black jacket over a white shirt.

> I have a dream. You say you don't want a big car, or a big apartment, but I already have a big apartment. My dream though is to be rich. I have been the same dream since I was young, I want to have a lot of money. Now I have a business, I am learning English to be successful, because today you need speak English if you want to be successful. My goal is to have one million yuan by the time I am 40. Now I am 29, so I have some time.

Several people agreed with the man, saying it was impossible to be Laozi in today's China. "It is too difficult to be comfortable," said one young university student.

"Being comfortable in China is not satisfying. You must always be striving for something." The explicit rejection of more traditional modes of social being was tied here to language acquisition, and as such creates a discontinuity between those who can speak English and those who cannot. To realize one's dreams, knowing a foreign language is deemed a necessity.

Language was not the only conduit for foreign cultural patterns; for many, foreign teachers acted as potential role models who could demonstrate forms of transnational subjectivity. As Li Kui, a high school student living in my apartment complex told me one day, "*The advantage of foreign teachers, the best part, is openness [kaifang] and fun [haowanr], these two things.*" Chinese teachers, he said, were too narrow-minded. The twinned values of openness and fun were often considered inseparable from English itself; people who spoke the language saw these attributes in themselves. Winston had the following to say about his first foreign teacher: "There was one guy, and this guy was a rock 'n' roller, he was a drummer. So I remember I would just go with him to buy CDs and we would go have coffee at McDonald's. And then being with him really changed my whole idea of learning English. I mean, speaking cannot really be learned from a textbook. You got to learn it from, like, movies and music and real life." Other forms of English media could also prompt cross-linguistic reflections. Fanny contrasted Chinese and foreign English textbooks, for instance. Chinese books tended to be, in her words, "*systematic and theoretical,*" while the foreign ones were relatively simple: they had less text and more pictures, activities, and exercises. "*Moreover, I think the things you study in China are never going to be useful. I studied a lot of English in China, but whenever I met a foreigner I still didn't know what to say. Foreign teaching materials are like, I need a sentence I use a sentence. In China, I want to teach you this, but in foreign countries, I want to teach you how to use it.*" Fanny valued foreign pedagogies and teaching materials very highly for these reasons, even if (as I will discuss in chapter 6) she did not always have great confidence in the foreign teachers themselves.

Lu described for me how her home was filled with English books, including dictionaries, novels, and magazines. She had published several essays in Chinese literary magazines and commented on the different styles of the works. "*Before, most of what I read was books and essays written by Chinese, and I thought in a very Chinese style. Then, I read some English books, and a lot were more profound than the Chinese authors.*" They were simpler, less verbose, and more direct. This new style of thinking and English composition, she argued, had made her a better writer of Chinese. Being bilingual, she told me, was like being two different people. "*Originally, I thought I was very happy that I can do something others cannot do, because I can talk to foreigners, despite the fact that sometimes I am a little nervous . . . This feeling of being two people, I'm not saying I feel like a British person,*" *but I'm saying if you can speak another language, you can understand that country's culture, their lives, and their customs a lot better. It's like, even though I've never lived in a foreign country, through my knowledge I can comprehend them.*" The idea that English expands not only one's opportunities but one's mind-set was common in these descriptions of language contact. Tiger, the Washington English manager, promised students they would develop a "two-version CPU" (central processing unit in computing) by learning English, "one version Chinese, one version English." Such transformational language was very attractive to English speakers. Selena, a graduate student in English literature at a local university, told me that studying English had made her into a more confident person. "I dare to compete and to struggle for it. I think that is the unique experience that I have." Similarly, Wan Jianhu, a vocational school English teacher, claimed that English gave her unique insights and abilities. "I have the language ability, I can feel the language, I can feel the meaning of the language . . . sometimes I can feel the meaning between the words." This sense of a deeper meaning to English and its transformative potential were common topics in discussions I had with English speakers. The language takes on the role of catalyst in bringing such desirable personal qualities into being.

Deriding the Local: Environment, Population, and Quality

Despite the potentialities of English, many Shenyangers are confronted with a sense of isolation from the broader world. At dinner one night with a diverse group of Chinese friends, conversation turned to the quality of life in foreign countries. Several of our group had been outside China and talked about the scenery, the shopping, dealing with foreign people, and other aspects of their experience. One woman at our table grew increasingly agitated over the course of the conversation, tapping her chopsticks loudly in her bowl and sucking in sharp breaths of air at each mention of the different cities people had lived. "*When I hear about these kinds of experiences,*" she broke in, "*I just want to go abroad. I hate this little place. Really, it's better to die abroad than to live in China.*"

That "*little place*" is, of course, a city of eight million people. But her description highlights the perceived limited social and chronotopic horizons of Shenyang in contrast to idealized, even paradisiacal, representations of foreign countries as wonderlands of possibility (V. Fong 2011). Another frequent shorthand for this perspective was the saying "*The foreign moon is fuller than China's*" (*Waiguo de yueliang bi zhongguo de yuan*). Dylan quoted this to me while telling me about the saga of the English school he tried to open with one of his friends. After its failure, he told me he was thinking of immigrating to England. I asked him why he wanted to go there. He responded: *"In this place there are no opportunities for development. And besides, the environment is so bad. The foreign moon really is fuller than China's. If I go, I won't come back. There's just nothing I can do here."* Life abroad really would be better than having to struggle all the time, he concluded. We walked a little further and discussed how he might apply to a foreign university. Even that, he argued, would be difficult. *"Look, now my English has gotten worse. Before, I could recognize ten or twenty thousand words. I was that good! But now? When I look at a book and I see a word,* 'Hey, you look familiar, but what are you? What does this word mean?'" Dylan felt trapped in Shenyang.

Juxtaposed to idyllic representations of life abroad, attitudes toward Shenyang as a natural, social, and economic environment were relatively gloomy. Talk often turned to the negative characteristics of Shenyang. The people are bad-tempered and of low quality. The city is dirty, congested, and backward. In winter, the temperature drops well into the double digits below freezing, leaving its citizens cold and cranky. The coal-burning power and heating plants leave a fine soot over everything and everyone. In summer, the city bakes under cloudless skies and relentless heat, parching the ground and drying rivers to a thin trickle. Torrential rains in the spring and dust storms in the fall round out the extreme conditions. Shenyang's economic foundation on heavy industry during the Maoist era, and rationalization policies that have closed factories and reduced the manufacturing workforce in the reform era, have created a rust-belt economy of limited opportunity. In short, Shenyang is a place to get out of, and many people talked of friends or relatives who had successfully relocated to major cities such as Beijing or Shenzhen, or managed to go abroad.

I met Huang Gufeng, an art teacher, randomly in a park one day just behind a large commercial shopping building. He saw my notebook and asked if I was drawing. Our conversation eventually turned to life in Shenyang, and Gufeng scowled with disgust. *"It's so dirty here. Look at the sky. Ten years ago, there were one hundred and fifty days of clear blue sky that year. Now how many? You guess. This year, this year, there were only three or four days of clear blue sky. Now, think about this, if you ask a child,* 'What color is the sky?,' *do you know what they say? They say* 'White!'" More coal for heat in winter, more cars driving on the road, more people, especially rural migrants, trying to squeeze into limited urban space. Gufeng argued that this flawed natural environment was the source of the people's shortcomings. He pointed out that foreigners look down on Chinese because they regularly spit on the ground—even the government tried to curb the practice during the SARS outbreak in 2003, he said.[2] *"But with all of the air pollution, what choice do people have?"* And to control pollution, the government closed down many factories, but this has led to situation of massive unemployment, with many households forced to sell their belongings on street corners to make ends meet.

Migrants to Shenyang were likewise almost always critical of the city and its people. Wan Jianhu grew up in a rural village and came to Shenyang after attending a teacher's college in a small provincial town. She recalled for me how, at college, she used to wander with her friends in the evening, locked arm in arm, enjoying the trees and grass around campus as they chatted about their lives. "But here, I can't find a place to have a walk. I don't think the—that the air is good, not clear, there are some noise, so I don't enjoy." When she first came to Shenyang, the behavior of people shocked her too. Growing up in her village, she told me, everyone was polite and concerned for each other's welfare. They would call out to each other, "*Where are you going?*" and "*Have you eaten?*" But people do not care for each other in the same way in Shenyang, she claimed. "If I show my polite, they will feel—they will feel a little bit strange, so, mmm, so I think now I have become a little impolite too sometime."

Charles once picked me up in his car, a luxury sedan with leather seats and tinted windows, to drive me out to his school for a visit. At thirty years old, Charles was a dynamic and engaging foreign language educator. He studied abroad in Malaysia for five years, worked as a businessman there, and eventually returned to Shenyang to open an English school with an old classmate. As we idled in traffic, the crisp air-conditioning completely distancing us from the noise and heat outside, he began listing off the disadvantages of life in Shenyang. First was the troubled economy and the low incomes of most workers. He estimated that for a household to obtain all its basic necessities would require at least 10,000 yuan a month. "But the question is how many people, how many percent of population in Shenyang can actually earn more than 10,000 yuan a month? Maybe like 5 percent, maybe 5 percent I think is quite reasonable amount. So, how do others live?" Next was the environment. Everyone wants to protect the environment, to reduce pollution, he said, but nobody wants to be the first to make a change. Charles included himself here, saying, "Even I don't want to make the change." So Shenyangers keep driving in their cars, throwing garbage on the street, and letting their air conditioners run. The government promises to find solutions, he told me, but they cannot solve the Chinese way of thinking. If twenty families living in one city block decide to collectively stop driving and protect the environment, then others might follow, but less than that and nothing will ever change.

As Charles ticked the problems off on his fingers he also identified the city's overheated housing market, the price of food, political inaction, and traffic. And then finally, he came to education and the fact that attending a good school is now entirely dependent on income and social connections. Schools that are "good"—which people define as producing students who score well on tests—are very selective in what students they take. They can charge parents whatever they want and set whatever standards they choose.

> So when they really want to enter this kind of school they have to pay a huge amount of money, so the school, the good school can get this money. That's why they still want to keep their reputations, to absorb more rich people to pay the money to their school, so that they can get more to spend. So it's became a circle, it's become a strange circle, a bad circle . . . And all the teacher, all the best teacher, will like to come to the school, because their pay is higher. So they got more good teachers, and they got more good students, and more good students they pay more money and they can hire more, even more good teachers.

Charles once again identified himself as part of this problem, since the reason his English school was successful was because children needed to take his classes in order to gain access to good schools. Yet, he asked, what could he do? If he did not make money from the students, another school would. It was the system, he argued, that was to blame, one that created a tiered structure of education. "We shouldn't divide people into different levels, especially in education, especially for students, right?"

These problems with education were symptoms of a much wider defect, Charles argued, rooted in intractable cultural practices and low personal quality.

> China is always a money-can-do-things society. So compared, even compared to Hong Kong, let's say you go to Hong Kong you say, "My son's examinations grade is not very good, so can he go to—he should go to a level-C school but can I pay some money to make my kids go to level-B school?" In Hong Kong is like not possible. No one's ever heard it before . . . But here? It will be like, "Oh, you want to go to that school? No problem. I'll check the connection with people and I'll check the price for you. After that I'll tell you, and then I will introduce you to meet, and then you can just make the deal." It's like happen to everyone, everyone knows it. So, it's like a whole society's freakish thinking way.

As we will see in the next chapter, Charles had much more to say about the Chinese art of social connections (*guanxi*) and the burdens it places on honest people. But I quote him at length here because he expresses so cogently the complaints most urban residents had about Shenyang and its people. Practically everyone agreed that, even if it was getting better in material terms (taller buildings, more shops and services, more money), Shenyang was still a bad place to live. Most agreed that life would be better somewhere else, perhaps in the nearby coastal city of Dalian, or a well-connected metropolitan city like Beijing, or abroad where the moon is fuller. The very dissatisfactions with life in the here and now informed the greater fantasies of what English could provide, a way beyond the limitations of daily life in a city so many looked down on.

On a few occasions, I interviewed Shenyang residents who had returned from other cities or countries, and some of their descriptions were tinged with sentimentality. One night over a few beers, Darren, the local Shenyanger who had worked in southern China for several years before returning home, told me about some of the nostalgia he experienced being away for so long. "Man, I love Shenyang. I was down south like two, three years and I missed it all the time. My family, you know, my friends, they're all here. But it's a dirty place. If I'm not from Shenyang, I won't like it here at all." It was, he admitted, a tough city to love.

A Life to Be Envied

The movement from China to another country is a crossing of the threshold in the ritual sense. It is transformative: whether they wish to be or not, those who return after time spent abroad are treated as different types of people. Numerous times during my stay in Shenyang, people would ask me what living abroad would do to them. Would they come back speaking English fluently? Would they learn to rely on Western foods like bread and cheese rather than rice and noodles? Would it change their ideas or points of view? I struggled to answer such questions, but many of those Shenyangers who had lived abroad constructed narratives for their more isolated peers about the changes that had occurred and how they were affected. Living abroad was a powerful source of symbolic capital for those who had returned to Shenyang, and their tales, both positive and negative, commanded attention from others.

One prominent area of discussion was food. Ideas of Western food in Shenyang are highly developed, but often based on assumptions deriving from domestic marketing campaigns rather than firsthand knowledge: Shenyangers assumed I ate hamburgers and pizza every day. People in Shenyang eat Western food a lot, but most of it comes from international fast-food chains or restaurants that serve local versions of Western food like fried chicken or pastries. Like others who have studied this topic (Hsu 2005; Y. Yan 2009), I found that many Chinese, especially adults, found Western food unpalatable. The flavors and textures were unfamiliar and off-putting, compounded by the difficulties Western restaurants had in obtaining fresh ingredients like cheese and bread. When an American student attending a local university revealed his plan to open a high-end coffee shop in Shenyang, several of his Chinese classmates scoffed. He intended to focus on premium ingredients while opening just a hole-in-the-wall storefront on a busy pedestrian street. The Chinese students countered that nobody in Shenyang actually likes drinking coffee—the taste is too bitter—but everyone likes the idea of other people watching them drink coffee. His business would not survive, they told me, without a large retail space and wide windows where customers could sit and be observed.

Food was therefore a topic of intense interest, particularly discussions of what Chinese eat abroad. Not only eating Western food but knowing about Western food practices could be an important source of distinction. When Jasmine married her longtime boyfriend, for instance, one of the guests at our table, a cousin of the groom, arrived dressed in a well-tailored black pantsuit. As each dish of food arrived, she quizzed the staff on its contents. *"Is there meat in this dish? What kind of meat is it? What about the sauce?"* She explained as she ate that she was vegetarian, a practice she had discovered while living abroad in Australia. Jasmine later laughed when she heard about this, saying that vegetarianism was just an affectation to let others know about her time abroad.

Mr. Lin, a businessman who traveled frequently, told me over dinner with friends one night how he rarely enjoyed dining out in the United States. He complained that the restaurants there are badly lit and too quiet. Mr. Lin then hunched his shoulders and lowered his face to his plate. *"Everyone eats like this. Everyone has their own plate and talks quietly. It's not much fun. And what if I want to try something you're eating? No, no, that's your food, I can't take it. I go to the restaurant and I buy a steak, because that's what everyone eats. It's this big, you know."* Mr. Lin cupped his hands together to illustrate the small size of the steak. *"One hundred dollars! For a little thing like that. And it's still raw inside, so I ask them to cut it open, you know,* butterfly, *and cook it again."*

Mr. Lin's complaints about Western food should not be taken as a simple critique of either the West or Western culture but situated within the broader discourses around foreigners and foreignness that circulate regularly in Shenyang. Foreigners are quintessential strangers who represent what is perceived to be the already accomplished modernity of Western countries (Henry 2013a). Talking about Western cultural practices such as food positions Shenyangers as either knowing insiders who possess knowledge and mastery of those practices or globally isolated outsiders who do not. Shenyangers like Dylan, who dreamed of going abroad but lacked the ability to do so, lived the West vicariously through their consumption choices, dining in Western restaurants and outfitting themselves in Western clothing brands. All of these consumer choices were made at a distance, as it were, inspired by an emulation of life abroad that could only be authoritatively discussed by those who had actually experienced it firsthand. Mr. Lin could feel free to complain about the food because he actually had the opportunity to live abroad and eat it.

The authoritative knowledge of Western cultural practice was commonly assumed to extend to English-language and foreign-language acquisition strategies. Recall, for instance, Tiger's exhortation to the Washington English students I recounted in chapter 1 to be willing to lose face—he implied that by living abroad he had lost his own attachment to face. One of Winston's stories echoed a similar feeling of alienation from Chinese culture where he talked about English phrasings entering his Chinese speech.

> I remember two years after my graduation I was speaking English too much, so my Chinese began to sound weird. There was a, like a classmates reunion, and I was the monitor of the class. So a girl in my class said, "Hey, we're getting together, you got to come because we don't have lots of boys." I say, "Okay." Then, while I was flipping down my phone, she said, "Are you going to make it?" and I said in Chinese, "*Wo hui nuli de.*" It sounds like, pretty retarded, you know. You know, *wo hui nuli de* can mean something like, "I will try hard." I was in the English thinking, but I just blurted that out in Chinese. It sounded very weird.

There was no sense from Winston that this Englishization of his Chinese language was somehow deficient or regretful; in fact, it was a story he sometimes used in class to illustrate to students just how going abroad would change them. Charlotte, the assistant manager of an English school, related to me some of the information she frequently shared with her students. "I've been Trafalgar Square. They've never been to Trafalgar Square. For them, Trafalgar Square is just a weird sound. It's just tra-fal-gar. No meaning! Tra-fal-gar. They know nothing but the sound. They know nothing about the history of the square, and I was there. I was really looking to tell them why they should visit, 'cause Trafalgar Square is like Tiananmen Square in China. And then they know more." Charlotte would often show pictures of the places she had visited to her English classes: the Tower of London and St. Paul's Cathedral, Times Square and Central Park in New York, the White House. These strategies served not only to connect her to foreign landscapes but to imbue her with tremendous respect garnered through her presence in those landscapes. In the times I did observe her classes, she never told the students that she could travel abroad easily because her father ran a successful export business and lived in the United States. But these stories put the possibility that many of the students attending those classes might be able to do so through the medium of language study within tantalizing reach.

Taken together, all of the stories I have related in this chapter construct an idea of language fluency and cultural accommodation through life abroad as a welcome form of personal growth and transformation. They distinguish Shenyangers who have experienced the roundness of the foreign moon firsthand from those who can only appreciate it from a distance. And through the overall narrative structure, in which foolish children gradually learn maturity and openness through language, while distancing themselves from Shenyang's limited environs, the transformation of a self rooted in foreign experience describes a life for others to envy.

But for those who have not been abroad, who feel trapped within the boundaries of an undesirable city, either through age or lack of opportunity or language ability, these narratives are fraught with anxieties about personal development and individual potential. As Sophie described at the beginning of this chapter, the oasis of modernity is still a far way off for those walking in the desert. Their stories may follow the structure I have outlined here, but reach a moment in which they can go no further, where change becomes ossified and people must resign themselves to the limits of their own lives. As Wan Jianhu said in finishing one of our interviews, "I can't remember before I learned English, what I thought about. Maybe I thought about settle down in one place and to live with husband and a kid, but after I learn English I think it's good to live in different countries or cities to have more experience. Because life is so short. You should try more. But now I can't." Instead, she taught English to others and tried to convey similar aspirations to her students.

The massive transformations within China as a nation are experienced by its citizens not as monumental exteriorized forces but in very personal ways. They affect everything from the most intimate and private social relations, including love and family life, to choices individuals make about their life course, their careers and aspirations. But people also see themselves as oriented toward these changes in multiply contingent manners, sometimes as active participants, sometimes as passive subjects. A close examination of how Chinese narrate their biographies and projected futures reveals deliberate attempts to locate themselves at the forefront of these ongoing national projects. Discussions of foreign languages and linguistic abilities accompany these personal changes, sometimes even acting to drive them forward. Here I have focused on the role English plays in these narratives, how language becomes part of a life trajectory dedicated to transcending and surmounting life in Shenyang and joining a more global order of social belonging in the shadow of China's own emerging modernity. Embedding discussions of language within such narratives also does the crucial discursive work of enregistering certain linguistic varieties with chronotopic value.

4

COMMODIFYING LANGUAGE
The Business of English in Shenyang

Foreign language study in Shenyang is suffused with numbers: books are entitled *100 English Idioms* or *200 Common English Verbs*, and courses are marketed on the basis of how many new words students will learn. People commonly use vocabulary estimates as stand-ins for measures of fluency, claiming to know one thousand, two thousand, or five thousand English words. I was asked several times by language students how many words they would need to learn before they would "know" English. Why this numerical obsession, bordering as it does on a kind of linguistic fetish? What does measuring language by words mean for teachers and learners, and for how foreign languages are consumed?

The answers to these questions can, I believe, be provided by a detailed look at the commerce of foreign languages in contemporary Shenyang. In 2013, the average Shenyang household had 29,074 yuan in disposable income (Shenyang Municipal Bureau of Statistics 2014). Annual tuition for an average English language school for a child is about 7,500 yuan, and this does not include special classes during the winter and summer school breaks, textbooks, dictionaries, and other educational materials. Obviously, then, with limited financial resources, a household must judiciously plan how to allocate its money toward a child's English education, and one of the key issues is that of comparability. Without detailed linguistic or educational knowledge themselves, how can students or parents compare two English classes? Or the advantages of taking a class versus reading an English book? Certainly one could look to price, but with limited ability to evaluate the authenticity or efficacy of the teacher, the pedagogy, or the accuracy of the language being taught, how can one know which is more effective or which is a better value?

The number of words that a class will teach or that a person will learn to speak allows an illusion of comparability across many different options, including books, software, tutors, and various types of English classes. English language schools, which are for the most part private businesses, latch onto such ways of objectifying their product and creating this sense of a better value. It is far easier and far more tangible to advertise a class as granting a student knowledge of a discrete number of words than it is to traffic in vague descriptors of fluency (although, as I will argue in chapter 6, this can still be accomplished through a complex semiotics of racialized imagery in advertising). In the context of Shenyang's linguistic educational marketplace, the word is not simply a unit of meaning within the densely interlocking system of values that is language, but a thoroughly commodified unit of measure through which students and parents can compare various educational options as forms of a product to be consumed by the learner as customer. This pervasive enumeration in turn leads to an understanding of language as composed of easily segmentable units of knowledge that can be accumulated, bit by bit, into spoken or written fluency.

However, the significance of counting words as units of measurement goes far beyond the immediate context of comparing language classes; it taps into new conceptualizations of language itself and its embedding in contemporary forms of neoliberal capitalism. Consider how the process of acquiring fluency in English has changed in the past forty years. Many of my older informants started learning English shortly after the beginning of the reform period of the early 1980s. At that time, there were no English schools or private classes, and opportunities to learn English outside of the public school curriculum were rare. Even there, limited classroom materials were available, and most of those were more deeply concerned with socialist orthodoxy (teaching the speeches of Mao Zedong in English, for instance) than pedagogical effectiveness. Bolton (2003, 248–249) provides a reprint of an English primer from 1960, for instance: below a drawing of Chinese children ripping apart a tiger, the English lesson reads, "Paper tiger, paper tiger. U.S. Imperialism is a paper tiger. We are not afraid of it. Look! We crush it at one blow!" (see also Adamson and Morris 1997). Many older informants' initial lessons came from listening to the BBC or Voice of America on the radio, trying to sound out the words and follow along. They bought English-language newspapers and magazines (but written by Chinese authors for a Chinese audience) and translated them, or studied publicly accessible textbooks and phonetic guides. Like others at the time interested in pursuits such as Chinese art or calligraphy, these learners were essentially hobbyists, cobbling together their language skills from a range of sources and materials.

In comparison, the educational environment today is one of professionalized, technologized, and commercialized acquisition. The foreign language industry in contemporary China is increasingly structured around very particular ideologies about what language is and how it may be acquired; the hobbyist has been replaced by the consumer, one who purchases acquisition within a marketplace of available commodities rather than leisurely assembling it at home. As Mary Crabb describes it, China's new educational environment is one in which "education and educational credentials have become market-supplied commodities, parents discerning consumers/investors in a burgeoning transnational educational marketplace and children determining figures in the realization of a cosmopolitan, middle-class Chinese modernity" (2010, 387; see also F. Liu 2015; Pérez-Milans 2013). Language accrues a certain materiality, what Michael Silverstein presciently calls its "thinginess" in saying that "linguistic forms and their deployability-in-context can take on the characteristics of sometimes alienable, sometimes inalienable possessions and their personally-controlled display or even bestowal" (1996, 290–291; see also Keane 2003). In other words, the simplistic objectification of the English language into an enumerated collection of words in China is a symptom of a larger political economy in which neoliberal systems of education reduce language to a commodity.

Since Bourdieu (1977) first described the competition among different varieties of a language as a linguistic marketplace, there has been a proliferation of research on the political economy of language (see Duchêne and Heller 2012; Gal 1988; Heller 2010; Irvine 1989; Jaffe 1999; J. Park and Wee 2012). In essence, what Bourdieu originally proposed was a rejoinder to Ferdinand de Saussure's notion of language as the product of a "collective mind," like "a storehouse filled by the members of a given community through their active use of speaking" (Saussure 1959, 13). Rather, as the Russian linguist V. N. Volosinov (1986) retorted, an utterance is more like an individual speaker borrowing from the stock in that warehouse and offering it in an exchange relationship with other speakers. Each act of speech is thus a reflection of the social relationships that enmesh those individuals together: relationships of class, gender, inequality, ethnicity, and so forth. Saussure's storehouse metaphor is an ideological construct legitimating the homogeneity of a single official, standard, and national linguistic code against which all others are measured. "Utterances receive their value (and their sense) only in their relation to a market, characterized by a particular law of price formation. The value of the utterance depends on the relation of power that is concretely established between the speakers' linguistic competences, understood both as their capacity for production and as their capacity for appropriation and appreciation" (Bourdieu 1991, 67). Different forms of speech thus embody different forms of linguistic capital, and the inequality of various linguistic forms (such as the devaluation of Dongbeihua in comparison to Mandarin Chinese) is the product of the social inequalities among the groups of people iconically represented by those forms (Gal and Irvine 1995; Woolard 2008).

Until recently, however, such research has always proceeded on the assumption that these relations were really only analogous, that language was only acting "as if" it were a commodity and codes were only acting "as if" they were currencies. Several scholars have, rightly, critiqued research on the commodification of language for mistaking the metaphor (language acting like a commodity) for the real thing (language being commodity) and thus implicitly accepting a neoliberal logic of value that is divorced from human labor (McGill 2013b; Simpson and O'Regan 2018). That essential confusion may stem from the inherent immateriality of language in most discursive contexts—materiality (and thus commodification) is only the product of significant efforts by capitalists and markets to monetize language as a product (Cavanaugh and Shankar 2014). This is akin to other natural products such as water. Although water may have a price, it is not a commodity in most cases (such as when it pours out of a tap) because it has not entered into capitalist markets of exchange. And yet, water does sometimes enter into such markets when producers subject it to human labor power, as when water is harvested and bottled for consumption.

Recent work on the semiotics of branding and commodity production has sought to divorce commodity formulations both from their exclusive link to durable products and from decontextualized notions of value (Manning 2010; Shankar and Cavanaugh 2012). As Agha (2011) points out, to reduce the formulation of a commodity to its use at one particular time (such as at the moment of exchange), or to limit it to only certain forms of materiality, ignores the ways in which commodities are produced as complex interweavings of varying sign values that are invariably transformed over time (see also Appadurai 1986; Kockelman 2006; McGill 2013a). In this sense, speech practices are no less commodified than a car or a watch. But it is also clear that these sign values are not intrinsic to the commodity (as Marx also realized so long ago) but are the emergent product of interactions between producers and consumers, buyers and sellers. My point here is that, similarly, where language was once an inalienable component of ethnic or regional identity, in the new global marketplace language has become a marketable and measurable skill, a resource that needs to be marshaled, incubated, and deployed to match market-oriented communicative needs (Cameron 2000; Heller 2002, 2003; J. Park 2010, 2015; Rahman 2009; Silverstein 2003b). It has, in other words, been commodified at some scales, particularly in cases where profit motivations have stimulated new rounds of investment and marketization in language teaching as an industry.

Nevertheless, most current scholarly interest is still only devoted to *consumption*, by which I mean how individuals, communities, institutions, governments, and corporations assign social value to various forms of language. When schools reward students, or corporations reward workers who speak in a particular way (e.g., Heller 2001; J. Park 2013), we are witnessing how these institutions consume the language varieties (and by extension sociocultural identities) available in the marketplace. In this chapter I am mostly concerned with the *production* of language as a commodity, the means by which certain forms of language are imbued with social value through the practices of marketing them to consumers. Uses of the phrase "language production" are often synonymous with the act of speaking, but here I frame that term within a broader political-economic framework by looking at the business of educating speakers. In the scramble to develop Shenyang's foreign language marketplace, school owners developed innovative strategies to build and maintain their businesses, strategies that themselves were crucial in reconfiguring the nature of language itself from something that is learned to something that is sold. The commodity logic of English extends far beyond their reach through uptake into almost all aspects of foreign language use in China, from public schools to testing to corporate management of linguistic (human) resources. It is no longer a stretch to say that English speakers in China are manufactured in much the same way as the vast number of goods bound from Chinese factories to Western marketplaces.

Private English Training Centers

It is difficult to convey just how ubiquitous private English schools are in Shenyang. In 2013 I did a walking survey of businesses within a four-block area near my apartment, located just west of the city's main downtown train station. I counted three Mandarin-English bilingual kindergartens, four children's English schools, two adult English schools, and two "training schools" that offered English classes in addition to other subjects (see figures 4.1 and 4.2).

Two of the four children's schools and both adult schools were branch operations of larger companies. And these were just the publicly accessible businesses fronting onto the main streets; most residential complexes have one or two teachers offering classes in their homes or in rented apartments for local residents.[1] In 2010 I accompanied a friend interested in opening an English school to a marketing presentation by an industry insider who had invested in several schools around the city. He told us that there were five major companies operating multiple branch schools throughout the city, but also hundreds of other smaller schools. Mr. Bai, the owner of Washington English, also told me that there were over three hundred officially registered English schools in the city, but the total number of schools, including those that operated as surrogates to larger schools as well as those that did not bother to register, was likely around a thousand.

FIGURE 4.1. A midsized children's English school on a popular retail street in Shenyang

FIGURE 4.2. Other schools in the same neighborhood: a children's English school and a private school that teaches English in addition to other subjects. On the third floor is a Korean language school.

Many of these schools are highly profitable corporate entities, bolstered by foreign capital investment and extensive managerial expertise. Others are relatively simple businesses or partnerships operated by a few individuals out of rented spaces. To develop a picture of what these businesses look like, I describe two of the major schools I worked with below: Hong Ri and Washington English. Both schools were typical in that sense that, although they served different markets, the educational delivery, marketing, working conditions, and corporate strategies were very similar to those of their direct competitors. Hong Ri was almost exclusively focused on children's oral English, while Washington English offered diverse classes with a range of objectives, including children's English, business training, and foreign language exam preparation. Later in the chapter I discuss some of the smaller schools and the many obstacles their owners experienced in trying to make them successful. These sketches are intended to give a picture of what life within Shenyang's English language industry is like.

Hong Ri

Throughout the time of my research, one of the largest English schools in Shenyang was Hong Ri. The company's many branch schools cater mostly to children's oral English, although specialized adult classes are offered at a few locations.[2] The school advertises widely and is a company generally recognized by most Shenyangers, even those without school-age children. Hong Ri was opened in the late 1990s by four partners: three Chinese and one American. The American recruited and managed the overseas foreign teachers while two of the Chinese partners handled marketing and finances. The fourth partner was the son of the sitting provincial education minister, and his role was to facilitate their relations with the government. His connections allowed Hong Ri to circumvent many of the visa and foreign worker restrictions that other schools faced at the time. For many years the school held a competitive advantage in that it could easily hire foreign teachers while other schools could not, and offered textbooks that other schools could not gain access to. These features allowed Hong Ri to solidify its position as a premier language school in the city. Hong Ri strives to maintain a general appeal to middle-class families throughout the city, and so tuition is generally quite low: as of 2015 about 150–180 yuan per week.[3] These amounts are affordable to even modest households, although several parents told me that they pooled money with other family members so that one child could tutor his or her cousins later on. At its peak in the mid-2000s, Hong Ri had about twenty-two thousand students enrolled and over four hundred teachers. As a large school, Hong Ri tended to set the tuition rates of many competitors as well, who would try to undercut them by perhaps 10–20 yuan per month. The school remains tremendously profitable (although I was never made privy to exact numbers) despite increasing competition; all of the partners have made several trips abroad, drive their own luxury cars, and maintain residences in very upscale neighborhoods.

During evenings and on weekends, Hong Ri is a frenetic playground of activity. Despite being located in neighborhoods all across Shenyang, the layout of each branch school is remarkably similar. The front entrance is typically crowded with parents who often wait outside during the forty-five-minute classes, reading newspapers or chatting with others. At the first-floor front desk, reception staff deal with questions and complaints, sell textbooks, and ensure that children heading up to the second floor for their classes are all registered students. Upstairs are the classrooms (usually four to eight of them), along with washrooms, a teacher's office, the headmaster's office, and sometimes a kitchen or cleaning closet. The teacher's office is a crowded affair of desks pushed into odd corners, lockers against one wall, coats, books, and papers piled everywhere, and always the comings and goings of teachers and students. Each Chinese teacher usually has a desk for planning lessons, correcting homework, and engaging in one-on-one tutoring sessions with students. Foreign teachers have no assigned desks, but often share a central table or sit at whichever desk is currently unoccupied.

On one typical evening, I accompanied Daniel, an American who had been teaching at Hong Ri for eighteen months (and was thus one of the more experienced foreign teachers), as he worked at one of the busiest downtown branches. He was scheduled to teach Susan's class of twenty-four students that night, and five minutes before the beginning of class, she came to him with the textbook open in her hands. "You will be teaching the 'be doing' sentence, so things like 'What are you doing?' 'I am riding my bike.' 'I am reading a book.' Okay? See here in the book, there is some pictures and a conversation we can practice. Maybe later we can play a game with the children and then sing a song." Daniel looked over the lesson in the book and nodded a few times, asking a question about something the students had learned earlier. Foreign teachers generally have about fifteen classes that they rotate among. Chinese teachers usually teach between two and five classes. Each class meets three times a week and receives one and a half hours of Chinese-teacher instruction and forty-five minutes of foreign-teacher instruction, although this did not always occur in practice due to the perpetual shortage of foreign teachers.

New classes are formed when students enter the school around the age of four or five and are assigned a Chinese teacher who will follow them through until they finish the series of oral English textbooks, usually about four to five years later. Some will also continue with more academic textbooks tied to the middle school curriculum, but Hong Ri's focus is on young children. In each class, new students might be added, and some will inevitably drop out over the years. If a class becomes too small it is combined with another at an equivalent level. Chinese teachers are responsible for student retention—the headmaster can impose a fine of several hundred yuan on a Chinese teacher's salary if too many students leave.

When the time for class to begin arrived, I followed Daniel and Susan down the hallway and into her classroom. There were about twenty-four students inside who stood up when we entered. Susan surveyed the students for a moment and then announced that class was beginning, before nodding to Daniel and allowing the students to sit. "Hey there everybody. How are you tonight?" Daniel belted out to the class. There were smiles and laughter from a lot of the children as he ran up and down the aisles of desks saying hello and high-fiving students as he asked them various questions. Susan stood quietly at the front of the room, occasionally moving to verbally discipline a student or answer a question in Chinese. Daniel took a ball from his pocket and told the children that whoever caught the ball had to ask and then answer a question. Toss. "What's your name?" Toss. "My name is Bill." Toss. "Do you like singing songs?" Toss. "Yes, I do." Later, Daniel modeled the "be doing" sentence from the textbook, and Susan added some translation for the students. They played a game that involved students drawing pictures of new words they had learned on the chalkboard, and sang a song before ending the class.

Like most of the other Chinese teachers I worked with, Susan evinced a deep connection to her students and responsibility for their learning and success. While much of the commercial apparatus of the English school is depersonalized, in that it is dedicated to maintaining student numbers and profits, teachers like Susan often spoke of their emotional attachments and personal feelings for students as individuals. Because teachers do not circulate among classes, many have taught the same students for years. Susan could recount each student's history, their successes, failures, learning attitude, and family circumstances from memory. She took time each day before class to decorate her classroom and blackboard with colorful drawings and figures, made up new songs to sing with the students, and worked hard to cultivate positive relationships with their parents.

Overall, the emphasis at Hong Ri is on creating a fun and exciting environment for students, especially through interaction with foreign teachers who joke around and maintain a boisterous demeanor. Although there are nominal standards for student achievement, students were rarely held back from advancing to the next level. Chinese teachers are rewarded for keeping their students enrolled rather than for attaining standards of linguistic proficiency, a task they accomplish by forming strong emotional bonds to students and families. As I was told by Chinese teachers several times, "*if the students are happy, then the parents are happy,*" and will keep paying their tuition. The focus of the business is less on educating the student than on reproducing the structure of consumption that creates the demand for its services.

Washington English

If Hong Ri is a mainstream school for ordinary middle-class urban Chinese households, other schools attempt to attract a wealthier clientele. Washington English has only one branch but is quite large in size, occupying three floors of prime retail space on one of Shenyang's busiest main roads, flanked on all sides by newly built residential high-rises and very close to a large shopping center. Inside there are four children's classrooms, eight adult classrooms, a theater, a computer lab, a library, and a large general-purpose room for lectures, English corners, and other events. The reception area contains plush couches for potential customers to sit on, three wall-mounted televisions tuned to international English news stations, and a coffee shop. Washington English was opened in 2004 by Mr. Bai, a middle-aged businessman with much previous experience in the industry, even though he spoke barely any English himself. He is a jolly and avuncular man in his forties, with wavy but neatly styled short hair and large glasses. He dresses in the conventional fashion of most Chinese businessmen, wearing either nondescript black suits or collared sweaters. Mr. Bai employs about thirty Chinese teachers and ten foreign teachers, as well as a large staff for marketing, sales, human resources, finances, and so forth.

Hong Ri's branches can be quite plain and utilitarian, but Washington English is meant to communicate luxury. Walls and floors are decorated with inlaid mosaics of colorful stones. Frosted glass with clear portions at the floor and ceiling form the walls of the classrooms, such that by standing on their toes students can see into classrooms from outside, or from one classroom into the neighboring one. Many of the walls and spaces are curved, giving the entire school a feeling of flowing movement from one area to the next. Foreign teachers are encouraged to take their breaks in the coffee shop downstairs, where they can be seen by both students and, through the large front windows, passersby on the street. In turn, students are encouraged to approach foreigners and talk to them, to try out the English they are learning in classes. The design of the school is intended, Mr. Bai told me during a tour, to be comfortable and leisurely, where students can drink their coffee while browsing through a foreign magazine or spend an afternoon watching English films.

Adult classes are generally small (usually only two to five students) and feature intensive interaction between students and teachers. Incoming students are interviewed by a "course consultant" who determines the student's goals and level of English before developing an individualized plan of study. Students combine classroom instruction with computerized learning modules that, in theory, teach them new words and grammatical patterns to be used in their upcoming lessons. However, the effectiveness of these technological methods was regularly called into question by the teachers themselves, who saw personal interaction as the only path to fluency. Tuition at Washington for adult students is 4,000 yuan for a three-month "pass," which students can then use to gain access to all of the school's facilities. With an average of eight hours of instruction per month, students pay about 170 yuan per classroom hour at Washington (in comparison to Hong Ri's average of 55 yuan per hour). Children's classes are similar in size and style to Hong Ri's, but far more expensive at 450 yuan per week.

With these higher prices, Washington sometimes struggled to attract students, especially to fill the children's classes. But over time Mr. Bai successfully integrated English education with study abroad opportunities and cultural contacts between foreigners and Chinese. At Washington English, foreign language is a carefully crafted aesthetic experience, one meant to be absorbed from one's surroundings and interactions with foreign others. Mr. Bai was most careful in the design of the school to orient the student not toward the classroom, but toward the symbolic ties English already has with modernity and cosmopolitanism. As with other luxury consumer goods, Washington English's product attempts to magnify its exchange-value (to create a sense of its English as being "better than others") by cultivating indexical links to other highly valued lifestyle formulations—such as coffee, foreign media, and technology—that are prestige consumables in China.

Teachers
Chinese Teachers

The one defining characteristic of almost all the Chinese teachers in private English schools is that they are women. During my original data collection period in 2005, Hong Ri's Chinese teachers were 95 percent female. Another children's school listed all of its eighty teachers in a promotional newsletter; only six were male. Washington English did not have a single male Chinese teacher. Male teachers are more common at higher levels of education, such as in university teaching, and are more likely to have opened their own schools. As we will see, though, male teachers can more easily draw on extended social networks for capital and expertise. The higher expectations placed on them as family breadwinners also often led them to manage their own businesses. The reasons for these disparities are complex and have a lot to do with gendered expectations in both education and employment. Of the two streams in Chinese education, arts (*wenke*) and sciences (*like*), women were often discouraged from the latter. In my experience of university classes for English majors, women usually outnumbered men two to one and language learning was often described as a gentle (*wenrou*) pursuit, something that required a woman's patience and grace.

The parents of students told me almost universally that they preferred female teachers for their children. Women were thought to be more kind, nurturing, active, engaged, and committed teachers than men. Women follow the child's progress more closely, I was told, and put extra effort into tutoring should the student fall behind. Headmasters and administrators recognize these preferences, often describing ideal teachers using similar feminized adjectives. Teachers, however, often complain of parents who are intrusive, bullying, and hypersensitive to their child's progress, a relation that seems to be linked to the gender dynamics of teaching as well: parents like female teachers because they are easier to push around. With less financial security, female teachers are more susceptible to threats from both parents (to withdraw their child from a class, for instance) and administrators. Female teachers are therefore often relegated to secondary roles in the industry, teaching children or review classes, while men are the school's "rock stars," leading large lecture courses or occupying managerial positions.

Beyond the gendered aspect to teaching, however, teachers' backgrounds are quite broad. They come from a range of socioeconomic and household situations, educational backgrounds, and places of origin. Typically, though, teachers at a school like Hong Ri are in their twenties, are unmarried singletons (i.e., they have no brothers or sisters), and have some kind of college or university education. Although many majored in English, it was common to meet teachers who had a background in disciplines such as foreign trade, economics, accounting, tourism, Chinese literature, sciences, and so forth. A handful of teachers are a few years older and married with a child of their own, but unless they have significant household resources for childcare, women generally leave teaching jobs to take care of their child full-time.[4] Teaching English is often thought of as a transitional job for recent graduates, a chance to earn some money before they need to take on the responsibilities of parenthood or move to a more promising career. Private school English teachers earn more money than their public school counterparts, but still not enough to provide for independence. New teachers usually sign a one-year contract that can be renewed annually, and it was common for teachers to renew between one and three times before moving on to something else. There was, though, little opportunity for promotion or advancement within the company.

About half of the teachers I interviewed were from Shenyang and the other half from other regions of China or from smaller prefectural cities nearby; teachers from rural areas were rare. Most of my informants agreed rural teachers would be unable to find employment in the industry due to the paucity of decent foreign language education in rural schools and the stigma of rural accents. Teachers are evaluated for their Chinese language skills as much as their foreign language ability or pedagogical training. Accent, whether unmarked Mandarin or marked Dongbeihua, was a major consideration in hiring decisions. Most students and teachers I talked to agreed that a teacher with a Dongbei accent would not be taken seriously. "Even [if] her English is perfect," Sophie said of a hypothetical rural teacher, "how can she talk to the parents? Are they going to trust in her?" Frequent comments such as these were made by teachers on the topic of voice: good teachers have a pleasing sound and accent. As Susan Blum (2004) observes, there is a complex politics of voice in China, with descriptions like "pleasant to hear" (*haoting*) encoding class, educational, and regional prejudices that typically favor standardized urban speech over vernacular accents. Without the knowledge needed to evaluate the teacher's English directly, many parents and administrators rely on patterns of spoken Mandarin as an index of teacher ability, so an eloquent Mandarin speaker is judged more favorably than a speaker with a rural accent, no matter her actual English fluency.

Those teachers not native to the city usually rented a bed in a nearby school-owned apartment converted to a dormitory, which provided a safe, cheap, and lively (if often crowded) environment to live in. But keeping many of the teachers together was also advantageous for the school. There was little privacy in the dormitory, and the most senior teacher living there usually reported to the headmaster about any developments in the lives of her colleagues—boyfriends, job opportunities, the various networks of friends and enemies—information that the headmaster could use to keep the teachers in line. When Jasmine, whose story I discuss in more detail below, was planning to leave Hong Ri to open her own school, she kept her preparations secret from the other teachers in the dormitory. Nevertheless, the headmaster guessed what was happening because Jasmine kept taking phone calls and leaving the dormitory to meet with her property agent and various other representatives, and thus refused to pay Jasmine's final month's salary.

Foreign Teachers

Itinerant native speakers who teach English in China are commonly called "foreign teachers" (*waijiao*). When English returned to the national curriculum in the late 1970s following the end of the Cultural Revolution, there were few qualified domestic teachers. The government began looking abroad to recruit foreign-language experts both to teach students and to train their own teachers in modern pedagogy (Deng 1997, 132; Porter 1990).[5] The number of such teachers increased steadily throughout the 1980s and 1990s, and then surged in the 2000s when private language schools were allowed to begin recruiting their own foreign teachers. Today, the number of teachers working for private English schools vastly outnumbers those employed in public schools and universities.[6] The government still mandates certain educational and teaching qualifications for foreign teachers, but given the right connections, these can be relaxed or ignored. In fact, by the mid-2000s, the vast majority of foreign teachers in Shenyang had no more than a general undergraduate degree. The number of foreign teachers in a city like Shenyang is, as one can imagine, always in flux, but there were at least several hundred employed in various institutions during my research at any given time.

I provide more detail on the lives of foreign teachers and the occasionally strained relationships with their Chinese counterparts in chapter 6. Here, it is sufficient to note that most foreign teachers are recent university graduates from a range of Western English-speaking countries such as the United States, Canada, United Kingdom, South Africa, Australia, and New Zealand. Many choose to come to China because of the potential for tourism and the exotic appeal of "the Orient," but underlying this is often a dearth of economic opportunities in their home countries. The numbers of men and women are approximately equal. They are typically recruited online, either directly or through a private placement agency, and their work visas are sponsored by the English school in which they will teach. The typical arrangement is a one-year contract with return airfare guaranteed on successful completion. Foreign teachers usually earn two to three times the salary of their Chinese counterparts for teaching about fifteen to twenty hours a week. Many teachers also earn additional money through freelance teaching or tutoring work that they arrange privately with individuals or smaller schools. Foreign teachers in Shenyang often enjoy a carefree and libertine lifestyle. Several clubs and bars cater to them almost exclusively, and their salaries are high enough that they can spend much of their free time drinking and socializing.[7]

Foreign teachers are valued predominantly for their oral language skills. Despite a range of national origins, and therefore a range of speech styles, as native speakers they are thought to provide the proper accents for Chinese students to model. They are also a guarantee of authentic language production, teaching oral English that is "real," and capable of evaluating the production of it by Chinese speakers. Importantly, though, foreign teachers are representatives of a globalized world of transnational connectivity that taps into Chinese desires for modern subjectivity. Schools therefore may survive or fail based on their ability to recruit and retain foreign teachers for their students, no matter the quality of their actual pedagogy, textbooks, or management.

Public Schools

Teaching English at a public school is a stressful job, and the teachers I interviewed often recounted the financial hardships of teaching and the vast commitments of time required by the profession. Unlike their private school counterparts, public school English teachers were not typically transient workers, often teaching at the same school for many years. As part of its Nine-Year Basic Education Law, the government issued new curricular guidelines for English language education in 2001, with English becoming a compulsory subject in grade three for all students (although many urban schools begin instruction as early as grade one) with at least eighty minutes of instruction per week. In grade five, instructional time doubles to at least 160 minutes per week until the end of secondary school (X. Cheng 2011; A. Feng 2009; Y. Hu 2007). In reality, the quality of foreign language education varies from school to school and can be impacted by a lack of qualified teachers, curricular pressures from other subjects, and unavailability of classroom technologies. Since student placement in secondary and tertiary education is dependent on examination performance, there is intense pressure to "teach to the test," and, as several teachers confirmed, the final year of junior and senior secondary school is devoted exclusively to test preparation (see also G. Hu 2002b; L. Mao and Min 2004).

Lessons are largely text-based, despite calls for increasing use of oral teaching strategies (G. Hu 2002a; M. Li and Baldauf 2011; Ouyang 2000). A typical class will begin with the teacher asking a student to recite a portion of the lesson from the previous class from memory. The recitation is then followed by a variety of activities such as vocabulary tests, oral recitations of the text (both individually and as a group), directed questions from the teacher about the text, explanations (usually in Mandarin) of certain vocabulary or grammatical features of the text, and the assignment of homework for the next lesson. Public school foreign language teaching is therefore highly structured, with a distinct focus on the flow of grammatical and lexical knowledge from teacher to student (Zheng and Davison 2008).

English teachers in public schools, like their counterparts in other disciplines, invest hours each day in preparing lessons, teaching classes, tutoring students, and grading student work, all for minimal financial compensation. But there is one area where English teachers have a distinct advantage over their peers: since English skills are highly desirable in the context of their weighting on college entrance examinations, English teachers are ideally positioned to supplement their meager salaries with specialized tutoring classes known as *buke* (pronounced as two syllables and literally meaning "mending class").

Buke are extra classes scheduled after regular school hours, usually for an hour in the evening or on the weekend, or intensive classes offered during the winter and summer holidays. Using the same textbook as the regular class, in theory students receive extra instruction, drills, and homework. In practice, teachers are often so pressed for time in the regular class that they finish their lessons in buke. English is not the only subject offered in buke, and students usually attend the buke of several teachers in the school, meaning that the teachers for English, chemistry, math, and so forth coordinate their schedules so that their individual buke do not overlap. The typical rate for buke in Shenyang is about 60–100 yuan per hour depending on the subject, the ranking of the school, and the perceived expertise of the teacher. Every public school English teacher I spoke to offered some manner of buke, and almost every language-learning individual I spoke to had attended buke at some point.

Buke have long been a part of the educational landscape in Shenyang and, indeed, in other East Asian regions, as evidenced by the *juku* and *yobiko* phenomena in Japan (Russell 1997) and similar programs in South Korea (S. Park and Abelmann 2004). A 2015 article in the *Shenyang Evening Post* reported on the phenomenon, highlighting the opinion of one parent confronted by a reluctant child: *"You have to go. Right now everyone is in buke. If you don't go, when you get to high school you'll be behind; even a top student will become a weak one."* Parents also fear that not enrolling their child in a teacher's buke would lead to subtle forms of discrimination in the regular class, such as making the student sit at the back of the room or giving her fewer opportunities to answer questions.

Buke is a controversial topic in contemporary Chinese education, the subject of media exposés and occasional popular outrage. Until 2005, teachers were allowed to host buke in their regular classrooms, but new educational policies went into effect that sought to curtail its use. Subsequently teachers moved buke either into their homes or into rented classrooms in libraries or English training centers such as Hong Ri. In 2013, the provincial Ministry of Education banned the practice altogether; nevertheless, both teachers and parents have colluded to maintain the practice in secret. The parents I talked to supported the right of teachers to offer buke and the necessity for their child to attend, concerned only that teachers be reasonable and fair in how the buke are conducted and the cost.

The public school teachers I talked to resisted government attempts to restrict the practice and justified their buke on three levels. First, the standard curriculum was too large to be successfully taught during regular classroom hours, so additional instructional time with students is essential. Second, teachers' advancement and remuneration are all dependent on student success in standardized examinations, meaning that additional instruction time for students translates into material benefits for their own careers. Third, teaching salaries are unreasonably small in relation to teachers' educational credentials and long work hours, and buke are the only way to supplement their incomes. After admitting that she offered buke to her middle school students, Teacher Wu had this to say about the practice:

> The government wants to ease the burden on students and make their lives less stressful. But in reality, if they [eliminate my buke], the students still have to take it, just not at school. They go somewhere else to take it, so they're still stressed out. Parents are stressed out too; they want their child to take buke at the school with their own teacher . . . The students who have buke in the school improve their test scores more quickly. Outside the school, well one, it's more money and that wastes a lot of the family's resources, and two, we say it's too commercial, a kind of business activity, right? They're just looking out for themselves, not the student's success. So my feeling is that nobody wins in this situation.

In other words, despite the obvious commodification of education and language present in the buke phenomenon, Teacher Wu grounded her actions in the affective discourse of the teacher-student relationship, namely, the teacher's concern for the student's welfare and success.

Opening a School

I met several ambitious individuals during my fieldwork who had opened English schools. My initial expectation in interviewing these individuals was that issues of pedagogy, curriculum, and teaching dynamics would dominate our conversations; after all, if the goal of teaching English is to instill a high level of fluency in the student, considerations of how to teach should be primary. And with so many schools in the city competing for the consumer's money, educational techniques would seem to be one area where schools could specialize and create some measure of competitive advantage. But this was rarely the case; in fact, most private schools adopted the same pedagogical techniques and textbooks as public schools (and each other), since in point of fact the ultimate goal of this schooling was better performance on nationally standardized tests. They might advertise their particular methods of instruction as being advanced, innovative, or superior to others, but little differentiation in pedagogy actually took place. Instead, in conversation after conversation, school owners emphasized the hard financial realities of their business. How much money does it take to open a school? How much to grease the wheels and appease the right officials? To attract and retain the best students? To attract and retain the best teachers? Despite the potential rewards of cashing in on their own fluency and making a fortune in Shenyang's English language fever, most of the owners' stories highlighted the numerous setbacks and frustrations. The barriers to entry are high, the potential pitfalls many, and several of their ventures were either failures or barely scraped by financially. Exploring these stories illustrates the pernicious financialization of foreign language teaching in Shenyang.

Bureaucratic Regulation and *Guanxi* Networks in School Administration

Officially, private English schools are classified as "people-run schools" (*minban xuexiao*) as opposed to "state-run schools" (*gongban xuexiao*), a category that includes many other types of private education in China, such as boarding schools and private universities (Crabb 2010, 390; Deng 1997; J. Lin 2007). Despite their private status, however, *minban xuexiao* are also subject to certification by educational authorities. Schools must submit financial statements, proof of teacher qualifications, curricula, textbooks, and other materials for approval on an annual basis, along with a substantial fee. Even then, the granting, denial, renewal, or retraction of a school license can occur for seemingly arbitrary reasons. School owners must therefore rely on networks of personal relationships, called *guanxi*, that can potentially allow them privileged access to these powerful gatekeepers.

Essentially a complex web of favors, gifts, and obligations between people related by ties of family, work, schooling, and residence, *guanxi* enables people to use personal contacts to navigate what would otherwise be a densely bureaucratic environment (Kipnis 1997; Lo and Otis 2003; Smart 1993; Y. Yan 1996; M. Yang 1994, 2002). While there is a tendency in the West to view *guanxi*, particularly as it relates to the entanglements of government figures and private business, as a form of corruption, most Chinese view it as an essential component of human interaction (Gold, Guthrie, and Wank 2002). *Guanxi* practices can shade into socially devalued corrupt practices such as bribery, but only when they are perceived to be devoid of feeling (*ganqing*)—in other words, only when the relationship between people is solely based on the instrumentality of the exchange.

When I arrived in Shenyang to do fieldwork in 2005, I spent several days settling into my apartment before making the trip to the local Public Security Bureau (PSB) office to register my residence. I was told there that new regulations had made it mandatory for foreigners to register within twenty-four hours of their arrival, and was slapped with a 5,000 yuan fine for my tardiness. Rather than pay the fine, my wife and I started calling around to the university, her family, classmates, and anyone else who might "know someone." I eventually got in touch with a former English student of mine who now worked as a police detective. He directed me to a friendly district-level PSB official who phoned the local office and told them to just register me and waive the fine. Through these types of networks and interactions, fees, fines, and regulations can frequently be reduced, mitigated, or simply overlooked. But, importantly, they depend on access through preexisting networks of contacts (such as the teacher-student relationship I was able to exploit). In contrast, people without connections, such as rural migrants and other outsiders, must either accept the regulatory environment as it exists or work hard to establish those contacts. Businesses like English schools often rely on a new class of social actors who can connect private enterprises with government regulators and facilitate the mutual exchange of gifts and favors (Hsu 2007; X. Liu 2002; Osburg 2013; Pieke 1995; Wank 1999). Successful use of *guanxi* networks has thus become a key factor in the conduct of business in contemporary China.

When Dylan, a university English teacher in his late twenties, decided to open his own school, he partnered with a former classmate who owned a suitable building; Dylan would run the school, and his classmate would handle the finances. They were immediately faced with two choices: they could register the school themselves, but at a prohibitively high cost of 100,000 yuan; or they could list their school as a branch of a larger school but still operate under their own name. Doing so would allow them to appropriate the larger school's license and reduce their up-front costs to 20,000 yuan, but half of their profits would go to the parent corporation. They desperately wanted to take the first option but did not have access to the necessary capital. In the end, Dylan and his partner appealed to a contact of his parents in the government, and his license was granted at a significant discount in return for 30 percent of the school's profits.

Charles partnered with another teacher to open their school in the newly built Yuhong district south of the city, largely serving upwardly mobile middle-class families. They submitted all of their credentials and materials to the provincial education bureau but were informed that the government had put a moratorium on licenses for new English schools. His business partner contacted her husband's former classmate, and through him was able to arrange a dinner with several government officials. They struck an agreement to pay a 100,000 yuan deposit to the education bureau, and in return the officials would allow the school to operate without a license until one could be obtained. Even after this success, however, Charles still had to develop and draw on his *guanxi* network; for instance, he gave regular gifts to the landlord of the building where his school was housed as a guarantee against substantial rent increases.

Another option is to avoid registering the school at all and hope to escape official notice. This is generally only possible with small schools operating out of a home or a rented apartment. Jasmine, in her midtwenties and recently married, had taught for many years at Hong Ri but was frustrated by her inability to become a manager or headmaster; consequently, she decided to open her own school. Jasmine had worked hard to develop relationships with her students' parents, and, in advance of leaving Hong Ri, she privately contacted each to announce her departure. But she also offered to continue teaching their child at her own school, charging a lower tuition than Hong Ri, at only 36 yuan an hour. In this way she was able to retain many of her Hong Ri students, while also attracting others from her neighborhood and by referrals from parents. Through a parent of one longtime student, she located classroom space on the second floor of a pharmacy, facing inward to a residential complex courtyard. Students entered the school through a stairwell at the back of the pharmacy, and her only advertising or signage was the red stencil characters of her school's name, Happy Dove English, on the classroom windows. To ensure that her school did not attract the attention of the education bureau, she also offered discounted tuition to members of the local neighborhood committee (the administrative unit of a residential complex), who agreed to let her business operate under the radar. Jasmine thus drew on multiple *guanxi* relationships cultivated with parents and the residential administration to develop a successful business, but any potential expansion was constrained by the need to remain unobservable by higher-level educational authorities.

Attracting Students

Jasmine recruited her students through existing relationships with parents established during her time at Hong Ri, but many school owners could not find students so easily. Small schools in residential communities can advertise within the neighborhood by, for instance, knocking on doors or setting up a display table. Larger, more commercial schools need to find other methods. Dylan first tried to recruit students by posting advertisements outside the university and handing out flyers in the neighborhood. This did not lead to many customers, and Dylan felt that people are so overwhelmed by flyers from many different schools that his was unable stand out. Charles estimated that handing out ten thousand flyers would lead to only one new student for his school—a financially wasteful strategy. Instead, *guanxi* networks can again play a large role in finding customers. Dylan later drew on his family networks to solicit assistance from several local public school teachers, offering them an inducement of several hundred yuan for every one of their students who registered in his classes.

I was often told that many of the qualities of the Dongbei personality lead to difficulties in doing business in Shenyang. A prominent feature of these commentaries is the conviction that Dongbei customers are always wary of being cheated, leading them to be suspicious, stubborn, and thrifty.[8] Charles told me that when he first opened his school, he adopted the same customer service attitude that he had used in his years doing business in Malaysia: friendly, smiling, accommodating.

But, he said, this only led parents to wonder how he was cheating them. And so the budding entrepreneur has to find ways to trick parents into committing to the school. Charles said that he eventually adopted a more aloof attitude toward his customers.

> You want to study here? You study here. If you don't want, go anywhere you like. I usually say the word like this . . . in a very tough way. And then I found out, the outcome is better, the result is better. They thought, "Whoa, you're being very *bold* [*niu*] . . . you're being sort of cool, a little cold face." I'm not doing any service talking with them in a very nice way, but in a very, very cold way. A little bit aggressive. And then, they think "Wow, you must have some stuff."

He also told parents that they were required to accompany their child to class once a month. This too was a trick, he told me, because parents would see this as a free English lesson for themselves. Had he offered this to parents, they would have been suspicious, but by making it a requirement they saw themselves as taking advantage of him. He also learned, at first, to tell parents that his classes were full and that he could not accept any new students; this convinced them that his school was better than others and only made them redouble their efforts to register their child.

Another strategy for attracting students was to emphasize certain curricular differences from other schools. Occasionally this was done through pedagogical discussions, and many schools advertised classes using "advanced" or "state-of-the-art" teaching strategies developed abroad, such as Total Physical Response (TPR) or Communicative Language Teaching (CLT). More common, though, was the attempt to differentiate the school's particular "brand" of English from that of its competitors. At its heart, a brand establishes some sense of similarity and coevalness among groups of commodities as tokens of a common identity or type (Manning and Uplisashvili 2007; Nakassis 2012). Branded commodities thus share in particular unique qualia that differentiate them from other brands, classifications that are established through a variety of marketing practices. When Sophie was working as a student recruiter for a newly opened English school, she explained:

> "Water" is the key word [to] seduce parents to send their child to your school . . . [Students] have learned in other English training centers, maybe they learned British English and say "wa-tuh." The headmaster tell us, "This is the key word—water, water, water." We had it on a piece of paper and carried it around in our hand. Water, water. When we met the student come to our school, we give them the paper and ask them,

"Read it." *However they say the word, we just tell them it's wrong* . . . I explain to the parents, "Your child's pronunciation is wrong. Your child say it the British way, 'wa-tuh,' not the American way, 'wa-ter.' It's out of fashion." . . . You spend twenty minutes teaching this, just correcting the pronunciation, and then the parent will think, "How good is the teacher, she works for twenty minutes just to correct his pronunciation." They think our school is better because we study pronunciation, but in fact, it's only one word. It's just one kind of lure.

In this case, the differentiation between the British and American accents is not treated as a phonetic or linguistic issue but as one of qualitative differentiation, with Sophie's school marketing itself as imparting the now fashionable American accent.

Advertising can promote a public image for a school, and many schools, especially the larger ones, used billboards, print, radio, and television spots. Others opted for the more dramatic practice of offering promotional events in public areas such as shopping malls, using this opportunity to show off the fluency students had presumably acquired in their classes. Mrs. Gao, the headmistress of a branch school in downtown Shenyang, often hosted promotional performances in a nearby pedestrian shopping district. Children took turns at the microphone on a small stage singing English songs or recounting in English how they were inspired by their teachers, while Mrs. Gao's staff walked through the crowd handing out flyers and answering questions. She confessed to me, however, how difficult it was to find children to participate; the students had busy schedules, and parents demanded compensation for having their child perform. Many of the children on stage were therefore students from an elite private school where Mrs. Gao's former classmate was a teacher.

Schools also made use of the English Corners I described earlier, where people gather to practice conversation. English Corners were originally the product of the enthusiasm for all things foreign and the relaxation of state control over private lives during the reform period of the early 1980s (see Link, Madsen, and Pickowicz 1989). Today, however, these nominally public events are often commodified as advertising opportunities for English schools. On Saturday nights in Shenyang's Zhongshan Square, located under a large, imposing statue of Mao Zedong, large numbers of people congregate for leisure activities such as dancing, games, and writing calligraphy on the ground with water brushes. At the northeastern edge of the square is the English Corner. People of all ages and abilities gather in small groups, moving from one to another, sometimes listening to a particularly fluent speaker, sometimes striking up conversations with strangers or joining discussions already in progress. As with Mrs. Gao's promotional performances, it quickly became clear during my visits that many of the most eloquent English speakers were not there merely to practice but to represent their schools. As one young girl sang the Carpenters' 1973 hit "Yesterday Once More" (a popular song for English students), an older woman standing next to her introduced herself to onlookers as the student's teacher and distributed her business card to anyone interested. On another night, a line of English teachers from a local school marched in matching professional outfits through the English Corner clapping and singing a song while the headmistress made a pitch to onlookers with a portable public address system.

Getting "bums into seats," as one foreign teacher termed the relentless pressure to recruit students, was a key concern for school administrators. Parents could be fickle consumers of the educational commodity, abandoning schools and teachers who charged too highly for an inferior product, or flocking to those that embodied new pedagogical techniques or commitment to their students. Such impressions had to be carefully produced and cultivated by owners through advertising and promotion. Their strategies for attracting students drew on commodified notions of language (as particularly branded systems of meaning) and customers (as wary actors who must be "tricked" into parting with their money).

Even after the walls are painted, the desks are arranged, and the students have paid their tuition in full, there is still so much that can go wrong. The careful *guanxi* relationships a school owner has cultivated may fall apart, or government regulations may change (as Charles discovered with the moratorium on new licenses). Too many students may leave, or teachers may be unreliable. One former owner I talked to lost his business when his partner emptied their bank accounts and left the country. All of these possibilities, and the rigors of actually running the school itself, mean that owners are kept busy and under tremendous stress.

Charles, Jasmine, and Mrs. Gao all experienced varying degrees of success in their business endeavors. Charles was able to buy a spacious apartment in the same neighborhood as his wealthy clients. Jasmine kept her school small, but made enough money to go abroad several times as a tourist. Mrs. Gao reinvested the profits from her school in real estate and owns several apartments throughout the city that she rents out to others. Dylan's school was, unfortunately, short-lived. The arrangements he had to make to receive his license delayed the opening of his school from April until June, at which point most parents had already planned for their child's summer break schooling. Despite his extensive contacts, Dylan was able to recruit only thirty students. He planned to go ahead, however, even if it meant the school would not make a profit in the first year. Unfortunately, two weeks after the school opened, the teacher he hired demanded a higher salary. Already stretched financially to the limit, Dylan refused, and the teacher quit. She convinced many of the students' parents to leave Dylan's school for a class she would offer privately in her home. With only a handful of students remaining, Dylan's school closed its doors after only two weeks.

The Industrialization of Teaching and the Manufacture of Speakers

Since the early 1990s, China has been undergoing a massive shift toward neoliberal forms of governmentality, financializing and privatizing many aspects of social life that, until recently, were provided or subsidized by the state such as education, health care, markets, job security, and so forth (Sun and Guo 2013; J. Yang 2007; L. Zhang and Ong 2008). In an era where English fluency has become a key component of individual success, it was inevitable that English education, too, would become subject to commodifying processes. In this chapter I have outlined the various ways that foreign languages are produced as commodities and the resulting semiotic ideologies that inform English language education. In the next chapters I turn to how those commodity formulations have been taken up by consumers as they engage with these learning processes. A few key implications of this commodification process stand out, however, and deserve to be spelled out more explicitly.

A commodity is not simply an object, much less a physical one, but an item of exchange produced through coordinated forms of social labor and embedded in economic systems of capital (Marx 1978, 302–308). In this sense, English in China certainly qualifies as a commodity given the financialization of the education sector and the various ways in which language is produced and marketed to the general public. This is not to say that language in general is always a commodity; only when the bare form of language (its use-value) is laminated with exchange-value in a distinct linguistic marketplace does it take on these enhanced commodity formulations. But these commodity formulations are, importantly, also semiotic relationships of indexical linkage to other elements of China's modernization process. We can see in the description of Washington English, for instance, both a product differentiation in terms of a branded luxury offering of the language and an attempt to associate that product with other co-occurring signs of sumptuous consumption: coffee, technology, architecture, leisure, and so forth. These networks of sign relationships are crucial to establishing the modernist chronotope of English as a future-oriented language.

We should also recognize how neoliberal forms of education transform both labor and language in the context of instruction. While one may conceive of capitalism as ruthlessly profit-oriented to the point that human relations of affect disappear from the marketplace (Jameson 1991), I have shown that in many ways teachers retain a Confucian idealism in terms of the deep emotional commitments educators feel for their students. Schools too must draw on *guanxi* networks founded on relations of kinship and friendship to successfully cultivate their businesses. Yet these affective ties do not exist separate from the market but are rather absorbed into it, recruited for the purposes of capital expansion (Hardt 1999; Richard and Rudnyckyj 2009). The affective labor of the teacher is exploited like any other form of surplus value by the corporatized school, just as *guanxi* networks are instrumentalized for productive purposes.

Finally, as I noted at the beginning of this chapter, one consequence of language's commodification is its conversion into an objectified, materialized form, exemplified by the ideological reduction of English to a collection of words that can then be counted, compared, and used as a measure of fluency. Becoming a speaker of English is recontextualized as a manufacturing process in which a collection of inputs is assembled into a final product: the fluent speaker. Ironically, it is only under relations of capitalist linguistic production that this outcome has become viable. The craft production of fluency during the early days of foreign language interest in the 1980s, where language learners were mostly isolated hobbyists studying as a leisure pursuit, was a notably inefficient and ineffective strategy. True competence could only be achieved abroad through intimate personal contact with native speakers. And although native speakers still play a prominent role in English education in China in the form of foreign teachers, they too have been incorporated into the productive process as manufacturing inputs.

The highly proficient speakers in China today, who snag trophies at English-language competitions or sing out the praises of their teachers during public promotional events, are products of a domestic system of industrialized language teaching and acquisition. Many have never been abroad, even if they hope to go there some day. This state of affairs has only become possible due to the commodification of English and its attendant alienability. By making language a consumable product through the highly complex systematization of expertise and the marketization of language knowledge—yoked, of course, to an encompassing national project and highly bureaucratic forms of regulation—the foreign language industry in China has made possible the appropriation of language from its former status as an emblem of ethnolinguistic identity and belonging. Instead, through complex relations of exchange, it stands ready to be consumed by student learners and thus incorporated into their own sense of self as participants in China's modernizing enterprise.

ON "CHINGLISH"

Stigmatization, Laughter, and Nostalgia

In preparation for the 2008 Summer Olympics, the Beijing city government and the Beijing Organizing Committee for the Olympic Games initiated several projects to standardize (*guifanhua*) and internationalize (*guojihua*) the city's English, the most visible of which was the Beijing Speaks Foreign Languages program (E. Fong 2009, 44; Pan 2015a, 11; Zhou and Wang 2013). These campaigns sought to improve English both in the capital city and around the country as a means of ensuring smooth and effortless communication between Chinese and outsiders. Taxi drivers were issued recorded English lessons on cassette to assist them in conversing with foreign customers. Over one hundred thousand foreign language–proficient volunteers were recruited to offer information, assistance, and translation. A 170-page booklet of English translations for common menu items was published and issued to restaurants across the city. And a hotline and website were set up for Beijing residents to notify authorities of public displays of bad English, colloquially known both in China and abroad as "Chinglish." Similar efforts were made in Shanghai in preparation for Expo 2010 (R. Zhang 2014). As several stories in the state media made clear, Chinglish was to be subjected to the same type of mass campaign that marked the socialist era, a large-scale and radical effort at reforming the nation's use of English on a wholescale basis.[1]

In retrospect, these campaigns appear amusingly earnest, if not even a little farcical. Surely international travelers did not arrive in Beijing and Shanghai expecting voluble small talk from their taxi drivers on the state of the weather, nor did the government truly imagine it could turn hundreds of thousands of ordinary citizens into fluent speakers practically overnight? Yet according to both official pronouncements and the many Chinese-language experts I interviewed, there were serious concerns about the consequences of ignoring Chinglish and a fear for the potential utter confusion of foreign visitors. How would abundant use of Chinglish reflect on the country in the eyes of these visitors? Chen Lin, a retired foreign language professor and consultant for the Beijing Speaks Foreign Languages program, was quoted in a February 27, 2007, *China Daily* news story as saying, "We want everything to be correct. Grammar, words, culture, everything . . . Beijing will have thousands of visitors coming. We don't want anyone laughing at us." Although ridding Beijing of Chinglish during the Olympics may have ostensibly been a precaution against misunderstandings by foreign visitors, as Chen's words make clear it was also about the potential of foreigners "laughing at us." Each individual instance of Chinglish was a mark against the nation itself, calling into question the global legitimacy of an ambitiously modernizing country.

The campaign against Chinglish that swept China in anticipation of the Olympic Games, and that is still a frequent topic of concern in classroom environments, the media, and casual conversation among English learners in Shenyang, highlights the manner in which individual and state desires are often entangled. For individuals to discover that their speech or writing was in actuality Chinglish was perhaps the most discomfiting news a Chinese English speaker could hear, implying as it did that that the language in use was not only semantically or syntactically wrong but, more importantly, that the speaker's status as an authorized user of the English language was illegitimate and false. This is echoed in the concerns above that the Chinese nation might be judged negatively by English-speaking foreign tourists. Discourses of education, self-improvement, quality, and national image are not dissoluble into individual and collective matters, as we saw with the chronotopic narratives I discussed in chapter 3. Here, I examine the category of language popularly known as Chinglish and what this stigmatizing label means for the speakers to whom it is attached.

Within the schools where I worked, I was often approached by teachers who were preparing public signs, announcements, lesson plans, and other documents that might be seen by foreigners to provide a final check of the language. Fanny was one such frequent visitor, and her time studying abroad seemed to only intensify her anxiety about potential errors. As I reviewed yet another lesson plan destined to be distributed to the other teachers, she commented, "I just don't want there be any mistakes."

Most discussions of Chinglish and other stigmatized nonstandard linguistic varieties are concerned with two dimensions: the unique features that characterize the variety and the sociolinguistic value of that variety in context. Take the research on African American English (AAE) as an example: William Labov's

(1972) early work on AAE in *Language in the Inner City* is roughly divided into two halves, one on the grammatical structure of AAE and one on the use of AAE in context. This complementarity has continued in more recent work, such as Mufwene et al. (1998) and Morgan (2002). What remains underexamined, however, is how various forms of talk *become* AAE, outside of the fact that AAE is what African Americans may speak. We know that a feature such as copula deletion (the grammaticality of, for instance, the sentence "she happy") is characteristic of AAE because people who identify as African Americans commonly use it, and thus AAE is both an identity and a comprehensive linguistic structure by way of its close association with a discrete speech community. A discussion of the structure of AAE is thus inseparable from speakers' own metalinguistic awareness of it as a distinct code.

Such relationships are less evident in cases where the ties between identity and register are not clear, and where the variety is highly stigmatized across a range of speech contexts (Bilaniuk 2006; Blum 2004; Cavanaugh 2012; Reyes and Lo 2009). "Chinglish-speaker" is not an identity category in China, and certainly not a label that anyone would want applied to them. Rather, the negative social value of Chinglish is a product of its application by authoritative language users to those who are less fluent. Chinglish is formed through the process of enregisterment, where discursive practices encode and systematize the evaluative judgments of entire speech communities, and then sediment over time into particular semiotic registers imbued with social value and identified with distinct social types (Agha 2007; see also Goebel 2008; Johnstone 2009). The metapragmatic statements that shape the perceptions of Chinglish may be explicit (such as "that's not real English") but are more generally embedded within other speech genres such as, in some examples I will examine below, jokes. In the case of Chinglish, the shape of the register is a product of decisions made, often haphazardly, by particular groups of listeners who possess a measure of symbolic authority, either by virtue of being native speakers of the English standard or by being associated with foreign sources of sociolinguistic authenticity (Cavanaugh and Shankar 2014; Coupland 2003). Membership in the stigmatized speech community of Chinglish users is not claimed by intentional use of the variety but instead assigned by others, reflecting and maintaining existing inequalities in linguistic capital.

Defining a Nonstandard English

Fifty years ago, the linguist Pit Corder proposed a means of categorizing two different types of linguistic disfluency that he termed "mistakes" and "errors." Mistakes, he argued, are the product of normal human linguistic performance, "slips of the tongue (or pen)" that result from our cognitive limitations (Corder 1967, 166). We mispronounce words, forget to conjugate verbs, or choose the wrong word to express our intent. In short, in the performance of everyday speech, we are imperfect speakers. But as evidence of our innate linguistic abilities these mistakes are not particularly significant. To adopt a semiotic terminology, the mistake has no obvious signifier; it is a failed attempt to create a meaningful sign. In most cases, listeners can effortlessly ascertain the speaker's intention and fill in the denotational blanks of these mistakes. But another category of disfluency, which Corder calls an error, is significant in that it points to some aspect of the underlying linguistic knowledge of the second-language speaker. For instance, Mandarin's lack of /θ/ and /ð/ phonemes (the *th* in words like "this" and "there," respectively) means that these English sounds are frequently pronounced as /s/ and /z/ by Chinese English learners (thus saying "sroo" instead of "through" and "muzzer" instead of "mother") (Deterding 2006; Jiang 1995). These are not "mistakes" in Corder's sense because they point to something important about a student's language acquisition and can be targeted by instructors for additional attention in class.

In all cases of second language acquisition, learners make errors based on the differences—and occasionally false similarities—between their native language (called L1 by applied linguists) and the target language (L2). Such errors, like the pronunciation differences above, are not random but evidence of a speaker's "interlanguage" (which Corder called a "transitional competence"), a dynamic intermediate system between two languages that often draws on the syntactic, semantic, pragmatic, and even phonetic properties of the L1.[2] As speakers become more proficient, this interlanguage increasingly comes to approximate, but perhaps never replicate, native speaker patterns in the L2. Beyond just the phonetic component, several other common patterns have collectively emerged in Chinese English learners' speech that are evidence of this kind of cross-linguistic transfer. Virginia Yip (1995) draws on a vast body of spoken and written data produced by Chinese students to propose several key ways in which Chinese syntactic patterns lead to unique characteristics of Chinese English. Among these is, for instance, the differing emphasis on "topic" and "subject" in sentence construction (see Goddard 2005, 130–132):

> *Zhe ke shu yezi hen da.*
> this (classifier) tree leaf very big
> "This tree, (its) leaves are very big." (Adapted from Yip 1995, 75)

As in this example, Mandarin tends to foreground topic information (the tree) rather than subject information (the leaves). In speaking English, Chinese students favor the production of sentences with this kind of topical foregrounding, such as "My aunt, everybody likes her" (Yip 1995, 89; see also Huang 2010). Adverbial phrases are often placed directly after the subject of a sentence, and the use of aspect markers rather than verb tense, lack of gendered pronouns, and restricted use of copula verbs in Mandarin all influence English production. The following utterances, drawn from my classroom data, are direct transpositions of Chinese syntax into English:

> "I very much like your clothes."
> *Wo ting xihuan ni de yifu.*
> "Mary yesterday go to the store."
> *Mali zuotian qu le shangdian.*

Clearly, then, there is an underlying grammatical basis to much so-called Chinglish.

Can we say then that Chinglish is merely the systematic errors Chinese learners of English make on the way to acquiring native-like fluency? Cross-linguistic influence is undoubtedly the source of many linguistic tokens labeled as Chinglish, and identifying them in this way provides a clear basis for systematizing a nativized Chinese variety of English that many linguists argue is valid in its own right (Wei Li 2016; Z. Xu and Deterding 2017; Z. Xu, He, and Deterding 2017). However, this systematicity breaks down when we account for the ways multiple and diverse groups of stakeholders, including Chinese linguists, Chinese teachers, Chinese students, foreign linguists, foreign teachers, and foreign visitors, use the term "Chinglish" as a label for a range of linguistic behaviors with very little consistency or even overlap between one definition and another. In this sense, Chinglish is a semiotized register rather than a coherent language variety, a way of talking about the language use of particular groups of people and what that usage may say about them indexically. When teachers, foreigners, and other language experts identify the "errors" of Chinglish—and this is separate from everyday "mistakes"—they are not pointing to an aspect of the students' interlanguage but to their identity as proper English speakers. This is clearly illustrated by the most common venue in which native speakers of English encounter Chinglish: on the internet. Thousands of examples float around on websites, e-mail forwards, blog posts, Twitter feeds, and Facebook updates, united only in taking these texts as a source of amusement and highlighting the peculiarities of language in the Chinese landscape. Using Chinglish simply to mean "nonstandard English spoken by Chinese people" is therefore grossly simplistic and ignores the tremendous variation among different groups of speakers and listeners in their application of the term.

Compare, for instance, the syntactic patterns outlined above with the pragmatic considerations of writing instructors. *The Translator's Guide to Chinglish* is a writing guide published by China's Foreign Language Teaching and Research Press and written by Joan Pinkham, a foreign language expert working in China. Intended as a handbook for steering Chinese translators away from incorrect Chinglish forms, it argues that "plain English" is "a language based on verbs. It is simple, concise, vigorous and, above all, clear. Chinglish is a language based on nouns—vague, general, abstract nouns. It is complicated, long-winded, ponderous, and obscure" (Pinkham 2000, 170). Pinkham offers some consideration of how Chinglish is produced, namely, through the transfer of Mandarin semantic and pragmatic norms into English, and thus implying that Mandarin too is a language based on vague, general, and abstract nouns. Significantly, though, many of the examples provided in the book would not look out of place in a native speaker corpus; indeed, several of Pinkham's Chinglish examples are explicitly drawn from English native speaker–produced texts, and advise Chinese translators to avoid phrases such as "image packaging" and "impression management" (Pinkham 2000, 174). These are familiar prescriptivist tropes in many such manuals, but while they may violate her directives for clear writing, they would also be familiar to Western management consultants and publicists—and no one is arguing that they speak Chinglish. So where does "plain" or "real" English end and Chinglish begin?

Any comprehensive theory of Chinglish needs to take account of humor as the framework through which many metadiscursive discussions and evaluations of Chinglish are conducted. As the Olympic officials realized, the stigmatization of Chinglish is underscored rather than mitigated by the perception of Chinglish as a subject of laughter. Laughter has often been positioned as a "weapon of the weak" in the study of symbolic relations of dominance, such as James Scott's discussion of Haji "Broom," a landowner who "swept up all the land in his path" (Scott 1985, 13–22). Scott characterizes the gossip and tall tales surrounding Haji Broom's purported avarice as "an exchange of small arms fire, a small skirmish, in a cold war of symbols between the rich and poor" (22), but the actual effect of these stories on the hegemonic relations of power in the community was minimal and symbolic, creating a moral discourse of appropriate behavior while failing to effectively sanction transgressions. In fact, rather than a "weaponized" discursive strategy of the "have-nots," humor has been seen, in more recent scholarship, to reinforce rather than subvert dominant ideologies (Billig 2005; Hill 2008; Kramer 2011; Pérez 2013; Santa Ana 2009). This is due to the inherent indeterminacy at the heart of humor, the way in which a joke straddles the divide between playful and serious. Jokes are only funny insomuch as they contain a kernel of "truth" about the status of relationships between various social groups dramatized in the joke itself:

linguistic, racial, gender, and religious prejudices can all reside in the space of the joke-teller's heartfelt denial "I was only joking."

We also need to view Chinglish within the attempts to study the plurality of "Englishes" that I noted in the introduction. The work of scholars like Braj Kachru and others in the tradition of "World Englishes" seeks to provide linguistic descriptions of national varieties of nonstandard English. Thus, a book such as *The Other Tongue: English across Cultures* contains chapters titled "Standard Nigerian English" and "Chinese Varieties of English" (Kachru 1992). Such documentation has continued in a host of other publications (Kachru, Kachru, and Nelson 2006; Kirkpatrick 2010) as well as the scholarly journal *World Englishes*. The implicit assumption of this work is that by recording the sociolinguistic and grammatical particularities of these varieties, linguists can push for them to be recognized as legitimate varieties of English rather than simply deficient forms of the native-speaking standard.

In decentering linguistic authority from formerly colonizing Western powers and recognizing the legitimacy of subaltern varieties of English, the concept of World Englishes offers an admirable political agenda. Nonetheless, it is difficult to apply this framework to the case of China, despite many attempts to do so (Bolton 2002; C. Cheng 1992; He and Li 2009; Kirkpatrick and Xu 2002; Z. Xu 2010). There are two key reasons for this. First, the concern in China has rarely been with creating, legitimating, or validating local forms of English. In Shenyang, unique Chinese patterns of English were widely considered deficient in a marketplace for language that takes foreign norms as an explicit model.[3] This valorization of internationally standardized English extends through every aspect of the acquisition and learning process. Despite the efforts of some Chinese scholars to promote "China English," in Shenyang, Chinglish was almost always a stigmatized variety in actual discursive interactions. Second, in everyday practice the forms of language classified as Chinglish have less to do with accurate or objective comparisons to native-speaker norms, and far more to do with the identity and status of the individual making the classification. The issue is not what is being said but who is saying it. Attempts to identify and categorize particular forms of language as Chinglish are therefore doomed to fail because Chinglish is less a coherent linguistic code than it is a regime of value applied to particular forms of language production and, ultimately, a form of language discipline constraining and evaluating the speech of various "unauthorized" groups of individuals. Chinglish is a discourse fraught with anxieties about what constitutes "real" English, the possibility of the speaker's English being inauthentic, and the implications for that inauthenticity regarding their own position as future-oriented modernizing cosmopolitan citizens.

English with Chinese Characteristics

Chinese speakers of English differ both in their levels of fluency and in levels of authority and technical expertise in English as an academic subject. At the most authoritative level are translators, professors, school administrators, and educational officials (who I will call Chinese foreign language professionals). Next are Chinese English language teachers working in public and private schools. Finally, there are the language students themselves, who can range from young children in bilingual kindergartens to adults in business English or examination preparation classes. Recalling here the variety of English registers I discussed in chapter 1—including examination, oral, and cool English—we also have to remember that a speaker's legitimacy can derive from a range of sources such as academic credentials or the symbolic appropriation of foreign cultural elements, thus implying that sociolinguistic authenticity can derive from multiple bases of authority. The discourse of Chinglish in China is similarly divided into multiple interpretive frameworks, often revolving around the identification of nonstandard English speech forms, discussions of descriptive terminology and classification, and the status of Chinese speakers of English in a global context.

Chinese Foreign Language Professionals

The first issue here is to understand how Chinese scholars talk about Chinglish and the politics of labeling speech varieties. Chinglish, in many quarters, is not only a stigmatized linguistic code but a stigmatized term as well. Virginia Yip's analysis, discussed above, uses the phrase "Chinese-English Interlanguage" rather than Chinglish to indicate that the nonstandard forms she analyzes are fleeting linguistic expressions produced by speakers on the road to fluency, rather than permanent features of a linguistic repertoire. Chinese scholars frequently differentiate between Chinglish (*zhongshi yingyu*) and a relatively stable Chinese variety of English, often called China English (*zhongguo yingyu*), which can stand on its own as a viable vernacular, a local instantiation of a global linguistic form (L. Han 2007; Xiaoqiong Hu 2004; Jiang 2002; Wenzhong Li 1993; Y. Wei and Fei 2003). They either reject the term "Chinglish" altogether or confine its application to the overtly political Maoist forms of English popular during the height of socialism. China English is, in contrast, a form of the language that is "mainly determined by the intrinsic way of thinking of the Chinese people and by China's unique society and culture" (Wan 2005, 42). In this formulation, China English uses Standard English to express uniquely Chinese concepts by way of transliterating Chinese words or phrases (such as "mah-jong" or "tai chi"), translating unique Chinese expressions into English (the "Four Modernizations" or "one country, two systems"), or coining new English words to express Chinese concepts ("barefoot doctor" or "bird's nest soup"). Much of the acceptable invention of China English, according to language professionals, is lexical and derives from attempts by Chinese translators to felicitously calque idiomatic Chinese phrases into English: "capitalist roader" and "right deviationist thinking," for instance, were invented to express the meanings of the Chinese terms *zouzipai* and *youqing*, respectively (C. Cheng 1992, 170). Note, then, that Chinglish is differentiated from China English not through any system of linguistic classification but as the product of a moral discourse about China's unique culture. Words that promote China are China English; words that reflect badly on China are Chinglish. Language that does not conform to Standard English conventions of expression, but "deforms" them in the process of expressing Chinese thought to a foreign audience is, conversely, negatively valued and labeled as Chinglish (Wan 2005, 41). Many Chinese educators have therefore targeted Chinglish by seeking to increase educational standards and refine pedagogy.

Chinese English Teachers

Chinese English teachers in private schools like Hong Ri and Washington English echoed both the concerns about Chinglish and the potential solutions outlined by foreign language professionals in China, but at the same time were less consistent in how Chinglish was defined. Many saw Chinglish as a stage that all learners pass through on their way to full fluency. "It's a stage, like crawling before you learn to walk," Fanny told me. At the same time, she could not tolerate Chinglish in those who should know better. "You listen to some people, they every day speak some kind of Chinglish. I want to cut it out! They should study harder . . . if listen to me, I tell them, English is an international language, you should speak it that way." Sophie was a bit less serious about Chinglish, saying that it "is a way to make fun of our own English." Nonetheless, "at the same time we give us an expectation that we hope we can get rid of the 'C' in front of the English, so finally we can speak English in the future." Yet she and all of the other teachers agreed that it was incorrect, and something that teachers should point out to their students. And many suggested various forms of exposure to naturalistic native language use as a potential remedy. Jasmine noted of her students that "if they can read a lot of article in English, their English can be better. They can have the feeling." This "feeling for English," the innate familiarity with the language possessed by native speakers, existed outside the goals of public school foreign language education in Shenyang, which was only concerned with the reproduction of grammatical rules and lexical items on examinations. In fact, public school teachers did not provide very strong opinions on Chinglish at all, often either denying its importance or providing relatively simple descriptions of it. Such responses make sense given that many saw Chinglish as an inevitable symptom of current instructional and pedagogical techniques in public schools that could be overcome only through the extra effort and exposure to native speech practices offered by private schools.

Nevertheless, opinions about what constitutes Chinglish were varied and diverse. Fanny described Chinglish as follows: "You say what you want to say, with your native logics, your native language structures, in different language." She continued:

> I'll give you an example. I think it is the English is badly influenced by the culture. Like, Chinese say, *women keyi chengwei pengyou* (we can become friends). We need that word, "can." But in English we don't have to say "we can become." I think "we can be" or "we become" is okay. So Chinglish is pretty much like translate each word in order. . . . And of course, we don't have the changes of set tenses. Because in Chinese we say, "we go shopping." We say, not "we will," but "We go shopping tomorrow. We go shopping yesterday." We don't have the change for the verb, like in English we have to change the verb tense. And another thing is, Chinese always tell you the conclusion, and don't tell you why we think so. Like, Chinese answer "okay" in response to "how's your holiday." One-word responses. "Did you enjoy your holiday?" "So-so." In Chinese it is okay to reply like that!

Note the vast linguistic ground Fanny covers in this very short extract. Her definition of Chinglish includes overly literal translation, improper use of verb tense, and the pragmatics of responding to questions. Quite notable here is her problematization of "we can become friends" not on the basis of its acceptability in English—which would sound perfectly ordinary in context—but on the basis of the sentence's grammatical transfer from Chinese. Several teachers similarly identified a phrase like "long time no see" as Chinglish because it was a direct translation of the common greeting *hao jiu bu jian*. Fanny's definition of Chinglish thus quickly becomes a laundry list of speech foibles that seem to her ear to flout native-speaker speech practices rather than being a comprehensive syntactic analysis of language transfer elements.

Jasmine described Chinglish as simply the product of inferior English knowledge, especially in students who are often too inexperienced to pay attention to linguistic differences. "You know, [students] can start the words according to its pronunciation, but they can't memorize its Chinese meaning. That's the hardest part. And also the grammar. The order of the words are different between Chinese and English. So sometimes they just translate the sentence in Chinese way, and they will think, 'Eh? We speak Chinese in this way.' Of course, because they don't know what's the difference between these two languages. They're too young to think about it." One of these differences Jasmine identified was the use of different verbs for similar actions in the two languages. "You say answer the phone, right? But we will say, *jie dianhua*. But in fact *jie* in English it is pick up or collect."

Sophie, in contrast, viewed Chinglish as a problem of older speakers:

> This problem [Chinglish] is not as serious, because some people, I think maybe their English is so good, but they just cannot pronounce some of the letters right, so that's not a big problem. And so, I think that usually happens among older generation, like people over forty years old or over thirty-five years old . . . I think, especially people belong to 1990s generation, usually since they were young they go to language schools to study English from foreign teachers. So usually I think among those generation this is not a big problem anymore. But for my generation, it is. So I don't think it's going to be a problem in the future.

Here, Sophie describes Chinglish as largely a phonetic problem, based on the inability of older learners to approximate a native-speaker accent, and one that will eventually die out due to proper exposure to native-speaker phonetic patterns.

These opinions on the nature and sources of Chinglish need to be contextualized by each teacher's background and goals. Fanny's zeal to "cut out" the Chinglish of her students is not only the product of the standardizing tendencies of Shenyang's foreign language education market but also of her own experiences studying in Britain. Valuing native-speaker standards increased her own social capital within a competitive market for competent teachers, where foreign degrees are prized over even the highest domestic credentials. Several teachers also made reference to Chinglish by comparison with Dongbeihua. Fanny, switching into Chinese, informed me: "*Actually my mother is from Beijing, but my father is from Changchun, so he speaks a regional dialect . . . At university, my professor didn't have an accent. My tutor, she didn't have an accent either. So, I think the higher a person's quality [suzhi] the less of an accent they have.*" The focus on Chinese accent and mispronunciation as indicative of Chinglish thus extends from similar concerns about nonstandard Chinese and the local accent. Sophie described her own quest for Standard English as follows:

> I don't want my Chinglish to disappear. I mean, my own English. I want it disappear when I need it to disappear. For example, when I need it to disappear, like, if I get a better job in the future, then if I talk with other people, I want to speak authentic English then, which makes me more professional. But, I still want to keep the Chinglish part when I can have

fun with it. For example, among my Chinese friends, when we speak English together, then Chinglish might be a fun thing to talk, to speak. So Chinglish can be fun, but if we have a choice that we can choose to keep it and we can choose to get rid of it, and then, that will be perfect. For example, I hope one day I will be like a Southern Chinese which can speaks Mandarin and Cantonese, and they can switch, whenever they want. Which means, the more language I can speak, the better I can be.

Sophie's desire for a kind of mastery over her Chinglish, the ability to switch it on or off, to have it disappear or reappear at will, is compared to Chinese speakers who can switch between Mandarin and Cantonese—or between Dongbeihua and standard Mandarin—at will in order to appeal to different groups of people. The value of such self-control over speech repertoires in Chinese was extended to Chinglish, where, even as a stigmatized variety, it sustains relations of intimacy and friendship.

Chinese English Students

In comparison to their teachers, Chinese English students—who tended to be younger and less sure of their own language abilities—were vaguer in defining Chinglish. When I asked Liu Boshan, the student who articulated the difference between mute and oral English in chapter 1, if he knew about Chinglish, he nodded enthusiastically and described how his teacher barred them from using it in class. But when I asked him what Chinglish was, he had to think for several moments. *"It's stuff we say every day, like when we're on the phone we say, 'bye-bye.'"* I asked him if he thought "bye-bye" was an unacceptable truncation of "goodbye," and he said he was not sure. Then he offered the idea that Chinese speakers using English informally tend to impose their own grammar on it. *"It's mostly accent, right? And when your language isn't one thing or the other, okay? For example, 'where are you going?' People say 'you go where?' That's not good."* Teachers' criticism of code-switching in class, of mixing Chinese and English, was internalized by Liu Boshan as representative of Chinglish and thus something to avoid.

Cai Yuhua, another university student, also exhibited a typical level of confusion about the subject. *"I've heard of what it means, but I don't really know it. I've just seen that kind of small book you can buy inside the bookstores on Chinese pronunciation, you can use it in conversation."* The book she showed me to illustrate this is titled *Richang Yingyu* (Everyday English), an ambitious 375-page compendium of English, featuring two to three phrases per page, as outlined in table 5.1.

Each entry in the book comprises a Mandarin sentence written in characters, its English translation, the English phrase rendered phonetically, the phrase

TABLE 5.1 Linguistic equivalences in *Everyday English*

我说四种语言	[Chinese characters]
I speak four languages.	[English]
[ai spiːk fɔː ˈlæŋgwidʒiz]	[Phonetic notation (IPA)]
艾斯鼻克弗兰归支兹	[Chinese character phoneticization]
ai si bi ke fu lan gui zhi zi	[Pinyin transcription of character phoneticization]

transcribed into Chinese characters that approximate the phonetic values of English, and then, finally, the characters transcribed in the Pinyin romanization system. These five lines constitute an intertextual complex combining various forms of English and Mandarin. No mere travel phrasebook, *Richang Yingyu* is an attempt to provide English that can be used in all manner of situations, from business ("I called her office twice but nobody answered.") to pleasure ("Can I invite you to have a dance?"), and even a section called "consolation English" that offers the phrase "You still have your wife and children." In using the book, Cai Yuhua participated in a kind of Chinese fantasy that "proper English" can be acquired through already familiar linguistic skills such as using Mandarin phonetic patterns (as in the phoneticization *ai si bi ke fu lan gui zhi zi*). The book also situates Chinglish as an issue of mere accent, rather than one pertaining to morphology or syntax, which are noticeably absent in *Richang Yingyu*.

Another perspective on Chinglish came from Fei Ge, who was in his late forties at the time I interviewed him. Fei Ge had been learning English informally for over twenty years since his time as a student of Japanese at Shenyang University, where his interest in English had been stimulated by BBC news broadcasts on the radio. Working with tutors and from books he had purchased, Fei Ge managed over the years to become a reasonably proficient English speaker. His pride, however, was his accent, and it was this, he argued, that differentiated him from other students who spoke Chinglish. Fei Ge liked to take me over to a newly opened foreign coffee shop in Shenyang so that he could order in English. Taking out his notebook, in which he kept track of English words or phrases he had heard on television or seen in public, he would point to each individual entry and repeat it for me out loud. "Bee-yu-tee . . . sa-lon . . . beauty salon." As I repeated it back to him, he would then take his pencil and make phonetic notations next to the word. "I speak everything, I want it sound beautiful. Like I born speak the language." Fei Ge also used an electronic dictionary in his quest for the perfect accent, a common tool for many language students in China. These small devices allow the user to input Chinese characters and receive an English translation. Fei Ge's even had a built-in speaker that would say the word for him, from which he would attempt to mimic the pronunciation perfectly.[4] For Fei Ge, accents act as acoustic icons, not simply arrangements of sound patterns but "transparent reflections of personal, social characteristics" (Cavanaugh 2005, 132). Fei Ge's perhaps overly fanciful dream to speak like a native speaker implicates an aspiration toward modernist forms of subjectivity.

Like their teachers, students identified a range of linguistic issues as characteristic of Chinglish, including accent, grammatical transfer, and inappropriate code-switching. They too were almost universal in the desire to eliminate these features from their own speech, consuming instructional books and software, DVDs, foreign media, and language classes as a means of doing so. But without the relative familiarity with native-speaker standards possessed by their teachers, students could only identify Chinglish on an ad hoc basis, as simply what they were told not to say. This often led them to fetishize certain linguistic markers as convenient indexes of standardization, such as a non-Chinese accent, rapid tempo, and knowledge of English slang and idioms. With accent considered the most reliable marker of validity, many Chinese English classes featured an inordinate amount of instruction in pronunciation. Students learn the International Phonetic Alphabet (IPA) from a young age, and most textbooks provide IPA renderings of words along with English spellings. Some private schools have classes specifically focused on pronunciation, where students spend their classroom hours repeating the teacher's words as accurately as possible and correcting minuscule variations in accent. This focus on accent reflected a common perception that speech intrinsically marked as "sounding Chinese" must represent the production of substandard Chinglish.

Foreign Perspectives

One evening, during an advanced oral English class at Hong Ri, an American foreign teacher named Gary elicited from the students simple narratives about their day. This was a means to introduce and reinforce past and future tense forms for the students who were, as usual, preparing for exams. Lily, a Chinese high schooler, responded hesitantly, often interrupting her answer to refer either to her electronic dictionary or to whisper a question to the woman beside her. "I with, ah, my friend . . . we go . . . ah, we at the restaurant have dinner, ah, together." Gary responded by asking her what they ate. "We go to restaurant. We eat, ah, cock." At this reply, Gary seemed somewhat uncomfortable and did not respond for a moment, and Lily attempted to expand on her answer. Gary then asked her to repeat herself, and Lily, perhaps sensing his confusion, audibly whispered to her neighbor, *"How do you say chicken?"* Gary could understand her Mandarin and filled in the conversational gap: "For that, we . . . yeah, we usually say 'chicken.' Cock is . . . well it's kind of like the same thing but you shouldn't use it that way. It's a, you know, it's a boy chicken. But the word is a little bit *yellow* [*huangde*]." Gary code-switched into Mandarin to punctuate his explanation, using a bit of Chinese slang that his students would understand: the word "yellow" is a Chinese euphemism for off-color or pornographic. His final comment provoked a great deal of amusement from the class, who probably recognized the nature of the linguistic confusion, in that Mandarin contains a similar metonymy between chickens (*ji*) and the male genitalia (*jiba*—but also shortened, often jokingly, as *ji* or *jiji*). Lily laughed too, but covered her mouth as she did so in an expression of embarrassment.

What happened in this case is that Lily's electronic dictionary supplied several translations for the Chinese *ji*, one of which happened to be "cock," and this was the word she offered to Gary and to the class. Afterward, Gary was amused not only by the content of Lily's answer but also by what he perceived to be the salacious juxtaposition of the word "cock" spoken by an otherwise demure female Chinese student. The story was also one he later used to entertain other foreign teachers in both the school's office and on informal social occasions. Other such Chinglish stories frequently circulated among foreign teachers after teaching hours, usually in relaxed settings like their apartments or bars. Gary's narrative retelling of Lily's Chinglish highlights inequalities and tensions within a common Chinese English language participation framework, where one particular group of people sit in judgment as knowing listeners and others as insecure speakers.

Going back over my recordings of where Lily uttered the phrase "we eat cock" to her foreign teacher, I later realized that responses by other students to Gary's questions were also riddled with errors. Even the utterance directly preceding Lily's marked phrase ("we at the restaurant") is a direct grammatical transfer from Mandarin and, by the strict criteria of many of the groups I outlined above (particularly Chinese teachers and students), would be considered Chinglish. Yet in the context of this classroom example, it went unnoticed. To think about it another way, had Lily phrased herself in a more innocuous manner, saying, for instance, "we eat hen," the sentence would likely have only been met with a teacher-initiated correction, and the class would have moved on without further comment. It was the content of the utterance itself, particularly its risqué qualities, rather than its linguistic form, that marked Lily's words as Chinglish. That identification was effectively dependent on the interpretive action of Gary as a native English speaker.

The idea of a native speaker, one who acts as a linguistic prototype for nonnative students of the language, has been the subject of intense discussion in the field of second language acquisition, with most recent research describing a continuum of "nativeness" related to the interactional expectations of participants and their familiarity with the linguistic varieties being used (Cook 1999; Davies 2003; Doerr 2009). Moreover, with the continuing spread of English as a global lingua franca among those who use it as a second or additional language, the centrality of the native speaker is gradually being displaced (Seidlhofer 2011). Whatever its ultimate utility in linguistics, however, the idea of the native speaker plays a key role in ideologically regimenting English as a coherent language in Shenyang, and positioning certain types of people as experts in its use. Judgments of whether someone is or is not a native speaker of a given language are, as Alan Davies (2003, 199) writes, always matters of identity: "That is to say that when judgements are elicited about people or about their language what is obtained is some view of the people themselves." The same can be said of how closely nonnative speakers are judged to be modeling the appropriate linguistic behaviors of native speakers.

Miyako Inoue has observed that, in the case of Japanese women's language, perception is an intrinsically political phenomenon, mediated by ideologies that socially construct speakers and listeners through various subjectivities. "A particular mode of hearing and seeing is, then, an effect of a regime of social power, occurring at a particular historical conjuncture, that enables, regulates, and proliferates sensory as well as other domains of experience" (Inoue 2003, 157). Like the novel tones of the early twentieth-century Japanese schoolgirls that Inoue analyzes, Chinglish is imbued with signification through the very act of its observation, or potential observation, by the foreign native speaker. In this case, the social power is not derived from inequalities of gender but from ethnonational origin, with foreign native speakers allowed to "hear" the Chinglish of unauthorized Chinese English speakers. To understand why Gary's story is funny is to exercise membership in a particular class of knowing English authorities. English conversations in Shenyang are overshadowed by an almost omnipresent native speaker even where none is physically present, one who might overhear and find the talk being circulated lacking.

But Chinglish is not only heard in Shenyang; it is seen as well. For many years now, foreigners living in or visiting China have been capturing and circulating on the internet photographs of so-called Chinglish signs, often of a nonsensical or humorous quality (Radtke 2007, 2009). In these cases, Chinglish is usually the product of mistranslation, as when the sign for "disabled toilet" is rendered as "deformed man toilet" (since the Chinese word *canji* means both a disability and a deformity). In my own fieldwork photographs is a picture of a sign from a Chinese restaurant saying "Be careful of landslide"; the crux of the mistranslation comes from the Chinese *dihua*, where *di* can mean both "ground" and "floor," and *hua* "slip" or "slide." Hence "slippery floor" can appear, through either the work of human or computer mistranslation, as "landslide." Significantly, most of the examples collected in print and on the web are not simply language mistakes (bearing in mind Corder's distinction between mistakes and errors outlined above) but have an underlying double meaning or significance. If the mistranslation in the case above were, for instance, a question of lexical ordering ("Careful be of floor slippery"), I likely would not have noticed it and brought out my camera. In other words, there is something here in the nature of the mistranslation that caught my eye and, in the thousands of other examples, the eyes of native English-speaking foreigners.[5] Chinglish images, like their spoken counterparts, are therefore not simply mistakes but errors, semiotically dense and metaphorically rich, evoking an alternative reading or interpretation of the text.

It is no surprise, then, that many foreigners in China feel a certain degree of loss and nostalgia over the government's efforts to eradicate Chinglish. In a published collection of Chinglish photographs entitled *More Chinglish: Speaking in Tongues*, Oliver Radtke, a longtime German resident of Beijing, weighs the possibility of ridiculing Chinglish, and by extension Chinese English speakers, against the benefits of recording it: "I am more convinced than ever that Chinglish has to stay. It's a window into the Chinese mind, a phenomenon that goes beyond cheap jokes and finger pointing" (Radtke 2009, 5). His book is intended partly as a tribute to Chinglish and partly as a historical document, in that it attempts to preserve a linguistic form he feels is endangered by overzealous public officials. Radtke's book also features an interview with the linguist Victor Mair, who maintains that Chinglish is valuable, not because it is humorous, but because it is revealing.

> As a scholar of Chinese language, one wants to get beyond the humor of a particular instance of Chinglish and figure out what caused it to happen in the first place. This is what I refer to as the *etiology* of a particular mistranslation. I don't think this kind of research is at all shallow. It frequently requires a great deal of effort and ingenuity to come up with a satisfactory, convincing answer. For the pure linguist, research on Chinglish is its own reward. (Mair, interviewed in Radtke 2009, 10)

The significance of Chinglish, for Mair, is what it can reveal to the scholar about the state of Chinese English speakers' interlanguage and the nature of cross-linguistic influence between the two languages. By understanding the etiology of how Chinglish is produced—in other words, by excavating its linguistic origins—the linguist can better understand the process of English acquisition in Chinese students. But one is also struck by the evident pleasure derived from this process—it is, after all, "its own reward"—and the sense that Chinglish is less a problem of translation than an intellectual puzzle to be worked over, pondered, and eventually solved by the linguist as detective.

In the vast majority of cases, though, these are not texts aimed at native speakers (or linguists) as a potential audience. There are, of course exceptions, and many online Chinglish images document signage in tourist locations or government offices; but texts intended for public consumption by foreigners, such as brand advertising, pedagogical materials, menus (in preparation for foreign visitors to Beijing and Shanghai), and so forth, are typically meticulously prepared. There is, however, another key audience for English signage, and that is a Chinese audience that associates English text with foreign authenticity (Pan 2010). Many of the instances of Chinglish I collected in China appeared in places that do not cater explicitly to foreigners, such as in the restaurant with the slippery floor, but they certainly catered to Chinese who considered themselves worldly and modern. English acts, in these cases, more as a signifier of foreignness than as a denotationally explicit message. As Jan Blommaert (2010, 29–32) argues, such phrases are emblematic in that they evoke complex associative meanings between the form of the words and social attitudes toward those forms, quite separate from their referential meanings (see also Blommaert 2015b). Similarly, nonsensical Chinese characters circulate in similar fashion in English-speaking countries, representing as they do mysticism, wisdom, and other orientalized attributes, quite apart from what they might actually mean.

Despite the lack of a clear set of diagnostics or descriptions of what constitutes Chinglish, native English speakers nonetheless demonstrate multiple interpretations of what Chinglish means in the mouths, or texts, of Chinese speakers. This was true of cases where foreigners were explicit addressees of Chinese speech, but also where foreigners act as omniscient overhearers of speech or text aimed at others. All of these interpretations are premised on the native speaker as ultimate arbiter of the linguistic standard and the meaning of variation from the norm. Chinglish can therefore be given a measure of structural coherence only by its incorporation into prescriptive—and thus ideological—systems of value. However, judgments about Chinglish, no matter the basis on which the ascription to this category is made, relate not to the content of the utterance but to the intersubjective relations between interactants, specifically their relative levels of authority, expertise, and social capital.

The Misadventures of Xiaoming

The hilarity with which many foreigners circulated stories of Chinglish speech or images of Chinglish text is part of a generalized narrative genre within which linguistic inequalities can be enacted. Chinglish jokes were also common among certain groups of Chinese, especially teachers, often used pedagogically to illustrate the dangers of Chinglish for projecting a fully competent transnational persona. In a planning seminar for the teachers working in his school, for instance, Winston once stressed the idea of naturalistic talk, and illustrated this with the story of a student who employed overly flowery language on a regular basis. "He wants to say, 'You look really good today, look really happy today.' Instead, he said, 'You look radiant today.' Am I? What, am I pregnant or something?" The student's error was not simply a question of Standard English but also referenced how foreign language examiners watch to see students using appropriate adjectives rather than just obscure or difficult ones, and Winston turned that into a joke for his teachers about how he received this particular compliment. Note how laughing at the joke positions both Winston and his teachers as participants in a shared framework of language proficiency—like the native speaker, they too are in on it. In another context, during an annual awards ceremony for Washington English teachers, Mr. Bai made a speech that included several English phrases, despite his own limited fluency. Several of the teachers seated beside me began to joke with each other over his pronunciation, saying that it sounded no better than that of some of their kindergarten students. Humor can thus operate at varying levels of expertise to establish linguistic authority and authenticity by one person over another.

Charles used joking narratives—in which jokes are embedded in other types of speech events in order to comment on broader contextual factors—about Chinglish to great effect. During one of his classes, I recorded several joking narratives he used to entertain the students, a strategy he told me was quite helpful for dealing with dense or boring material. In other words, these jokes were diversions he used to lighten up the mood and get students laughing. But, as he pointed out to me several times, they were also pedagogical, insofar as they were meant to teach the students the value of their language lessons by highlighting the negative effects of Chinglish. In this way, jokes are powerful speech acts because they straddle a line between public and private, serious and playful (as in the cliché "I was just joking . . . but seriously"): a form of ideology hiding in plain sight, allowing a certain nonserious deniability about the content of the narrative while still making the crucial point that language locates individuals within a socially meaningful cartography encompassing the values of power, modernity, agency, or, for those disfluent in the dominant modes of talk, their opposites (Hill 2008). As Joel Sherzer writes, jokes are forms of speech play that "involve complex manipulations of linguistic, interactional, and cultural relations" (2002, 36; see also Basso 1979). They draw on, and are made meaningful by, the surrounding discourse context and act as vehicles for serious forms of social commentary, but served in an easy-to-dismiss, lighthearted idiom. These speech acts therefore serve to create, maintain, and reinforce relations of inequality among different registers.

The stories Charles told fit within a genre of humorous narratives frequently found in oral discourse and popular media in urban China. They recount the adventures of people out of place: farmers in the big city, provincials in the capital, ordinary Chinese people abroad. Often the protagonist of this type of story is simply referred to as Xiaoming (literally, "little bright"), a generic name with no discerning individual properties for the character other than that he or she is Chinese. Xiaoming narratives tend to dramatize contexts that the audience would find familiar but that the protagonist finds alien and strange, such as a peasant eating in a fancy restaurant for the first time or contemplating people playing golf. For an urban audience these are all perceptually familiar activities; even urban citizens who have never played golf can recognize the game and imagine themselves behaving appropriately in that context. The fact that Xiaoming often behaves inappropriately (in one story I heard, clapping and cheering wildly as a golfer is about to swing, which leads to him being ejected from the golf course) incorporates the listener as a knowing member of the audience. In this sense, Xiaoming narratives are a kind of othering device within an increasingly stratified society, identifying the opposing social categories of urban citizen (*shimin*) and backward peasant (*nongmin*) and placing the listener firmly in the position of the former. On this particular day in Charles's class there were seven students in attendance, all teenagers preparing to enter their final year of high school before university—and thus were all cramming for the all-important university entrance examination. Two of the jokes he told are as follows:

> *There's a very simple joke, okay? There's a single word, a word, an* expression *that says* "look out." *Just a very old joke, okay. Xiaoming . . . he went to America. When he got to America he lived in an apartment building, and in the building he lived on the first floor. Then one day, he heard from outside someone shouting, "Look out!" He thought it meant look outside.* Look . . . out . . . *He thought it meant look outside.* Something like "Look out of the window." Yeah? But actually, *in reality we all know what this means, right? Then, he looks outside. He opened the window and looked outside.* "There's nothing going on." Nothing special. *There wasn't anything special out there. And then . . . HUA! A bucket of dirty water. A bucket* dirty water, *just* pour down. *Just came down. It spilled all over his body. He thinks it's strange, why did this person ask me to look outside? Did she pour the water on me on purpose?*

> *Xiaoming, it's Xiaoming again. He goes to America.* Xiaoming was taking driving lesson. So, the day he went to the driving exam, the driving test, to get the driving license . . . *Then, Xiaoming gets in the car. The exam-*

iner sits beside him, beside him in the passenger seat. Xiaoming is very afraid. Very nervous. He starts driving. He drives straight ahead. He sees ahead there's a sign, traffic sign. On it is written, the meaning is you must turn left. There's a sign, okay? When Xiaoming sees this he's just so nervous, and he asks the examiner beside him, "Left? To the left?" The examiner says, "Right." So Xiaoming turns right, so he failed.

There is a great deal of code-mixing throughout these extracts. Charles intentionally told most of the jokes in Mandarin but highlighted key parts in English. Prosodically, the Mandarin was spoken rapidly, but his English speech slowed down, adding additional stress and emphasis so that students could follow more easily. The change in rate of speech also marked translation boundaries, alerting his audience that a different language was coming. Many of the code-switches anaphorically refer to the preceding words, translating Mandarin portions into English for the students. This provided students with two channels of related information, allowing them to pay attention to new English words or phrases while still ensuring comprehension in Mandarin. The code-switches also mark important pedagogical content: Charles highlights an expression on which the joke hinged ("look out"), similar to other expressions he had taught in the preceding hour, such as "out of date" and "necessary evil." In the second joke, he emphasizes several new words introduced earlier in the lesson, such as "afraid" and "nervous." Therefore, while it might appear that Charles is abandoning his role as teacher by shifting into a jocular tone, left implicit is the fact that students are still being instructed, just in a more indirect way.

Beyond these stylistic considerations, the narrative content is also important. Both jokes feature the foreign as the backdrop for the events. Since studying abroad was the ultimate goal for many of the students, distancing the setting of the joke from the students' immediate social environment engaged them within a fantasy structure of future possibility—the hope of going abroad—while also exploring the negative consequences of not being linguistically prepared—namely, being laughed at. Situating the stories abroad also severs the audience's connection to the setting as knowing social actors. While Charles had lived abroad for several years, none of the students had experience outside of China. Whereas other popular Xiaoming narratives in China might dramatize the plight of peasants in the big city—toward whom the audience can relate as actors familiar with both settings—in Charles's narratives the audience must take his word that the surrounding social contexts are as he presents them (the disposal of dirty water over a balcony, or the experience of a driving exam).

Charles's expertise was not simply the product of his status as narrator; in other parts of the class, he worked to establish his own credentials as a navigator of multilingual discourse contexts. In the following extract from the same class, Charles used the word "beware" as a springboard for an extended narrative about an experience from his time in Southeast Asia.

> CHARLES: *I remember a while ago, okay, I was in a, uh, staying in a place in Singapore [or] Malaysia. At the time, uh, then, I just saw a lot of, um, inside the homes, one of the homes had a yard, had a yard, a big yard. And there was a big iron gate, a gate, really high, like this* [raises arm], *and the fence around the yard was for raising dogs, raising those kind of dogs, not like a* puppy, right? Not a puppy. *Not that kind of nice dog. Yeah?* [inaudible] *They were all that kind of dog, okay?*
>
> STUDENT: *No owner?*
>
> C: *I didn't know either, because I've never raised a dog like that. I don't know. I wasn't prepared, yeah? Then, inside they were raising two or three dogs, inside the yard. So obviously the dogs were there to watch the gate, right? And on the gate they had put a* notice, yeah? [Writes on whiteboard.] They put a notice on the . . . on the gate.
>
> S: *Watch out for?*
>
> C: *Yes, on the notice was written, English and Chinese, [because] in Singapore there are two kinds of language*, in Singapore there are two major languages. English and, uh, Chinese, *right? So,* in every notice, they write two different kinds of language, which means the same. *They wrote* beware of dogs. *So actually, what is this announcing? It's announcing* be aware of . . . [Writes on whiteboard.] Be aware of, *make you pay attention. To what?* Dogs. *Pay attention to what?* Dogs. *Then underneath they wrote four Chinese characters: ferocious dogs are inside.*

Charles's story serves to demonstrate his ability to understand Singapore's cultural and linguistic environment, knowing the languages in use and how to respond appropriately within that context. Charles correctly interprets the sign's indexical reference to be wary of specific dogs within the area circumscribed by the yard's fence and not, by way of possible contrast, dogs in general. He thus narrates himself as a knowing actor in this story, one who understands not only the semantic meaning of the sign but also its pragmatic implications, and implicitly signals his own ties to the foreign as a distinct social and cultural milieu.

To return to the two Xiaoming jokes Charles told earlier, their foreign setting authorizes Charles as the narrator because of his foreign experience, while deauthorizing the audience's ability to critique or contest the joke's metapragmatic message devaluing Xiaoming's Chinglish. The students may desire to go abroad, but are "not-yet" participants within this linguistic chronotope, and must defer to Charles's evaluative judgments of Xiaoming's behavior and mistakes due to their own lack of expertise. And it is these errors that Xiaoming makes in English that form the crux of each joke: misunderstanding the directive to "look out" and confounding the two meanings of "right." But note, ironically, that the crucial misunderstanding in each case is not a question of phonology or syntax—traditional linguistic vectors for Chinglish errors described above—but semantics and pragmatics. Xiaoming does not err in understanding the referential content of the English phrases. They are ambiguous, and Xiaoming merely picks the wrong semantic interpretation. In other words, we must come to grips with the fact that Xiaoming's problem in these jokes, and by extension the students' problem, is not with the form of English itself (Chinglish or Standard English) but with something more abstract: the socially acquired knowledge of how certain words and phrases can take on different meanings in different social contexts. This is knowledge that largely comes from living in and experiencing the language in context, by being abroad, rather than from the classroom; it is knowledge gained by use rather than study.

This would seem to undermine the logic of studying English in Charles's class; indeed, why bother to learn from him if such pragmatic knowledge is ultimately unattainable in China? But Charles's Xiaoming narratives enregister these errors as indicative of a particular social type who uses English inappropriately—a person who speaks Chinglish and not English, and is therefore ill-equipped to maneuver within the global domains he describes. The goal of language education, the transformation from flawed students of foreign culture to transnationally mobile social actors, is embedded within the narrative as a higher order of indexicality. Charles's narratives are thus models of virtuosity. Multiple interpretations are layered together: a lesson for the students, the importance of English in navigating complex multilingual environments, and Charles's own expertise in guiding students toward this destination.

Far from a legitimate register or local variant, Chinglish in the Chinese context represents a personal failure of modernization, a sociolinguistic blight to be cordoned and eliminated. Imperfect English is thus pathologized in reference to a globalized world of English discourse, a form of disorder rather than difference, highlighting the illegitimacy of the stigmatized Chinglish speaker to participate effectively in this speech community and in turn reinforcing the authority of those who "know" English to evaluate the speech of those who do not. The source of Charles's knowledge becomes unchallengeable on any other basis, such as perhaps checking a dictionary or a textbook, because the jokes hinge on pragmatic contextual factors that are bound within the narrative itself. But more importantly for Charles, Xiaoming narratives naturalize a particular logic that underwrites the entire private language-learning enterprise in China, the idea that students need to pay for classes to speak perfect English lest they be relegated to backwardness and irrelevance. The implications for the students may not be immediately obvious, but they are nonetheless clear: study English well, or look what might happen.

Power, Authenticity, Expertise

So what is Chinglish? Is it an artifact of grammatical transfer? Vague, general, abstract nouns? A localized Chinese variety of English? A bad accent? Unfortunate translations? All of these? None? Who gets to decide? What seems to be at issue in each case is not actually the language itself, which really acts more as a proxy for the unequal relations between speaker and listener, the judged and those who do the judging. As Judith Irvine (1989) has observed, the mastery of linguistic codes has economic and social value, and in their performance we recognize the authority of experts (based on a "chain of authentication" from the expert's attestation to our validation of it) who are capable of using and judging the use of a particular code (see also Bourdieu 1991, 57–61). All English language production in China is mediated by these distinct power differentials. Expertise in English, and thus the authority to judge the acceptability of the utterances of others or to relegate them to the category of Chinglish, maintains divisions between native speakers, Chinese foreign language professionals, and students. While the actors within this participation framework engage with each other in frequent conversations, it is Chinese students who produce Chinglish and linguists and teachers who interpret it, Chinese students who must monitor their own speech and experts who have no fear of their own mistakes. In an echo of what Bourdieu (1991, 137–139) terms "strategies of euphemization," involving the self-censorship of language users according to their rank in the chain of authority (from native speaker on down), the magic of Chinglish is the ability of this discourse to mask relations of inequality as (often humorous) differences of language form rather than the judgment of experts sanctioned by the authority of their expertise as native speakers or language professionals. The symbolic violence demanded by this censorship "can only be exercised by the person who exercises it, and endured by the person who endures it, in a form which results in its misrecognition as such, in other words, which results in its recognition as legitimate" (Bourdieu 1991, 140). Chinglish does not exist in the words themselves; words only become Chinglish when heard and interpreted by a particular audience in a particular way. The incredible power of the native speaker's gaze is evident in the way Chinglish was banished for the Olympics as a preemptive strike. The state attempted to eliminate Chinglish before it could be publicly viewed or heard, to foreclose the possibility that Chinglish texts could be resignified as a fault line within China's chronotopic modernity. It is the very anxieties of status in the neoliberal order of globalization that imbue Standard English with such prestige in China and erad-icate the potential ontology of a localized variety of Chinese English.

This disparate array of linguistic features that potentially qualify as Chinglish would lack any coherence as a distinct code without the unifying presence of the foreigner as language expert. To return to Pit Corder's distinction between a mistake and an error, it is the figure of the foreigner who provides the Chinglish utterance's signification. What is important is not the content of the utterance itself but the interpretive action of the listener who formulates the category in the act of perceiving it and who can identify the words as either a meaningless, insig-nificant mistake ("we ate hen") or as a meaningfully significant error ("we ate cock"). The listener's judgment is dependent on a claim to authority, either by being a native speaker (as in the case of foreign teachers) or by having their ex-pertise guaranteed by other credentials (being a foreign language teaching pro-fessional or experience studying abroad, for instance).

Chinglish is an interactive phenomenon, formed within the ongoing metadis-cursive evaluations of speakers and listeners in relation to each other. The social valuations of various registers may be shared, but the right to label certain utter-ances as belonging to one or another register is reserved for those "in the know," who through the proper deployment of semiotic resources (university degrees, time spent abroad, clothing, mannerisms, highlighting of friendships or foreign links) can assert their authority to interpret the words of others. All of these in-dexical associations tie individuals to a notion of foreignness, thus metonymi-cally reproducing the perceived "natural" order of international relations where the West serves as a linguistic model for developing regions. These judgments do not exist solely within the confines of singular communicative events, but circu-late (both orally and virtually) as discourses within an increasingly globalized speech community. Circulation promotes a coherence, an identity of particular forms of talk as a distinct sociolinguistic register iconically appended to a distinct kind of speaker: inarticulate, localized, backward, and so forth. The consequences of this identification are no less severe for their incorporation into genres of hu-mor and joking, or for the evident pleasure of their foreign observers and profes-sional interpreters (linguists and teachers). Even the most affectionate laughter, the kindest nostalgia, can still put people in their place.

RACIOLINGUISTIC IDENTITIES

The White Foreign Body of the Native
English Speaker

> Strangely, the foreigner lives within us: he is the hidden face of our
> identity, the space that wrecks our abode, the time in which under-
> standing and affinity founder. By recognizing him within ourselves,
> we are spared detesting him in himself.

Julia Kristeva, *Strangers to Ourselves*

It is fair to say that the relations between Chinese and foreign teachers in Shenyang are characterized by a deep ambivalence. While many teachers develop warm and lasting intercultural friendships with each other (and indeed, this was true of my own time teaching), the symbolic capital possessed by the native speaker nevertheless means that these relationships are always underscored by inequalities that are not just financial but structural in nature. As I noted before, foreign teachers receive significantly higher pay (and additional perks like return airfare and extra vacation) unavailable to Chinese teachers, even those who have studied abroad and earned degrees from foreign universities. Foreigners also experience a higher degree of freedom in the workplace: their teaching is not as carefully monitored or evaluated, they can skip classes without serious penalty, they generally do not have to plan their lessons, and they are not held responsible for students who miss classes or are failing. Chinese teachers find themselves constrained in just these ways. But the ambivalence goes deeper than mere professional differences, and in this chapter I will argue that it is ultimately rooted in the peculiar role that foreigners, or more specifically certain *kinds* of foreigners, play in Chinese modernism.

In August 2010, a reporter for a Liaoning provincial newspaper encountered two white foreigners relaxing by the side of a major pedestrian shopping street. One was sitting on a skateboard and bleeding from a scrape on his leg; both were drinking beer on a hot and sunny day while onlookers sat nearby, staring curiously at these two outsiders. With one of the foreigners' Chinese girlfriend interpreting—who was left conspicuously unnamed in the article—the reporter interviewed the two foreign teachers before filing a story for the newspaper entitled "Foreigners in Shenyang Make More Than 4,000–10,000 RMB Every Month." The article's focus on salary is not in itself surprising given the wide disparities in pay that have emerged since the reestablishment of private enterprise and markets in the 1980s. A typical university graduate might have expected between 2,000 and 3,000 yuan a month at the time, but even 10,000 yuan was not a shocking number to a public inured to hearing about million yuan bribes and other backroom deals. Indeed, the author justifies these numbers with a classical saying: "Foreign monks give better sermons" (*Wailai de heshang hui nianjing*), usually taken to mean that an outsider will naturally be better paid. But what was of real interest for both the reporter and his readers—the topics that actually dominated most of the article itself—were questions about who these foreigners were: "Where do they work, how much can they earn, do they make enough money, and are they happy in Shenyang?" Several urban residents (*shimin*) were also interviewed. Some noted that the high salary was a consequence of the "dignity" of the teachers' status. Others speculated that perhaps the foreigners suffered the same "bitterness" and high demands that Chinese employees did. The tone was not of outrage at these high salaries, but curiosity: Who are these people, and why are they here? Are they like us, or are they different? In other words, the emphasis of the article was not simply on knowing more about the lives of foreigners in Shenyang (their money, their purposes, their impressions of China) but about making them knowable social actors, to attribute to them familiar motivations, desires, and objectives.

In this chapter, I argue that categories such as race, foreignness, and the East-West dichotomy are discursively produced through complex semiotic processes such as those displayed in this newspaper article. The precise natures of the foreigner and the Chinese are created within local-level interactions involving a range of material and nonmaterial resources. In numerous interactions, Chinese people drew on circulating images and discourses as models of identity defining the nature of both these foreign others and themselves (see also Alim, Rickford, and Ball 2016; Bashkow 2006; Basso 1979; Roth-Gordon 2017; Rutherford 2003). A key concern was not the simple emulation of foreign subjectivities, as though this were a strict case of colonial mimesis (Bhabha 1994), but to both understand the virtues and flaws of each and ultimately surmount them, to remake the modern self as a dialectical resolution of the East-West binary. My goal in this chapter is to examine how the body of the foreigner comes to act as an iconic representation of the related values of whiteness, modernity, fluency, and cosmopolitan subjectivity.

I also aim to explore a central paradox of the semiotics of voice and intentionality, namely, the dynamic in which speakers are always, and at the same time, both willful participants in interaction and also characterological types, that is, semiotic representations of something else (Agha 2005; Barker, Harms, and Lindquist 2014; Duranti 2015; Inoue 2006). How we can be both agentive actors, controlling the flow of discourse with others, and agentless figures trapped by and suspended within the representational economies around us is a central question of contemporary anthropology. To be an individual is to inhabit a particular present, mediating and modulating visions of the self in an ongoing flow of conversation. But to be a figure is to inhabit a prescribed role within higher-order, and less time-sensitive, cultural imaginaries such as gender, class, or modernity (see Keane 2007). In this instance, I want to explore how foreigners are often emptied of individuality by the circulation of performative and discursive scripts, reduced to a role and a social type, and alienated from their own social productivity. When foreigners are, for instance, invited to a restaurant opening, requested to address an academic conference, or asked to judge a televised competition, they are acting within generally accepted frameworks that see them as willing participants within the dramatology of everyday life, adding their own symbolic weight to an interaction and sealing it with an authenticity derived from their sociological status as esteemed outsiders. Contesting these prescribed roles, as many foreigners often did, provokes discussion and, occasionally, revision of expectations, but more generally is perceived as morally problematic, as a failure on the part of what they represent (such as "Western culture") rather than their own agentive opposition to the dynamic of interaction.

Such reductions flatten the diversity of the foreigner as a category of person. No longer simply a national outsider, the "foreigner" is perceived as a particular racialized, gendered, and classed figure in a process Gal and Irvine (1995) term "erasure." In short, the foreigner is often portrayed, in media, in advertising, and in meta-semiotic discourses of their significance in fields such as teaching, as white, male, and rich. This is not to say that Shenyangers do not recognize members of other groups as foreigners, but that they see the former as the paradigmatic representation of this class of people, and as such, one who embodies the indexical values that the category entails. It is within the absences from explicit discourse, as Jane Hill (2008, 32–33) reminds us, and the natural inferences we make as properly socialized participants of speech communities, that racial ideologies often hide. When Jasmine asked me if I knew a *bairen* (white person) who might be willing to teach part-time at her school, I asked if the teacher had to be white. Jasmine paused for a moment and then answered, "*Well, any kind of foreigner is okay, but . . .*" and then shrugged her shoulders. That "but," invoking as it does the ideal type she was referencing, serves to reinforce a particular model of the foreigner even as it concedes the diversity contained within it.

I believe this erasure is significant for two reasons. First, emptying foreigners of agentive individuality makes them complicit within the discursive formation of chronotopic modernity. Foreigners are necessary to the English language enterprise in Shenyang not merely because they are native speakers but, even more importantly, because they are catalytic intermediaries. The path to modernity exists *through* them and the template established by the West, and their presence (or absence) authenticates (or delegitimates) the actions of Shenyangers who engage with this discourse. In effect, the foreigners' own intentions are immaterial to this process. Second, though, such erasures also make them ripe for appropriation. Without individuality, the foreigner is a caricature of the semiotic values attributable to "the West" (again, as a discursive construct), allowing a subject position that Liu Xin, in the context of post-Tiananmen economic reforms, calls "the otherness of self" (X. Liu 2002; see also Chen 1995). Racialized categories of otherness become potential resources for thinking about and producing the self within a society otherwise ideologically conceived as homogeneous. And as a proxy for the foreign, English acts as a convenient order of indexicality within which these selves can be produced.

Articulations of Race and Ethnonational Belonging

People often told me that China does not have racism because China has only one race. Such blithe disregard for the realities of both diversity and racism in China—despite abundant evidence to the contrary (see Blum 2001; Carrico 2017; Y. Cheng 2011; Dikötter 1992)—is symptomatic of a more general occlusion of race as a symbolic trope of difference and inequality in contemporary Shenyang. Ethnonational consciousness in China is a sentiment reserved for "barbarians" at the periphery of the modern nation-state in contrast to the Han Chinese, who officially comprise 91 percent of the population. As many have observed, the Chinese term *minzu*, usually translated as race, ethnicity, or nationality, is typically reserved for nonmajority, non-Han racial others, the so-called ethnic minorities (*shaoshu minzu*), who are concomitantly portrayed as poor, rural, and marginal (Gladney 2004; Harrell 1995). In both the geographical and political topography of the modern Chinese state, minorities are peripheral even as they have been recruited into broader national discourses that imagine the Han as a nexus for the dissemination of civilization to border areas (Fiskesjö 2006; McCarthy 2009; Mullaney 2011; Mullaney et al. 2012). At the same time, the Han themselves (a convenient heuristic for those at the center of the nation-state rather than any "real" term of biogenetic distinctiveness) receive little attention as a distinctly ethnic population.[1] "The widespread definition and representation of the minority as exotic, colorful, and primitive homogenizes the undefined majority as united, mono-ethnic, and modern" (Gladney 2004, 51).

And yet at some level, Chinese are aware of themselves as an ethnonational group in opposition to the outside world. This mind-set was often indexed through the distinction between second-person-plural foreigners (*nimen waiguoren*) and first-person-inclusive-plural Chinese (*zanmen Zhongguoren*) in conversation: you foreigners act one way, we Chinese another. The latter term is significant in that it draws on an inclusivity/exclusivity distinction in the Mandarin pronoun system; the inclusive *zanmen* includes all addressees (all of us), while the exclusive *women* omits one or more (some of us).[2] Pragmatically, *zanmen* (or the more colloquial *zan*) can also be used to mark intimacy, informality, and emotional commitment to shared experience (H. Zhao 1987). In situations where interactants build social ties with each other through collective social action (such as eating and drinking), the phatic qualities of *zanmen* emphasize the close bonds between them. Thus, the use of the inclusive *zanmen* as a modifier of "Chinese" invokes an essentialized, racialized ethnonational identity built on common narratives of genetic, linguistic, historical, and cultural convergence and similarity, and positioned in explicit contrast to the collective properties of foreigners as a whole. Although the Han majority stands as a unified but deracialized placeholder within discourses of Chinese nationalism, Han Chinese themselves become racialized subjects in contrast to those representatives of global normativity known as foreigners.

The term *waiguoren* (literally, "outside country person") means "foreigner" in Mandarin, with *waiguo* (foreign) and *guowai* (abroad) acting as adjective and noun, respectively.[3] In theory these terms would be fairly obvious to define and use in context, but they are actually quite complex and dense semiotic categories. What is foreign when all people and objects are linked by networks of hybridity? Many of the commodities branded as foreign in China are actually made in the vast manufacturing hubs of Guangzhou and Shenzhen, while foreigners occupy a range of categorical "othernesses," including biogenetic, cultural, legal, historical, political, and so forth. What unites various classes of people and objects into these categories? Additionally, the foreign is not a neutral term of outsiderness but one laminated with sociohistorical values. Especially within the context of Shenyang's limited social horizons, the foreign acts as a signifier of distinction within an unequal economy of sign relationships (Bourdieu 1984). Foreign clothes, foreign talk, foreign foods, foreign architecture, foreign academic credentials, and foreign people all exceed the value of their Chinese counterparts in various ways. Many of the narratives, objectives, and actions I have discussed so far in this book are motivated by a desire to possess and harness this semiotic power, to adopt and appropriate the prestige of the foreign for oneself. The foreign is therefore both a sign of, and a conduit to, the modern as an overarching discursive and semiotic category; it is a convenient heuristic that gives coherence to otherwise unstable and fragmented realities. Consequently I propose to treat "foreigner" and "foreign" less as descriptions of real categorical differences between certain types of people and certain types of things and more as semiotic registers, an entanglement of people and things, all bearing the foreign as a stamp of exoticism (Dikötter 2006). And these entanglements are consonant with discursive practices that excavate and systematize the features of the categories being proposed.

A relevant (and deeply interconnected) example of these processes can be found in the notion of authenticity in China. Beth Notar's (2006) analysis of ethnic Dali tourist markets notes the opposition between fake (*jia*) and true (*zi* in the Bai dialect), a product of both the tourist trade and the newly emergent consumer culture bringing exotic commodities (liquors, medicines, clothing, food) from outside Dali to market (see also Chubb 2015; Y. Lin 2011). While many treat authenticity as a quality attributable to the essence of an object, the "spirit of the place" from which it comes, Notar argues that, for Dali market women and their transnational tourist customers, authenticity is a product of "narrative value," the stories told about the objects being sold. Thus, in order to hawk their mass-produced bracelets to tourists as tokens of antique Bai craft production, market women constructed narrative histories of the object, placing its origin in the hands of former generations of ethnically identifiable producers. These narrative strategies were accompanied by material practices such as darkening the bracelet over a candle flame and then polishing the raised surfaces to give the object the appearance of tarnished silver. "What is strange about this phenomenon of authenticating narratives is that a fake object, accompanied by a false narrative, could become truer, more authentic, than an actual antique" (Notar 2006, 81). Authenticity is therefore a semiotic register combining discursive and material practices to construct a simulacrum of the antique, the success of which determines its value in the market for tourist souvenirs. As we saw in chapter 5, a similar process is apparent in the delegitimation of certain types of discourse in China as Chinglish rather than authentic English, a designation crucially dependent on the position of the listener within China's English language participation framework and his or her ability to embody the signs of foreignness successfully. Just as authenticity does not inhere in the bracelet's history (its reality as a mass-produced object) but in the attributes created for it through narrative and material practices, the racial, ethnic, and foreign qualities of people are emergent from processes of discourse and representation rather than any naturalized individual essence.

So what comprises the semiotic register of the foreigner? A casual glance at representations of foreigners in China reveals that foreigners are stereotypically represented by a generic phenotype: white, usually blonde-haired and blue-eyed. Although other depictions exist, as in advertisements for global sporting brands that often feature athletes of color, they are usually of recognizable individuals (like Michael Jordan or Tiger Woods) and markedly stand out against the panoply of otherwise grinning, smiling, and laughing white people hawking every product or service imaginable. English school advertising is a prime example (see figures 6.1 and 6.2).

Billboards for English schools grace many public places throughout Shenyang, often bounding construction sites or lining heavily trafficked streets. The faces in the stock photographs are predominantly white and typically blonde, and if they do contain any measure of diversity it is usually in the form of an Asian person. But this too is part of the structure of the message, since the goal of English language acquisition for Chinese people is to take their place within the global system.

A similar example can be found in television dramas, which increasingly feature the white foreigner as a stock character.[4] Speaking in halting but complex and grammatically well-formed Mandarin, these characters represent the West as a field of power and wealth even as they comment on their own inability to comprehend Chinese culture. If men, they often exist as a romantic foil for their female Chinese interlocutors, acting as libidinal commentary on transnational capi-

FIGURE 6.1. Advertising for Yinglun Foreign Language Training in Shenyang

FIGURE 6.2. Advertising billboard for Pattison English

talism itself; if female, they usually act as an eroticized exotic for the Chinese gaze (S. Lu 2000). But as Louisa Schein has argued, white female bodies on display in China are not strictly a matter of sexualized desire but act as points of condensation for a range of values marked as new and modern (Schein 1994; see also Johannson 1999). Therefore, whether male or female, the foreigner as television character acts as "repertoire of knowledge . . . for cosmopolitan citizens charged with the millennial mission of propelling China into a global future" (H. Lee 2006, 516; see also Song 2015; Sun 2002).

If the white foreign body is paradigmatic of both English and modernity, it stands in contrast to other racialized bodies that represent less developed temporal states. The linguistic capital of native English-speaking foreign teachers articulates with a more embodied form of racial capital, in which white skin acts as a metonymic representation of globalized social value. Other bodies could be treated quite negatively in my experience, and I witnessed several occasions where Chinese described the supposedly inferior racial characteristics of African or non-Chinese Asian individuals—particularly those who were Japanese, which derives from an antagonistic historical relationship.[5] And these negative evaluations translated too into the relative measures of success that particular foreigners had in cashing in on their linguistic capital. Teachers of color were considered notoriously problematic by school administrators because they would inevitably be the subject of complaints by suspicious parents—how can someone "like that" possibly be teaching my child "good English"?[6] White teachers, in contrast, had relatively few problems, and even the worst ones could bounce from job to job, school to school, and still make a living despite their lack of ability.

What Are Foreign Teachers Good For?

The exact nature of the conflict between foreign and Chinese teachers became evident when I invited some of the Washington English teachers out to lunch as a way of thanking them for their assistance. Fanny, the head teacher, Bliss, the most senior teacher (who was addressed by the others as "*elder sister*"), and four others accepted. But when I walked into the teachers' office that day, hungry and ready to leave, only Fanny was at her desk. We made some small talk, but Fanny seemed grumpy and guarded. The other teachers drifted in (and sometimes out) gradually, and though we were half an hour late, I finally managed to lead them to a "traditional" Dongbei restaurant two doors down from the school. Unfortunately, I had neglected to examine the restaurant's reputation, and was disappointed to discover that I had chosen a restaurant with quite possibly the slowest and surliest service in the city. We could not even get hot tea brought to our table. Bliss leafed indifferently through the menu, and Fanny read a newspaper. No one was talking.

As it turned out, I had stumbled into an ongoing conflict between the foreign and Chinese teachers that had, that very morning, come to a head. Bliss eventually explained that when a foreign teacher does not show up for a class (the words she used were "gets lost," as though the foreigner had taken a wrong turn on the way to work), none of the other foreign teachers are willing to fill in, so a Chinese teacher has to do it instead. The Chinese teacher might have only minutes to prepare a complex lesson, the students would be invariably disappointed (and occasionally combative) at being taught by a local, and no one had any illusions that they might be paid extra for the additional work. And so the Chinese teachers had been coordinating a form of passive resistance to the practice: if a foreign teacher was late or missing, they would collectively disappear from the office, leaving to use the washroom or to check on a student. The marketing manager had complained to Mr. Bai, claiming that this was causing students to leave the school, and that morning Mr. Bai had announced that Chinese teachers who refused to fill in would lose their jobs. "It's not our fault," Bliss concluded, "it's the foreign teachers' fault. Why do we have the responsibility?"

This led to a long conversation about foreign teachers and their role in English language teaching. All of the teachers agreed that they worked harder than the foreigners, putting more effort into their teaching, lesson planning, and prep-aration. Bliss contrasted her efforts to take teaching seriously with foreigners who are "just here for fun." When one new foreign teacher arrived recently, Mr. Bai asked Bliss to go to her class and observe her teaching. The foreign teacher had asked each student, "What kind of life do you want in the future?" As Bliss nar-rated: "Then, one student say back, 'But teacher, what kind of life do you want in future?' She [the teacher] say 'I don't know.' What is that? 'I don't know. I don't know.' What is that? *She doesn't prepare completely for a class, then how can she teach it?*" Fanny concurred, describing foreign teachers as "useless. I think for-eigners can teach nothing actually." "Not even oral English?," I asked. Fanny ex-plained that, since native-like English fluency can only come from living abroad, Chinese students should focus on actually getting there, and the barriers to that are international language examinations like the International English Language Testing System (IELTS) and Test of English as a Foreign Language (TOEFL) that govern entrance to foreign universities. But foreign teachers have never taken these exams, nor do they have any experience with Chinese learning styles. "[Foreign-ers] take IELTS speaking [as] speaking, rather than an examination . . . But we learned the language, so we know how the others learn the language."

To illustrate this point, Fanny explained that in the speaking portion of the IELTS students must respond orally to a set of randomly selected standardized questions asked by the examiner. Both the British Council, which administers the test, and certified examiners, who evaluate the students' performance, describe the speaking portion as interactive, "as close to a real-life situation as a test can get," as one textbook, parroting the British Council's official guide, put it.[7] To pre-pare their students, foreign teachers usually open a discussion with the students. They introduce topics such as "technology" or "parents" in class and then solicit responses, often asking the student to expand and elaborate. But as often hap-pens with such open discussions, the focus of the class can drift. "The first five minutes they stick to the topic. And then five minutes later they go nowhere. That means the student only spend the first five minutes in the class talk about examination-related questions. And then?" Fanny asked, clapping her hands loudly. "Nothing." In contrast, she argued that Chinese teachers know students are looking for "tricks" or "shortcuts," such as analyzing the potential questions and sorting them into types with distinct answer templates. Chinese teachers then provide students with strategies for answering each type of question. "It's like a domino . . . If you prepare for one question, and then, pitter-patter, pitter-patter, they can do everything." While foreigners attempted to engage students in conver-sation about various topics, modeling the ostensible purpose of the examination—to elicit so-called natural speech—Chinese teachers recognized the contrived na-ture of the conversational frame itself. They taught the students to realize that what appears to be natural speech is actually a highly structured examination with clear evaluative criteria, and then helped the students analyze the particular rules and conventions of this interaction.

Nonetheless—and this was perhaps the most frustrating element for the Chinese teachers—students demanded native speakers. As Fanny explained, "[Students] are so believed in the foreigners, and you know some of the students, they came here and say, 'I don't want a local, okay? I pay like three hundred for an hour, I want a native speaker.' Even though they are so basic, they cannot say a word. 'Okay, I give you a suggestion? . . . If you like to spend three hundred or more an hour to speak five words with a native speaker, you go!'" To explain the reasons for this, Chinese teachers often deferred to the iconization of English fluency in the form of the foreigner's white body. While introducing me to his class, Winston joked that the students would be more awake because he had brought the "*white monkey*" to talk with them that day. Others attributed student interest in foreign teachers to their "*white faces*." In our discussion of foreign teachers, Fanny conceded that there was one instance in which foreign teachers are valuable: the practice exam. "You practice several hours with the local teacher, and then you go to the foreigner, you stare at their white face and look into their blue eyes . . . and make yourself nervous. The more nervous you are in the practice examination, the less nervous you are in the real one." These appeals to the foreigner's default appearance as the source of their power and fascination for students conflate linguistic and racial capital, identifying their appearance as a key component of their linguistic capital.

The conflict between the Chinese and foreign teachers at Washington English was far more than simple office politics or even a more general antipathy toward an intrusive foreign presence. It was, crucially, about what kinds of people the foreigners are, their motivations, desires, strengths, and deficiencies. Are they serious teachers or just there for fun? Do they help the students or hinder them? Even though students might insist on the presence of a foreign teacher as a necessary stamp of legitimacy on their own learning, the Chinese teachers, those with an already achieved level of proficiency with the language, called into question the efficacy of foreigners as teachers. But while the foreigners' innate linguistic authenticity (their "native-speaker-ness") could be viewed as a threat to the livelihoods of Fanny and the other Chinese teachers, there is a greater instrumental role for the foreigner in language education beyond simply modeling correct forms of accent and grammar. The foreigner offers a pathway to modernity because the productivity of their own racial subjectivity can be appropriated by the Chinese language learner.

What Do Foreigners Say Foreign Teachers Are Good For?

I often asked foreigner teachers what they thought of being a language instructor in China. Did they see themselves, as Fanny did, as useless props for students' consumption? I was surprised that foreigners only rarely got upset by the question; in fact, the most common answer was something like, "Maybe . . . I don't know." A general sense of confusion pervaded the expatriate experience in China in the sense that, although foreign teachers were aware of, for instance, the conflict between themselves and the Washington English Chinese teachers over responsibility, they saw these as predominantly interpersonal conflicts rather than as representative of a more structural inequality based on symbolic and linguistic capital. Teaching is a job, and not always a particularly lucrative one from their perspective, and so larger questions about race, social roles, and the performance of modernity are of little interest.

They were, however, cognizant of the nonlinguistic aspects of student attraction to and fascination with foreigners. Teaching was often described as "the dog and pony show" or a "song and dance" to highlight their role as entertainers. Foreigners knew they were there in their capacity *as foreigners* rather than, for the most part, as educators. There was little emphasis by the various English schools on professionalization, training, or even class preparation. Indeed, of the forty or so foreign teachers I met or interviewed during my fieldwork, only five held professional teaching certifications.[8] Patricia, an Australian teacher in her fifties, summarized her experiences working at eight different schools in the city over several years. "They don't particularly care too much about their curriculum. As long as they've got students coming in the door, paying the money, and finding teachers with a fair face who can speak English, whether or not they're educators or whether they're bums or whoever they are, they'll give them a job." Kevin, a white South African in his thirties with eight years of teaching experience in Shenyang, told me about the shock of his arrival at his first teaching job. "When I got here, no one sat me down and laid it out for me. Like, this is what you're here for. The day we got here we were just shoved into a classroom. Five minutes before the time class starts they hand you a book and say, 'These are the words you're teaching today.'" He also told me about the numerous times he was pulled out of class to act as the "public face" of the school. "They would take us to do a little show, you know, to open a school, just to stand there, be the foreign face. So they can all see they have foreigners there at the school. It's a big draw." Others described this role as being the "token foreigner" in everything from school awards ceremonies and graduations to restaurant openings and weddings.[9] We can note here the metonymic reduction of the foreigner to a face, and stereotypically a white one, that can be used to sell the school's services.

The exact reasons these white faces were in such high demand, however, was less clear to the foreigners. When I asked Donald, a twenty-two-year-old American teacher and aspiring businessman, why foreign teachers were so desirable, he responded: "The Chinese really look up to Western cultures I think, especially the U.S. and their way of doing business and stuff. Their ability to make money—I think they really like that. I mean all Chinese people think that foreigners are rich. They see a white face, they think you're rich. Doesn't matter what they know of your background or anything. They instantly assume that you have money, and that's something they all aspire to. It's as simple as that I think." Note Donald's resistance to the attributions of wealth he received from Chinese students. He had only recently graduated from university, and so still thought of himself as a "poor student" despite the capability for mobility that had brought him to Shenyang. But he also generalizes his own engagements and experiences with China as symptomatic of the Chinese perspective as a whole: the man who wants to make money in China sees in the Chinese a desire for what he represents.

Kevin liked to see his own teaching as an antidote to "traditional" Chinese educational practices "where it's just facts, facts, facts get crammed in your head so you can write the test." Some of the foreigners' popularity, he argued, is the product of a more relaxed teaching style in contrast to the boredom inherent to the rote lessons of the Chinese teacher. "[The students] are always very happy when I get there and, you know, clown around. They have a good laugh. It's a bit of a break from their normal school life . . . Our way of teaching is a lot different I suppose. You just have fun with them." The Chinese way, he explained, was so work-intensive it left students with none of the energy required to really invest in learning a language. Patricia was even more critical, saying that it left students without key skills in critical thinking and expression: "They have almost zero imagination. And I think they're trapped inside this terrible education system their parents give them. They don't have any thinking for themselves, you know you ask them, 'If you won a million renminbi what would you do?' 'I'd buy a house.' 'What else would you do?' 'Cellphone.' Their imagination is not real good." Foreign teachers therefore often positioned themselves not simply as teachers but as conduits for a diverse set of values glossed as "Western" and "modern." If the Chinese educational system sucked all of the creativity and imagination out of students, the foreigner's teaching style—humorous, fun, energetic—could ideally inject it back into their psyches.

This role, however, was crucially dependent on an essentialized, racialized difference between foreign and Chinese teaching styles that effectively erases both the range of foreign teaching styles and the diversity of Chinese teachers themselves, many of whom had studied abroad and graduated from foreign universities. As countless Chinese teachers made clear to me, it was *their* job to teach critical thinking, expressive skills like speaking and writing, imagination, and creativity to their students. It was because the foreigners were lazy, uncommitted, and untrained (again, a discursive erasure of their diversity) that these skills were not being taught.

It is in the conflicting perspectives of teacher roles and goals that many of the disputes and tensions between foreign and Chinese teachers reside. Patricia, the Australian teacher, told me several times how frustrated she was with the jealousy she experienced from Chinese teachers, especially toward her salary (even though such jealousy might be justifiable, given Patricia's own lack of teaching credentials). This was even more remarkable given the similar experiences between Patricia and Chinese teachers in terms of work conditions. "I was doing twenty-four teaching hours a week, and they required me to go into the office from eight a.m. to four p.m., and I just wasn't able to do that. They'd also ring you up half an hour before a class and say, 'Oh, can you do a class here?,' or they'd ring you up two hours before and say, 'Can you come here?,' and that's, well it's just dysfunctional." In other words, despite Patricia being uninvolved personally with Washington English, her complaints and rationale for disliking her Chinese coworkers echo the very reasons Fanny, Bliss, and the other Washington English teachers were upset with their foreign coworkers. Each group not only saw the other as representative of a casual and sometimes even detrimental approach to teaching, but also claimed that they, and only they, were capable of delivering a quality education to the students.

I spent far less time interviewing foreign teachers than I did their Chinese counterparts, and so this section has been, by necessity, brief. The dominant themes of the expatriate teacher experience that I have outlined here can be confirmed by other work in the field (see for instance Stanley 2013, 125–167). It is on these themes, rather than on an exhaustive ethnography of foreign perspectives, that I want to focus. If we contrast the descriptions by Kevin, Patricia, and Donald of their jobs with the Chinese teachers' comments in the previous section, we can see a powerful tendency to elucidate differences based on naturalized constructions of ethnicity rather than individualized experiences. Foreigners are "fun" in contrast to a presumed Chinese tendency to be serious. Chinese teachers are "rigid" and Chinese students "unimaginative" in contrast to their Western counterparts. These oppositional frameworks are even deployed in contexts where the experiences of foreign and Chinese teachers are actually very similar. Next, I turn to an extensive account of how these oppositional discourses were used by various participants in a staff retreat organized by Washington English's owner, Mr. Bai, to generate accounts of selfhood using the other as a narrative foil.

Outward Bound

In the summer of 2005, I was approached by Lisa, a Washington English office staffer, to translate a word for her: *tuozhan*. After checking our dictionaries, I was at a bit of a loss; the word literally means "to expand," but I had no idea in what context she was asking the question. Lisa explained that the word described an event organized by a local human resources training company that the school planned to offer for all Chinese and foreign staff. Participants would travel by bus to the nearby Qipanshan scenic park for two days of activities, camping there overnight. It would be a fun event, she claimed, like a vacation from work to build morale among the staff. Lisa suggested the translation "outward bound adventure," which she had found online. Fanny later told me *tuozhan* meant "to change your mind, make it bigger, like wash the brain." When I asked Mr. Bai if I could attend, he was very enthusiastic, hoping I would serve as a model for the other foreigners. He was very excited about the program because it had been adopted from American corporate training materials, so he was optimistic that "the games," as he called them, would bring together the foreign and Chinese teachers and resolve some of the conflicts between them. He also hoped it would lead to increased productivity, employee loyalty, and satisfaction for everyone. Soon after this, posters appeared around the school advertising the retreat, prominently featuring the tagline "I am the superman!" with the familiar "S" emblem of the titular superhero in the background (figure 6.3).

In smaller Chinese type, the poster explained the purpose of the event:

> During World War II, many ships in the Atlantic were attacked and sunk, and a great number of crew members fell into the sea. Due to the cold water and distance from land, most of them lost their lives. A handful of people, after experiencing this long ordeal, were able to survive, yet most of these survivors were frail older people. The key to their survival was their excellent psychological quality. When disaster struck, their first thought was: I have to live! Later, it was proposed to use both natural conditions and man-made facilities for seafarers to perform mentally challenging activities and raise their psychological quality. This developmental training was the prototype for "OUTWARD BOUND," which means the desire of a small boat to leave its safe haven, to accept all challenges, and to overcome all difficulties!

Below this, in gradually expanding text, were the following slogans:

> We cannot control others, but we can control ourselves.
> We cannot predict the future, but we can make use of today.

FIGURE 6.3. The "I am the superman" advertising poster for the outward bound adventure. The real name of the school has been obscured in this image.

We cannot have everything go right, but we can be conscientious in
  everything we do.

One of the key terms in the poster, and in much subsequent discussion of the event, was *xinli suzhi*, which I have translated here as "psychological quality" and deserves some explanation. The choice to highlight psychological quality as the determining factor in the Western sailors' survival (rather than, say, toughness or resilience) transfigures this ostensibly foreign story into a form of Chinese moral discourse (Oxfeld 2010). As discussed before, the discourse of *suzhi* is intimately tied to modernization processes in which new forms of neoliberal citizenship are emerging. The properly socialized modern subject possesses this element of "quality" in abundance, marked by modern forms of thought and behavior, in opposition to "low-quality" citizens who embody outmoded and traditional lifestyles. Quality in this sense is not an objective measure, but the traits that mark and separate certain kinds of modern individuals from others who have either failed to achieve, or are not yet ready for, global cosmopolitan citizenship. The term "psychological quality" thus indexes the mental mind-set of new citizens, not beholden to the past but, as proper neoliberal subjects must, boldly seeking their fortune in a challenging world and not shrinking from the prospect of failure. Left unsaid are, of course, the social determinants of this new subjectivity, insomuch as people of quality are more likely to come from wealthy urban households than poor rural ones. The outward bound adventure was set within this framework of continuous self-making and self-improvement so characteristic of China's neoliberal experiment. As with Clark Kent's phone-booth transformation into his alter ego, Superman, the poster promised that participants would return from the event a new kind of person, ready to deal with life's challenges.

On the morning our adventure was to start, I met with about sixty other employees at the school, including four foreign teachers, all male, all in their mid- to late twenties: Corey, Leo, Peter, and Dale. Corey and Leo were Australian, Peter and Dale American. This constituted just under half of the ten full-time foreigners teaching at Washington at the time. The others later told me they refused to participate both because they were busy and, as was the case with their Chinese counterparts, Mr. Bai was not paying them to go. Leo had also invited his Chinese girlfriend, Rachel, along for the trip; she was close friends with Peter's girlfriend, May, a Chinese teacher at the school.

Inside the teachers' office, one of the office workers was handing out T-shirts with the school's logo on the front, and I was given one to wear. We boarded chartered buses and traveled about an hour beyond the city limits. Our destination was a heavily wooded area in the Qipanshan scenic area, consisting of a wide clearing, a central building with a large room that doubled as cafeteria and meeting space, and a series of smaller cabins and Mongolian-style yurts with wooden bunks for us to stay the night. As we disembarked from the buses, we were met by a line of Chinese "coaches" (*jiaolian*) in military parade rest stances, dressed in camouflage fatigues bearing U.S. Special Forces badges on their arms. The coaches immediately called our group to attention, barking out orders in Chinese: "*Attention! Line up! Turn to the right!*" The Chinese staff very quickly formed into ranks; these orders were familiar to them from numerous "learn from the soldier" days in high school and university. Two Chinese teachers were singled out for not accurately following the commands and were ordered to do ten push-ups each as the rest of us looked on. After lining up, standing at attention, and being inspected by our—as I began to think of them—new drill instructors, we were ordered to drop off our bags and then reassemble in the courtyard to prepare for a day of team-building activities, including obstacle courses and physical challenges.

On our return to the courtyard, names were read aloud from a list, and the coaches directed us to line up behind a series of pylons representing our teams. I was teamed up with the foreign teachers, May, Rachel, and three other Washington English Chinese teachers, one of six teams in total. At first there was a lot of enthusiasm on our team; we high-fived each other as each person joined the line. The coach assigned to our team, Wang Jingyou, was a fit and handsome young man with short-cropped hair, a recent graduate of Shenyang Physical Education University. He took us to a picnic table and told us to come up with a team nickname (we chose the Mobsters), a song, a chant, and a banner to carry with us. Each of us had to wear a headband with a nickname given to us by our teammates written on it; if we used a person's real name or forgot our song or chant, we would be "fined" (*chengfa*) in the form of push-ups, to be performed in front of the coach. We had to elect three officers: a leader, a secretary, and a safety officer (a position to which I was duly appointed). We joined the other teams in the courtyard and sang our song, shouted our chant, and before long were marched off into the woods. Our first challenge required us to use two lengths of rope and two bamboo poles to lift a bucket from within a large circular area without touching the ground. For half an hour we discussed, argued, and attempted unsuccessfully to find a way to lift out the bucket, until our time limit expired and our coach explained that the ropes needed to be twisted around the rim of the bucket, after which it could be lifted from outside the circle. Another activity asked us to build a bridge from rope and bamboo, which we also failed to accomplish.

There were several discussions led by our coach that morning on topics such as teamwork, goals, cooperation, and confidence. For instance, teamwork, Jingyou informed us, consists of three parts: the desire to work together, confidence in each other, and heart. The method for the team achieving its goals requires foresight, confidence, and action. At one point, Jingyou asked us to line up our water bottles on the ground, then, staring disdainfully at the result, ordered us to try again. Even a small action, he said, like lining up our water bottles, should be done correctly and with care. Later in the day, we performed a series of "trust falls." Unlike that staple of Western corporate retreats where people merely fall backward to be caught by a fellow team member (thus demonstrating trust in the fact that the teammate will catch the person), ours were done from a three-foot platform, with the rest of the team waiting in two columns on the ground below, arms stretched out toward each other to catch the falling person. Several of us did so successfully, but one teacher curled up in a ball as she fell backward and crashed through our arms. Jingyou criticized us for backing away and being too frightened to catch her. As safety officer, I was fined twenty push-ups for my carelessness. But the teacher's fall also unnerved several of the other people on our team, and one by one they refused to go. This prompted Jingyou to launch into an extended discussion on the issue of trust, and how we had failed because our trust and confidence in each other were not up to the proper standard.

As the day progressed, a considerable degree of friction began to emerge in our team. All of the instructions were given by Jingyou in Mandarin, and then translated by one of the teachers to the foreigners (as I madly took notes on a small pad of paper). At one point, Corey became frustrated and shouted out, "Hold on! Hold on! Can someone just tell us what the fuck is going on?" Jingyou forbade swearing, cigarette breaks, and washroom breaks without permission; Corey and Leo would therefore frequently disappear into the woods or behind a building to smoke. At lunch, Corey and Peter wanted to purchase beer for our table, but another coach explained that the refrigerator of beer in the dining hall was locked—we would only be able to celebrate when the exercises were over.

These simmering conflicts finally erupted during one of the afternoon events. Our team was brought into a clearing with an upright metal pole, about ten feet in height. The pole was lined with rungs on each side and had a small platform at the top, so that a person could climb up and, in theory, stand atop it. From a nearby tree hung a trapeze-like bar, roughly three feet from the platform and at chest height for an individual standing on the pole. Ropes dangled from pulleys fastened high above us in the trees. Jingyou explained that each team member would don a harness attached to the ropes. These ropes would be held by our teammates, in order to ensure we could not fall—requiring a daunting level of trust. Each person would then ascend in turn to the top of the pole and jump to the bar before being lowered gently to the ground. This was a test, he said, of our bravery and commitment to the team.

Several of us completed the task successfully, but Leo could not make it to the top of the pole; he had torn an ankle ligament several years previously and did not want to reinjure himself. As he climbed back down, Jingyou ordered him back up to try again. "*You need to encourage him more!*" he urged those of us on the ground. A few of us took up the cheer of "Leo, *let's go!*" Leo told his girlfriend, Rachel, to translate the information about his ankle to the coach, and then, back on the ground, told us that he was leaving to smoke a cigarette and use the washroom. Corey and Rachel moved to join him. Jingyou shouted after them in Mandarin to return, as they had not asked permission to leave. Corey swore back at him in English, and they all walked away. We continued the event, but when Corey returned after a few minutes, Jingyou ordered him to do twenty push-ups. Corey became furious and started swearing more at Jingyou in English, and eventually turned his back. "That's it, I'm out of here." He called to Leo and they left with Rachel, catching a minibus back into town. I remained with Peter and Dale, the two young American foreign teachers, and the other Chinese members of our team.

Jingyou watched them leave and then gathered the rest of us together and squatted down in the grass to help us "analyze" (fenxi) what had just transpired. "*I understand that you foreigners [nimen waiguoren] are different from us. The West is different from the East. In the West, people have freedom, but no discipline. You are used to doing as you wish. But we Chinese [zanmen Zhongguoren] understand that you can't always do what you want. You should learn a lesson from this.*" Jingyou indicated the targets of his last piece of advice by gesturing toward me and the other remaining foreigners. He asked the Chinese teachers on our team what had gone wrong: Why had some of their teammates acted selfishly and abandoned us when they knew it would hurt the team? After a few moments, one of the Chinese teachers ventured that the foreigners' temperament was different from theirs, and Jingyou nodded enthusiastically in agreement. It was the inability, he argued, of Corey and Leo to accept criticism (about their smoking, for instance) and their insistence on being stubborn that caused them to leave. Instead, people need to be flexible. Jingyou told us that in university he had two foreign friends.

> Some foreigners, like my friends, are indeed very good. They come to China and they like China. They want to stay here and learn from Chinese. They study hard. Even though my English isn't good, they were patient and I could learn from them too. Just like any group of people, there are different kinds of foreigners . . . Those who left should think about this: What do they stand for? Although you all did well, three of you [Corey, Leo, and Rachel] were not members of the team . . . My job is to encourage you, to make you more confident. A coach is a mirror in which you can see your success.

Jingyou's heartfelt conversation with us about the breach in our team did not resolve all the tensions, and much of the earlier enthusiasm vanished from both the remaining foreigners and the Chinese teachers. We completed two more challenges (successfully, I might add), but Jingyou's prompts to cheer on our teammates or call each other by our assigned nicknames met with less and less enthusiasm. Despite this, he declined to fine us with push-ups for ignoring his directives.

After a simple dinner eaten with our team, we were called back to the central building as the sun was going down. The room had been transformed, with tables and chairs pushed back against the wall, and a stereo blasting pop music through a speaker system. All of the coaches, Jingyou included, lined the entrance, clapping and cheering as we came in. The head coach, a handsome man slightly older than the others, took the stage and began singing along with an inspirational pop song, *Fly Higher*, with lyrics such as "*I want a life that's more brilliant, a sky that's more blue. I know the happiness I want is in a higher patch of sky.*" Those of us in the audience waved our hands and sang along. As the music continued, the head coach announced we would be playing a game. Each person was to cross the floor from one side of the room to the other using a "*unique walk*" expressing our own individuality. We crossed the room one at a time, and the coaches turned back any person they felt was not being distinctive enough, telling them to try again.

The evening was wearing on, and I was exhausted from the day's activities, but we were not finished yet. The head coach now directed us to form two teams and line up on opposite sides of the room. He solicited volunteers to act as team leaders, and April, one of the Chinese teachers, and Dazzle, an office accountant, were selected. The game, as it was explained to us, was for each team to count up from one, with the first person in line saying "*one,*" the second "*two,*" and so forth, continuing down the line to the last person. The team that could do this the fastest would win the round. There would be ten rounds, and after each, the losing team would have to bow and congratulate the other team while the leader would do push-ups as punishment. The instructions came very quickly, and I was not entirely sure I had heard correctly because, as I understood it, the punishment would double for each lost round: ten push-ups to start, then twenty, then forty, eighty, and so on. My comprehension turned out, however, to be correct.

April marched up and down our line, urging us to practice, and we shouted out our numbers in succession while a coach timed us on a stopwatch, informing us after each try that our time was not fast enough, that we would fail and April would be punished. Then the first round began, with me in the lead— someone had proposed that "*one*" would be the easiest number for a foreigner to say. At some point down the line, someone called out the wrong number, and my team began shouting "*Again! Again! Start again!*" We were the slowest, and we bowed to the other team, shouting, "*Congratulations to you!*" while April did her ten push-ups on the floor in front of us. We practiced again, and lost again, and April did twenty push-ups. We practiced again, then won twice in a row, and Dazzle did his push-ups, although he began showing clear signs of exhaustion toward the end of the second round. As we practiced yet again, I was growing increasingly bored of this, as I thought it, pointless exercise, which had already lasted half an hour. But when we won again, Dazzle got down to do his forty push-ups. He was not in the best of shape, so he began struggling almost immediately. With great effort he heaved his body up each time, panting for a few seconds, then collapsed to the floor, only to start again. Several of the staff began shouting encouragement. One of the office managers came out to kneel beside Dazzle and offered to take his place, but the head coach refused and ordered the manager back into line. Minutes passed, and Dazzle's push-ups came less and less regularly. Shouts, encouragement, and conversation buzzed around me. The head coach took the microphone on stage again, addressing Dazzle's teammates. "*Look at him. Do you see him? Your captain is suffering for you. He is taking your place, suffering this pain, because you failed him, you lost. Do you want it to be this way?*" From the floor, Dazzle began crying out, "*Don't worry about me, this is good for me.* I'm sorry that I'm a little fat." After another minute he was sobbing on the floor, unable to lift himself again. The head coach continued from the front of the room: "*Look at him. He's your captain and he suffers for you. Remember your mother? This is how she suffered for you, to give you a good life, to give you food and the things you need to live. Remember your father? He suffered too.*" Other Chinese members of the staff began crying too. The office manager got up again but instead of taking Dazzle's place began doing push-ups on the floor next to him. Others started to join him. Two teachers joined hands under Dazzle's chest and tried to help raise him off the floor for more push-ups.

At this point, I felt as uncomfortable as I ever would during my fieldwork, completely repulsed by the spectacle in front of me. I recall staring at the head coach with as much animosity as I could muster, but I was only one face in the crowd, and most of the staff around me were focused on Dazzle and his plight on the floor. This was, I am sure, the inevitable outcome of the game we were playing: at some point one of the team leaders would break down and be unable continue with the physical toil of the punishments, engendering these emotional responses in the others around me. I certainly cannot testify to the emotional state of all the other participants, but my own revulsion did appear to be in the minority. I do not claim that this was due somehow to my enlightened position as foreigner, company outsider, or anthropologist. Certainly the responses of others should be read with an understanding that the outward bound adventure was mandatory for staff and that contesting its dominant narratives might have endangered their jobs. And as we will see below, the messages of the event were not uniformly accepted by all participants. Nonetheless, I took advantage of my critical distance from the social fabric of the school and any possible negative consequences from Mr. Bai to get up and leave. A coach tried to stop me and pointed back to the line, but I pushed past him into the cool night air. Dale followed after me, but Peter stayed behind with May to watch the drama unfold. Dale smoked a cigarette on the way back to our cabin, as we both tried to give voice to our conflicting emotions and impressions. He looked overwhelmed. Later, Peter joined us (the cabin now only sparsely filled after Corey and Leo's departure). He described how, after we left, the game ended and then all of the Chinese staff were blindfolded. They were asked to hug another person and imagine it was their mother or father and thank them for the sacrifices they had made. "It was like one of those cults. When you join, first they want to break you down, like get rid of your confidence. And then they build you back up emotionally." We decided to leave the next morning by minibus as well.

When I returned to Washington School two days later, the staff in the teachers' office were gathered around a computer viewing the hundreds of pictures taken at the camp. They showed me photographs of the final challenge from the second day, after I had left, that involved moving the entire staff from one side of an eight-foot wall to the other. In the picture, a few of the staff members were boosting people with their hands, while others perched at the top of the wall and reached down to pull people up. Even Mr. Bai showed up at the end, and one photograph pictured him being hauled up the wall.

I still felt deeply unsettled by what had transpired, and ventured to some of the teachers that I was uncomfortable with what had happened to Dazzle. Peter's girlfriend, May, was sitting at her desk, and I asked her how she had felt during the retreat. "You know, I can understand why the foreigners leave. Sometimes that day, it felt a little strange. Even me, when we were putting on the, um . . ." May mimicked the act of covering her eyes, and I supplied the word "blindfold." "Yes, the blindfolds, even then I feel very uncomfortable. But, you know, we Chinese understand this kind of thing." May mentioned that her first month of university was taken up with military training (a practice that continues today) and said that this had shaped the Chinese experience. Western culture does not encourage people to meet challenges at any cost, while Chinese culture forces people to endure suffering for its own sake. Peter would probably disagree with her, she said, but the foreigners left because their culture is different—it prevented them (and by extension me) from understanding the event's true purpose. Fanny joined us and echoed this point: "*Outward bound* has two purposes. One is to teach you the discipline. The other is to know that you are part of a team, that one person can't do what they want, can't be selfish, or it will hurt the team. The foreign teacher just think, 'oh, it's a fun day.'" This led May to respond, "*You see, you foreigners just don't understand. We Chinese know* what is the discipline."

In her ethnography of a Japanese confectionery manufacturer, Dorinne Kondo (1990, 76–115) provides an account of an ethics school where the company's owner sent employees to assist them in transforming their lives. For six days she participated in lectures, exercises, meditation, chanting, and a regimen of chores, physical hardship, and ritualized corporal punishment. Several elements of her description bear eerie similarity to my own experience, leading me to wonder whether the training company borrowed this template from Japan rather than, as Mr. Bai claimed, from the United States. Kondo too was given orders by the camp's leaders on her arrival, was disciplined for tardiness and sloppiness, and participated in tasks organized by squads whose members were all accountable to each other, but interspersed with leisurely, even sometimes silly, activities. She too was taken aback by the emotional reactions of her fellow participants to what she found to be frankly manipulative tactics (see for instance Kondo 1990, 98). But Kondo also describes how, over the course of the retreat, she gradually began to not simply learn the ethics lessons being taught (about sacrifice, resolve, filiality, mutual support, and strength of character) but to internalize them as well. She found herself responding with visceral feelings—disgust, sentimentality, sincerity, unity, and ecstasy—to various events and activities without intending to, developing a kind of emotional discipline. The ethics retreat employed work, hardship, confession, and play as technologies of self-transformation that drew on deeply conservative notions of ideal Japanese personhood: discipline, punctuality, respect, and loyalty. These values made the retreat immensely popular with Japanese family businesses.

What is remarkably different between our accounts, however, is the symbolic medium within which these practices were embedded. While Kondo's ethics retreat was animated by a nostalgia for traditional Japanese values, the outward bound adventure employed the foreign as a coherent symbolic backdrop.[10] It is no coincidence that the adventure was suffused with images and signifiers of foreignness, from the coaches' American military uniforms to the English used in advertising the event, its comic book theme of "I am the Superman," and its recruitment of Second World War sailors as models of psychological quality. The event itself was organized by an English school, and Mr. Bai made a point to invite the foreign staff and promote their attendance. On a deeper level too, many of the themes, narratives, and lessons were predicated on a kind of idealized Western worldview, such as trust falls and the silly walk exercise that encouraged us to see ourselves as unique individuals rather than to subsume our desires to the group. But despite the overt "foreignness" of the adventure, it was also melded with traditional Chinese themes and values, as though the foreign, as an ideologically coherent cultural framework, were teaching them how to be Chinese. Jingyou's lessons for us—unity, cooperation, teamwork—were not simply aimed at creating a more docile workforce for Mr. Bai; they were predicated on, and framed within, very Chinese moral discourses of social value, including self-sacrifice, filiality, and virtue. When Corey, Leo, and Rachel left the team, Jingyou's analysis of the event involved a juxtaposition between Chinese, who have discipline, and the foreigners, who have freedom. This was immediately contradicted, however, by the description of his foreign friends who were "very good" and exhibited the hallmarks of discipline so pivotal to Chinese cultural identities, as well as the fact that this lecture was delivered to the very foreigners who remained loyal to "the team."

As we can see, the event itself, the reaction of the foreigners to it, and the sustained reflection of the Chinese staff afterward led to extensive discourses on the nature of foreignness—the characteristics, motivations, and, ultimately, failings of foreigners—and Chineseness as alternative models of selfhood. In being told who we were—our values, knowledge, and characteristics—our varying ethnonational identities were essentialized, standardized, and homogenized, creating a coherent picture of culturally localizable selves. May talked about Chinese as those who can endure suffering and the foreigners as those who cannot, while Fanny portrayed foreigners as selfish in opposition to Chinese, who subsume their individual desires to the needs of the team. Ironically, it was through participation in an overtly foreign self-making exercise that the Chinese teachers derived important lessons about themselves as properly socialized Chinese: disciplined, hardworking, responsible, indomitable. We should also read the responses of the Chinese teachers in light of the ongoing conflict between them and the foreign teachers over responsibility. When Fanny outlined the lessons of the adventure as including the realization that, as a member of a team, one cannot be selfish, this is an obvious echo of our other discussions about foreigners as being in China "just for fun" and the attendant lack of seriousness they brought to their jobs.

If we return to the logic of the poster advertising the outward bound adventure, one of the goals was to develop the same "psychological quality" as foreign sailors who had survived the icy waters of the Atlantic in wartime. But both the goal itself—quality—and the means to do so were translated into a local idiom, a hybridized discourse at once strange and familiar. This dynamic echoes an approach to modernization formulated over a century ago in a China just coming to grips with the perils of European imperialism: *zhong xue wei ti, xi xue wei yong*, or "Chinese learning as the essence; Western learning as the means" (Adamson 2004, 27; Spence 1990, 225). The maxim exemplifies the tension between what Bruno Latour (1993) describes as contradicting ideologies of hybridity and purification at the heart of discursive modernity. Even though "we," as moderns, attempt to keep cultural domains such as science and society or human and nonhuman separate (purification), categorical autonomy is always threatened by emerging practices that mediate between them (hybridity). In this case, China's modernization in the nineteenth century was predicated on an attempt to keep the Chinese and foreign separate, to maintain the essence of the former in the minds of students while employing the technologies and teachings of the latter. Note how both China and the West are posited as coherent, fixed, and essentialized categories of being, collapsing and erasing the diverse histories contained by these terms. As those early Chinese modernist reformers discovered, and as the outward bound adventure illustrates now, Chinese and foreign act as dialectically entwined discursive categories: always opposed, yet always hybridized. At one point Jingyou described his role as that of "*a mirror in which you can see your success.*" He might have been describing more broadly, however, the role of the foreign in contemporary Chinese self-making. It was through the foreign, held up to the Washington English staff members as a mirror, that they articulated the values and qualities of their own Chineseness.

Ai Hua and the Dialectic of Mutual Desire

When I first went to Shenyang to study Mandarin, my classmates and I were frequently frustrated by public interactions that always appeared to be highly scripted. "*Are you from Canada? That country has a large area but a small population.*" "*America? Very rich and powerful.*" These conversations, held with taxi drivers, shop owners, restaurant servers, and university students, were so rote that we feared we would never hear a new word or phrase. And so some of us were led to a kind of language game in which we pretended that we were from other countries. When asked, we would say we were from Brazil, Iceland, Luxembourg— each place smaller and more remote than the one before, but each rich in new conversational possibilities ("*Are there trees in Iceland?*" "*How do you say 'hello' in Luxembourgian?*"). This gambit ended for me one day, though, when I told a market vendor I was from Russia, and she immediately switched into fluent Russian. I could only offer the contrived excuse that I was from a part of Russia where nobody spoke the Russian language, and retreated from her raucous laughter.

But why were these conversations so scripted in the first place? My argument in this chapter has been that foreigners occupy a central place in the Chinese discourse of modernity, as catalyzing intermediaries between past and future. If the revolutionary changes effected throughout China's society in the postsocialist reform period have given rise to a new form of subjectivity characterized by individualism, cosmopolitanism, and openness that Lisa Rofel (2007) dubs "desiring China," it is a subjectivity intimately premised on fantasies of the world outside (see also Farquhar 2002; Kipnis 2012; Y. Yan 2009). The foreign, this categorical representation of that externality, is a power to be evoked, absorbed, and appropriated before these new Chinese citizens can come into being. Foreigners are valuable, therefore, not for their individuality, but as stereotyped figures or stock characters—in other words, for what they represent rather than who they are (Henry 2013a). The rote conversation invokes the foreigner's place (structurally, temporally, and geographically—in other words, chronotopically) within an economy of desire, of modernity in its discursive mode. The characteristics of the places so invoked (big, rich, powerful, with a tightly controlled population) are the desirable elements of a future China, a similarly modern, "high-quality" place to live. Foreigners are thus recruited into conversations that enact and confirm the trajectory of Chinese life courses and the development of the nation.

Another common question that appears constantly in foreign-Chinese interactions, a trope that, again, is often spoofed and joked about by foreigners who are subject to it, is "Do you like China?" How vague; what kernel of emotion is the questioner attempting to elicit through the use of "like"? But on the basis of the discussion in this chapter, we might profitably rephrase it as "Is the structure of desire that motivates our own quest for modernity mutual? What authenticities do you seek to engage in with us?" Remember here how Jingyou referenced his own engagements with foreign friends who "*like China*" as he discussed our efforts to determine what "we" stood for during the corporate retreat. The desiring subject does not desire alone, and implicit within the mirror metaphor is the sense that the object of desire should reciprocate that desire back to the subject. There is an obvious parallel here to Lacan's psychoanalytic depiction of the formation of the subject as a product of the dialectic of desire between self and other, that "the subject depends on the signifier and that the signifier is first of all in the field of the Other" (Lacan 1998, 205). And it is that mutual constitution of ego and other through the mirrored gaze of the self's desire that leads, Lacan argues, to alienation. Herein lies a central paradox of this kind of semiotic self-fashioning, because as much as new Chinese subjectivities were being created through the use of the foreign as a kind of intermediary, thus alienating their own social productivity to the outsider, there are limits to what can be achieved. Those limits are partly articulated through the essentialized biological properties of race, such as skin color. As "nonwhite," Chinese can never become wholly foreign to themselves and thus can never wholly surrender their own agency to shape the contours of China's future. Those limits cut both ways—a foreigner can never become wholly Chinese, no matter how strong their desire to appropriate and emulate the symbolic apparatus of Chinese personhood.

In 2005, Shenyang Television broadcast a variety show featuring an interview with Ai Hua, a well-known actress and star of several nationally televised shows in China. But Ai Hua is not just any Chinese actress—she is, as China Central Television's (CCTV's) website describes her, "the white-faced Chinese actress," an American woman who also goes by the name Charlotte MacInnis. Ai Hua grew up in Beijing and attended a Chinese public school while her father worked for a joint-venture company. With her bilingual language skills, blue eyes, and blonde hair, Ai Hua became a television sensation in China in the 1990s and a regular contributor to national celebrations such as the annual Spring Festival gala, watched by millions across the country. As CCTV's website goes on to say, "She is beloved by the Chinese people, and they have accepted her as a Chinese, not a foreigner."[11]

The interview ranged over a variety of topics, but kept returning to the theme of Ai Hua's love of China, prominently encoded in her Chinese name, which literally means "Love China."[12] The host asked Ai Hua to sing Chinese songs, reprise famous lines from her acting career, perform a Chinese comedy routine, and even demonstrate some of her skills in tai chi. After each demonstration of her Chineseness, the audience erupted in applause and praise. And yet, one moment stood out in the program: during the question-and-answer period, a man near the back of the audience was given the microphone. "*Ai Hua,*" he said, "*we can all see you are like a Chinese person, but maybe there are some things you still don't understand. I'm going to say a word; can you tell me what it means?*" And then the man uttered the phrase "*Guang guang di,*" a bit of Dongbeihua slang that means strong, tough, and excellent. Ai Hua admitted to the man she was stumped. The man explained to Ai Hua what it meant, and then sat down again, smiling, before the show moved on.

I read this encounter between the Chinese-speaking foreigner and the foreign-fascinated Chinese as an assertion of a fundamental and unassimilable difference; an assertion, in other words, of the limits of intimacy with the foreign (see Ang 2001). At some point, the difference between self and other has to be reestablished. By asking Ai Hua to enact, almost step by step, her desire for China, the audience could forgive themselves for equally desiring the foreign. But just at the moment where Ai Hua's Chineseness seems most certain, she is reminded by the audience member's question of her foreignness, becoming once again Charlotte. Assimilation is offered with one hand, and then snatched back at the moment of its near-realization with the other. It seems to me that Ai Hua was offered the same transaction that Chinese English learners feel themselves subject to—by denying her the final measure of affinity, despite her obvious overtures of desire, she was barred from native Chineseness in the same way that Chinese speakers of English cannot fully participate as the equals of native speakers. And more than a simple communicative medium, the English language is the paramount currency of this Chinese-foreign economy of desire.

A peculiarity of China's English language adoption has been the almost complete lack of popular resistance. While occasionally arising during periods of anti-Western sentiment, counterdiscourses to the prevalence of English in China's language environment are notably muted. One possible reason for this is that discourses of culturally homogenized modern "Chineseness" are so powerful that they cannot be endangered by the presence of a foreign language alone (see Chun 2017; Ong 1997; Tu 1994). But as I have tried to demonstrate, it is also because "the foreign" is such an integral part of neoliberal self-fashioning in the modern Chinese city. As a potential subject-position from which to rewrite (or in this case, revoice) the self, the foreign is available in the guise of the highly appropriable white body of the English-speaking foreigner, and especially the foreign teacher, informing both the critiques of the Washington English teachers toward their foreign counterparts and the outward bound adventure. This is also the source, I have argued, for the kind of performative conventions of foreignness in contemporary China like attending, witnessing, and, thus, sanctioning events that further that modernizing agenda, such as English school openings, a part of the more general dramatological aspects of modernity: the way in which people are made modern through their actions (consumptive, behavioral, lifestyle) and ways of speaking. In this sense, the role of the foreigner is scripted, not in the sense that a speaker's words are controlled by someone else, but that they follow and conform to certain discursive expectations formed within already circulating narrative tropes. If the word is, as Bakhtin (1981, 293) says, half someone else's, we might profitably ask: Which half? For in the end, the identities and languages of Chinese and foreigners in China are so entangled that they cannot be purified except in those few moments where, as Ai Hua discovered, the categories are, for a brief moment, made whole.

CONCLUSION

Reflections on a Global Language

In 2007, Li Yang, the proprietor of Crazy English, the learning system that encourages students to shout out their lessons as loudly as possible, was heavily criticized online after posting photographs to his blog showing hundreds of students bowing down to him after a lesson. Much of the opposition revolved around the accord, using a traditional gesture of deference and respect, granted to an English teacher at the expense of Mandarin. Li faced further public condemnation after details of domestic violence against his wife emerged and a divorce settlement that saw him lose custody of his children.

Then, in 2014, China's State Council announced a sweeping reform of educational assessment and university admission in the public education system (State Council 2014). A key element of these reforms is a decreased emphasis placed on foreign languages in the NCEE, the national university entrance examination, with 50 of English's 150 points shifted to Chinese language instead. Beginning in Beijing in 2017, the policy will eventually be duplicated throughout the country. In a review of these decisions, the Chinese linguist Zhao Junhai argues that "the once favorite 'son', i.e. English, may lose its predominance in the Chinese foreign language landscape and its importance may be diminished in exams. These changes are likely to cause a series of chain reactions since the dominant position of English largely lies in its weight in various levels of exams, with the [NCEE] having the greatest impact" (J. Zhao 2016, 38). English schools may close, and teachers may be laid off, he noted, although the reforms are reportedly popular with students. These incidents have prompted a range of commentary across China, both online and in the mass media, about the future of English in China: Is the English fever over?

Ironically enough, I heard almost the same assertion weeks after arriving for the first time in China; a foreign teacher told me I had missed the heyday of English teaching in the late 1990s and that I should be ready to move to the next language hot spot, perhaps in Southeast Asia or Eastern Europe. Nevertheless, there were signs throughout my fieldwork that the terrain was shifting. I heard arguments among parents about just how useful English might really be. Several of the language schools began to experience financial troubles as the language teaching market became saturated and expansion slowed. A handful of schools closed outright, and others began to shutter smaller branch operations. Other schools began to diversify into teaching French or German. Although English is still the most popular foreign language for students taking the NCEE, the state has lately begun to expand the number of options available, including Japanese, German, and Spanish, particularly as those relate to expanding trade and global soft power.

These indicators, anecdotal though they are, may presage a transformation of the English language industry in Shenyang to come, but it is important to appreciate the difference between the marketplace for language instruction and the more cultural dimensions of linguistic desire that I have articulated throughout this ethnography. A change in the economics of language schooling is an inevitable consequence of a maturing market. Similarly, the relatively minor reduction of English's weighting on university entrance exams underscores changes to the underlying ideology of education, but does not necessarily herald the doom of foreign languages in China or the elimination of English's linguistic capital. Nevertheless, in this conclusion I would like to survey the ground traveled in this ethnography and highlight some of the issues I have brought to the fore. There is much still that could be said about language, education, and modernization in China, and I hope to point the way forward to further research on these topics.

Modernity as Chronotope

Over twenty-five years ago, Heidi Ross described English in China as a "barometer of modernization," arguing that the language was accorded high status and importance when integration with the global community was prioritized, and low status when the foreign was perceived as a threat (Ross 1993). One could therefore see, in the 1980s and 1990s, foreign language learning as a proxy for broader political trends. In the time since, and as I hope this ethnography shows, the neoliberal restructuring of Chinese education and society, accompanied by intense anxieties about social class and economic positioning, has altered this calculus.

English now *is* modernization, or at least one of many potential ways of unlocking the perceived promises of a prosperous future.

As I outlined in the introduction, modernity has often been treated as the inevitable conclusion to various economic and political developments: the rise of nationalism and the nation-state, the capitalist transformation of the economy, and so forth. In theory, it is these substantive material changes to the bedrock on which culture is built that alter outlooks, everyday politics, and forms of interaction between people as newly emergent modern citizens. These changes are also, as it so happens, tied to the histories of Western nations, and much research over the past few decades has been dedicated to asking what the precise properties of modernity are and whether developing nations must mimic the preestablished template in order to become developed themselves, or if there are "alternative modernities," models of becoming that vary from or directly oppose some or all of those features (Knauft 2002; Ong 1997; Thomassen 2012).

In this book I have resisted an accounting of the financial or material metrics of either a Western-centric modernity or some kind of East Asian alternative modernity, accompanied by judgments as to whether this or that modernity has been achieved or if it is only to be realized a certain number of years in the future. As I argued in the introduction, modernity for the people I worked with was always in a state of becoming, tantalizingly close but always just beyond reach. Evidence of modernity's imminent arrival appeared everywhere in the form of taller buildings, global brands, more wealth and faster movement. But no matter how many bullet trains ran or coffee shops opened, modernity is still, in Lisa Rofel's (1999, 9–10) poignant words, "a repeatedly deferred enactment marked by discrepant desires that continually replace one another in an effort to achieve material and moral parity with the West." What matters, then, is not concrete evidence of modernity but the social practices—conversation, for instance, or consumption—where we find modernity creatively imagined and performatively instantiated.

As a consequence, I have dedicated quite a lot of space in this book to stories of how people situate themselves with regard to the social transformations that surround them. Are they leading the way into the future, or do they feel stuck in the past? Narratives of modernity implicate both their tellers, locating them within one or another spatiotemporal scale of development, and the nation as a whole. For a person to describe, for instance, their relative level of quality was to designate also the quality of their surroundings and the people inhabiting them. Modernity is therefore best regarded, I have argued, as a chronotope and best analyzed through its discursive enactments, through the way people talk about the changes around them and the circumstances of their own lives.

Scales of Social Action

The usage of some terms in this book have been imprecise but unavoidable in so far as they were deployed as common analytics by the people I was working with. As I argued in chapter one, terms such as English, Mandarin and Dongbeihua do not reflect identifiable and coherent linguistic systems but instead social evaluations that regiment forms of talk into particular registers. Another set of linked terms that require similar problematization are those of global and local. English is a global language in the sense that it is a language spoken, natively or by second language users, throughout the world. Dongbeihua is also a local language in so far as its usage indexes a sense of belonging at a regional scale. But it would be wrong leave it at this and imply that the two are categorically different, that they represent separate linguistic ends of a geographic scale. One can hear Dongbeihua spoken far outside its presumed regional limits, and indeed I have listened to many Shenyangers abroad speaking Dongbeihua with each other in a way that evokes strong emotional ties to home. It is, instead, more accurate to say that use of English posits action and belonging of a higher sociocultural order and that of Dongbeihua within more limited local ones.

These scales do not exist outside of interactional contexts but are instituted through them. What I mean by this is that global and local do not exist as static, opposed, and discontinuous geographic zones, which presumably shape the practices of language within them. Global and local are instead, as Arjun Appadurai (1996) noted, the product of human activities such as performance, representation, and ritual. He argued that practices such as naming, warding, demarcating, or situating structures, lands, and resources act as technologies of localization that provide a means of recognizing spatially proximate others as essentially similar to oneself—in other words, as locals. More recently, Jan Blommaert (2015a) has argued that global and local do not derive from separate ontologies but are rather different scalar representations of human endeavors and interactions (see also Moore 2004). Global and local are simply different perspectives on the same activity. When a Shenyanger uses English in interaction, it may index global identities or activities, but the interpretation of that indexical order also takes place at the local level, in dialogue with the person hearing and responding to those choices (Henry 2016; see also Büscher, D'Hondt, and Meeuwis 2013). Similarly, local language choices may spill out and impact larger national and global imaginaries, as when Zhao Benshan's Dongbeihua comedy skits were broadcast to a national and, given the networks of Chinese overseas migration, international audience. The global (whether it be worldwide relations of power or capital, histories of discourse, language ideologies, and so forth) always informs what might appear to be relatively isolated local practices, and these global systems can only ever be the product of (although perhaps more than the sum of the parts of) local interactions.

As we saw in chapter 3, narratives of language acquisition can bridge individual and collective desires, bringing personal experience in line with what are perceived to be broader social trends and developments. When the "I" of the language learner alternates with the communal "we" of the nation, speakers are holding two widely divergent scales in dialectical tension with each other. That sense of collectivity is also held in contrast to a globally sited indexical order materialized in the figure of the foreigner, the fluent native speaker. In the context of this ethnography, we can see this in the way that Chinese English speakers seem always aware of the native speaker's potentially disapproving gaze as they speak, and therefore carefully monitor their own language production. The very idea of speaking correctly, of not making mistakes, implicates the global order of language. But it goes even further than that: the foreigner, as Kristeva observed in the epigraph to chapter 6, lives within us. As we saw with the discussions around the outward bound adventure, it is through the foreign and the medium of a global language that people came to understand themselves as locally situated social actors. The characteristics of the Dongbei person (the living Lei Fengs of chapter 1) or the Chinese as a sociocultural collectivity, are imagined in dialogue with other scales of social activity.

The implication of this multiscalar perspective for research on languages is twofold. First, an ethnographic perspective that articulates speech with cultural practice is necessary to understand the indexical orders at play. Focusing merely on the form of one or more languages or registers favors a decontextualized and reified interpretation of fundamentally dissimilar linguistic structures (English and Mandarin, for instance) rather than the fluid shifting I have documented here. What interpretation of that speech means at each scalar level can only be achieved when the ideologies and frameworks of the speakers themselves are also targets of investigation. Second, the entire linguistic environment must shape the scope of research as well, since, as I have shown, different languages or registers can indexicalize differing scales of activity. Studies of English in non-native-speaking settings that marginalize other languages as unimportant or separate from the topic are therefore missing a substantive element of the equation.

An Anthropology of Global English

It is still common ethnographic practice to render all speech in written English, with no specification of what language was actually being used, in what setting, with which other interactants, and how informants may have switched between multiple languages during the speech event. Such practices obscure both a key element of the ethnographic record and the agency of people who must navigate complex sociolinguistic environments. How people speak and why they make the choices to speak those ways are relevant to our understanding of a range of anthropological issues and debates.

A similar oversight is present in a linguistic anthropology that is skewed toward minority languages and regional dialects, ignoring the majority languages that are increasingly required for everything from national citizenship to global mobility. The now mundane nature of talk between individuals from different countries or regions, requiring a common set of linguistic resources among all speakers, is reorganizing everything from educational priorities to how individuals use language on a daily basis. But for all of the work that draws our attention to language ideologies, we still seem to invest the native language, the language of home and intimacy, with authenticity, with representing a speaker's true essence and intention. Second languages are at best useful skills and at worst instruments of ongoing colonialism. There is a great deal of truth in those perspectives, and yet, as I have shown, as sites of intense desire, global languages are worth looking at from the viewpoints of the people learning them.

We should pay more attention to the role that global languages play for those who are, as Niko Besnier (2011, 6) terms it, "in the global but not quite of it." Anthropology, with its fine-grained analysis of individual engagements with social process, is well suited to such projects. It should be clear by now that the use of global languages is not a straightforward indicator of a person's social position or educational background. Rather, they are resources through which speakers can reconfigure their identities and selves in relation to a changing world. For Shenyangers, who experience spatial difference in chronotopic terms, global languages are also a form of spatiotemporal practice. Speaking English acts as a kind of deictic projection of the speaker into a future of global engagement, wealth, and unhindered social movement.

To the Chinese students and learners with whom I did my research, English was multiply evocative. A foreign language linked the speaker to the ongoing changes at the very heart of Chinese society: changes in the organization of space, temporality, economics, and personhood. It allowed speakers to participate, if only fleetingly and imaginatively, with a shared identity of cosmopolitan mobility that foreigners themselves seemed to effortlessly exhibit. Over time, it could come to transform the very way in which people thought of themselves as individuals, their senses of cultural belonging and affiliation. "In speaking," Winston once told, "well me, I'm Westernized, I will look you in the eye. But most Chinese will tend to look at their fingers, at the ceiling, outside at the window." The aspiration to see himself as different from others, to have abandoned local attachments and forged ahead into a global future, is accomplished through the medium of speech and, significantly, through particular language choices. If English can have such a profound impact on the Chinese sense of self, then a foreign language is never wholly foreign.

Notes

INTRODUCTION

1. The history of English throughout China's recent history has been well documented by several scholars, including Adamson 2004; Bolton 2003; Gil and Adamson 2011; and Pride and Liu 1988.

2. On the role of English in China's education system, see Cowan 1979; A. Feng 2009; Y. Gao, Orton, and Lo Bianco 2009; Gil 2016; Pan 2015a; Ross 1993; and Wenfang Wang and Gao 2008.

3. For an overview of English education in Korea, see J. Park 2009; S. Park and Abelmann 2004. For Japan, see Seargeant 2009; Stanlaw 2004. For India, see LaDousa 2014; Proctor 2014.

4. For an analysis of the English curriculum and foreign language policy in China, see X. Cheng 2011; A. Feng 2009; G. Hu 2005; Y. Hu 2007, 2008; L. Mao and Min 2004. For a description of contemporary pedagogy, see Pérez-Milans 2012; Ruan and Leung 2012; Zheng and Davison 2008.

5. Pan 2010, 2015b both provide many examples and an analysis of public uses of English script from Beijing.

6. See for instance Davidson 2007; Dick 2010; Divita 2014; Eisenlohr 2004; McIntosh 2010; Perrino 2011; Wirtz 2011.

1. DIRTY TALK

1. Manchu would have been a key part of the linguistic environment in Shenyang during the imperial era, but it has long since disappeared from the city other than in a handful of inscriptions on historical stone tablets. There may be some remaining speakers living in isolated rural areas, but I never met a single person in Shenyang who could speak any part of the language, and it has no impact today. For more on the language's contemporary status, see Janhunen 2005.

2. The relevant alveolars are z-, c-, and s- in pinyin, [ts], [tsʰ], and [s] in the International Phonetic Alphabet. The retroflexes are zh-, ch-, and sh- in pinyin, [tʂ], [tʂʰ], and [ʂ] in the International Phonetic Alphabet.

3. There is one exception, in the third line where Xue Cun uses a standard pronunciation of ren, but that is to accomplish a rhyme with the word "stitches" (zhen).

4. The other subjects are math, Chinese, and either an arts or science component.

5. For a comprehensive overview of washback in language testing, see L. Cheng, Watanabe, and Curtis 2004. Specific examples of washback from English-language tests in China can be found in L. Cheng 1998; L. Cheng and DeLuca 2011; and Green 2007.

6. I once took the 2012 English NCEE—which is usually published shortly after the examination is written nationwide to allow the next cohort of students to study—with a group of high school students. I could only complete the reading and practical language knowledge sections, but on those sections I only scored about 85 percent—not high enough, I was told, to get into a top university. None of the students found it odd that a native speaker of English would not receive a perfect score—all recognized the contrived nature of the examination.

7. Neither of these questions appeared on the NCEE itself, but I am arguing that preparation for the test is just as important as the test itself in shaping the context of register production.

8. A fuller discussion of these strategies and their use in practice can be found in Henry 2016.

9. I have not discussed the impact on Shenyang of other foreign languages, which share many indexical associations with English. Despite a range of multinational companies opening subsidiaries in Shenyang's Special Economic Zone, however, English remains the dominant foreign language in both public and private education. Some foreign languages, such as Japanese, which remains associated in Shenyang with the Second World War and experience of colonization, are positioned differently in the indexical field.

2. THE MORAL ECONOMY OF WALLS

1. For examples, see the excellent illustrations in Sicheng Liang 1984, 36–121; and Knapp and Lo 2005.

2. Interestingly, this aesthetic is only partially represented in Shenyang's own imperial palace, which was the residence of Manchu kings before their conquest of the Chinese empire to the south and the establishment of the Qing dynasty in 1644. The central feature here is the king's parade grounds and the arrayed tents of his Banner forces. After the move to Beijing, Manchus quickly adopted Chinese architectural norms.

3. With the exception of Beiling Park in northern Shenyang—site of several historical tombs—these walls were removed in preparation for an international horticultural exposition in 2006.

4. For a phenomenological description of what life in *hutong* was like prior to their demolition, see Q. Yang 2015 on Beijing *hutong*.

5. Yunxiang Yan (2009, 243–271) provides a good overview of the development of fast food in China since the 1970s. Particularly interesting in this case is the identification of American fast-food chains with new kinds of modernist social behavior described as "civilized" (*wenming*), such as customers clearing their own trash and keeping the space neat.

3. BETTER TO DIE ABROAD THAN TO LIVE IN CHINA

1. An early description of this phenomenon can be found in Theroux 1988, 115. See also S. Gao 2012.

2. On how SARS informed ongoing discourses of Chinese backwardness, see V. Fong 2007.

4. COMMODIFYING LANGUAGE

1. As I describe in chapter 2, most residential complexes feature security gates that admit only residents or invited visitors. I was not able to gain access to most of these complexes, and, in any case, many of these small classrooms are not marked or advertised.

2. There have been several periods of expansion and contraction since the start of my fieldwork in 2005. At that time there were fourteen branch schools within Shenyang and three outside. In response to market pressures, Hong Ri subsequently closed the three distant schools but has expanded within the city to thirty branches. Several changes in ownership at the school have also occurred.

3. Tuition rates can be highly variable, according to the location of the branch school and potential discounts that certain parents might be offered. The numbers I offer here are current as of 2015 and derived from checking with contacts in the industry and media reports at the time. As with many goods and services in Shenyang, tuition rates are subject to high rates of inflation, almost doubling since my original research in 2005. Also,

given the increasing levels of economic inequality, prices at the luxury end are increasing even more rapidly.

4. As the one-child policy continues to shift and evolve due to pressures from China's burgeoning middle class, more and more families will likely have multiple children. Currently, however, a single child is still the norm.

5. For more comprehensive descriptions of foreign language education and the uses of foreign teachers during this early part of the reform period, see Maley 1983 for a foreigner's perspective and Yu 1984 for a Chinese one.

6. The Ministry of Education reported 18,428 foreign teachers serving in higher education nationally in 2018 (MOE 2019).

7. A more extensive discussion of the foreign teacher lifestyle can be found in Stanley 2013.

8. For more on this dynamic, see my discussion of cheating and deception in Henry 2009, 25–29.

5. ON "CHINGLISH"

1. The campaign against Chinglish was also widely reported in the Western media, including CNN and the BBC. The Foreign Affairs Office of the People's Government of Beijing Municipality published a Chinese menu English translation guide in 2007. See also the Beijing Speaks Foreign Languages website at bjenglish.com.cn.

2. The classic work on interlanguage is Selinker 1972. For a more recent appraisal of the concept, see Z. Han and Tarone 2014.

3. The case is slightly different in places such as Hong Kong and Taiwan, where nativist forms have had both a longer history and a greater sociopolitical confidence in national autonomy. See for instance Pennington 1998; Bolton 2003.

4. Smartphone apps that perform this function are now widely available.

5. It should be clear that I too am implicated in the structure of inequality within the Shenyang English speech community, a dynamic I could not escape even as an "objective" anthropologist. As I discuss further in chapter 6, the foreigner (and his white body) is always already incorporated into a certain subject position. These considerations were not evident at the time and only became recognizable after a period of distance and reflection.

6. RACIOLINGUISTIC IDENTITIES

1. The presumed homogeneity of the Han ethnic population is becoming increasingly unstable. In 2009, a young mixed-race Shanghai woman named Lou Jing achieved national attention while performing in a popular televised singing contest. Her obvious phenotypic differences caused a great deal of online commentary, often of a quite retrograde and negative nature, while Lou Jing asserted her own version of ethnic belonging based on her linguistic and cultural heritage: having attended a regular Chinese school, speaking Mandarin with a Shanghai accent, and experiencing all the normal qualities of a Chinese childhood. Lou Jing thus drew on cultural and linguistic similarity to claim her legitimate place on the stage despite her apparent phenotypic "non-Chineseness." Such challenges to China's racial orthodoxy will no doubt become more common in the future.

2. This pronoun usage is not as popular outside of northern China, and is frequently glossed over or even omitted from standard reference grammars. It is, however, a key deictic feature of Dongbei speech. See H. Zhao 1987 for a more comprehensive discussion of both grammatical and pragmatic uses.

3. Another colloquial term is *laowai*, combining the respect term *lao* with the character for "outside." Other related terms, such as the many collocations of *yang* ("ocean"), as in *yangren* ("ocean person") or *yangguizi* ("ocean ghost," often glossed as "foreign devil"), were understood by Shenyangers but had little contemporary relevance in discourse.

4. Two very popular examples from the time of my own fieldwork were *Woju* (Snail House) (airing in 2009) and *Ma Dashuai* (the name of the eponymous main character) (2004–2006). Both featured white male characters who, despite the libidinal temptations they pose for main Chinese female characters, redeem themselves through righteous actions that resolve the main conflicts of the series. Although foreign female characters were once a staple of 1990s and early 2000s television dramas such as *Yangniu zai Beijing* (Foreign Babes in Beijing) and *Shewai Baomu* (Nannies for Foreigners), my impression is that roles for foreign women have declined in recent years.

5. Anti-Japanese sentiment is particularly acute in Shenyang, which was the center of Japan's colonization efforts in the 1930s and 1940s. Much like the discourse of foreignness I recount here, anti-Japanese rhetoric is the product of entangled macro-level state discourses, such as Shenyang's 9.18 History Museum commemorating the Japanese invasion and the numerous television dramas of this period, and micro-level private interactions. There were several small-scale anti-Japanese riots during my fieldwork that damaged local Japanese businesses.

6. For more on racialized constructions of "good English," see Cho 2012; Urciuoli 1996.

7. A more extensive discussion of the speaking portion of the IELTS exam and its rationale can be found at http://takeielts.britishcouncil.org/prepare-test/understand-test -format/speaking-test.

8. In my case, I was hired by an English school despite having no former teaching experience and no Teaching English to Speakers of Other Languages (TESOL) certification. Despite this, I and the other foreign teachers at my former school were all designated as "foreign experts" on our residence visas.

9. In 2005, Jasmine asked me to host her wedding, a job that combines the role of officiant and entertainer. I happily obliged and did, for the most part, a respectable job, but I suspect that her request to me was born not out of any perceived skill on my part as a master of ceremonies but out of my status as a foreigner, a choice that was the topic of much conversation by attendees after my duties were completed.

10. As Karen Kelsky (2001) points out, in Japan the foreign is much more likely to be ideologized as an escape or alternative to Japanese cultural practices rather than, as here, a conduit for rediscovering one's own.

11. See http://www.cctv.com/program/upclose/20051226/100732.shtml.

12. Or at least partially means that. Hua is a common shorthand for China and Chinese but can have other referential meanings. Ai Hua's older sister also grew up in Beijing and was given the name Ai Zhong. Together, then, the sisters are Ai Zhonghua, which means, unmistakably, "Love China." For more on the indexicality of Chinese names, see Henry 2012.

References

Abelmann, Nancy. 1997. "Narrating Selfhood and Personality in South Korea: Women and Social Mobility." *American Ethnologist* 24 (4): 786–812.

Adamson, Bob. 2004. *China's English: A History of English in Chinese Education*. Hong Kong: Hong Kong University Press.

Adamson, Bob, and Paul Morris. 1997. "The English Curriculum in the People's Republic of China." *Comparative Education Review* 41 (1): 3–26.

Agha, Asif. 2005. "Voice, Footing, Enregisterment." *Journal of Linguistic Anthropology* 15 (1): 38–59.

——. 2007. *Language and Social Relations*. Cambridge: Cambridge University Press.

——. 2011. "Commodity Registers." *Journal of Linguistic Anthropology* 21 (1): 22–53.

Alim, H. Samy, John Rickford, and Arnetha Ball, eds. 2016. *Raciolinguistics: How Language Shapes Our Ideas about Race*. Oxford: Oxford University Press.

Anagnost, Ann. 2004. "The Corporeal Politics of Quality (Suzhi)." *Public Culture* 16 (2): 189–208.

Ang, Ien. 2001. *On Not Speaking Chinese: Living between Asia and the West*. London: Routledge.

Appadurai, Arjun, ed. 1986. *The Social Life of Things: Commodities in Cultural Perspective*. Cambridge: Cambridge University Press.

——. 1996. *Modernity at Large: Cultural Dimensions of Globalization*. Minneapolis: University of Minnesota Press.

Austin, J. L. 1962. *How to Do Things with Words*. Cambridge, MA: Harvard University Press.

Bakhtin, Mikhail. 1981. *The Dialogic Imagination: Four Essays*. Austin: University of Texas Press.

——. 1986. *Speech Genres and Other Late Essays*. Austin: University of Texas Press.

Barker, Joshua, Erik Harms, and Johan Lindquist, eds. 2014. *Figures of Southeast Asian Modernity*. Honolulu: University of Hawai'i Press.

Barmé, Geremie. 2008. *The Forbidden City*. Cambridge, MA: Harvard University Press.

Bashkow, Ira. 2006. *The Meaning of Whitemen: Race and Modernity in the Orokaiva Cultural World*. Chicago: University of Chicago Press.

Basso, Keith. 1979. *Portraits of "The Whiteman": Linguistic Play and Cultural Symbols among the Western Apache*. Cambridge: Cambridge University Press.

——. 1996. *Wisdom Sits in Places: Landscape and Language among the Western Apache*. Albuquerque: University of New Mexico Press.

Bauman, Richard, and Charles Briggs. 1990. "Poetics and Performances as Critical Perspectives on Language and Social Life." *Annual Review of Anthropology* 19 (1): 59–88.

——. 2003. *Voices of Modernity: Language Ideologies and the Politics of Inequality*. Cambridge: Cambridge University Press.

Besnier, Niko. 2011. *On the Edge of the Global: Modern Anxieties in a Pacific Island Nation*. Stanford: Stanford University Press.

Bhabha, Homi. 1994. *The Location of Culture*. London: Routledge.

Biggerstaff, Knight. 1961. *The Earliest Modern Government Schools in China*. Ithaca, NY: Cornell University Press.

Bilaniuk, Laada. 2006. *Contested Tongues: Language Politics and Cultural Correction in Ukraine*. Ithaca, NY: Cornell University Press.

Billig, Michael. 2005. *Laughter and Ridicule: Towards a Social Critique of Humour*. London: Sage.

Billings, Sabrina. 2013. *Language, Globalization and the Making of a Tanzanian Beauty Queen*. Bristol, UK: Multilingual Matters.

Blom, Jan-Petter, and John J. Gumperz. 1972. "Social Meaning in Linguistic Structure: Code-Switching in Norway." In *Directions in Sociolinguistics: The Ethnography of Communication*, edited by Dell Hymes and John J. Gumperz, 407–434. New York: Holt, Rinehart and Winston.

Blommaert, Jan. 2010. *The Sociolinguistics of Globalization*. Cambridge: Cambridge University Press.

——. 2013. *Ethnography, Superdiversity and Linguistic Landscapes: Chronicles of Complexity*. Bristol, UK: Multilingual Matters.

——. 2015a. "Chronotopes, Scales, and Complexity in the Study of Language in Society." *Annual Review of Anthropology* 44: 105–116.

——. 2015b. "Meaning as a Nonlinear Effect: The Birth of Cool." *AILA Review* 28 (1): 7–27.

Blum, Susan. 2001. *Portraits of "Primitives": Ordering Human Kinds in the Chinese Nation*. Lanham, MD: Rowman and Littlefield.

——. 2004. "Good to Hear: Using the Trope of Standard to Find One's Way in a Sea of Linguistic Diversity." In *Language Policy in the People's Republic of China: Theory and Practice since 1949*, edited by Minglang Zhou and Hongkai Sun, 123–142. Boston: Kluwer.

Bolton, Kingsley. 2002. "Chinese Englishes: From Canton Jargon to Global English." *World Englishes* 21 (2): 181–199.

——. 2003. *Chinese Englishes: A Sociolinguistic History*. Cambridge: Cambridge University Press.

Bourdieu, Pierre. 1977. "The Economics of Linguistic Exchanges." *Social Science Information* 16 (6): 645–668.

——. 1984. *Distinction: A Social Critique of the Judgement of Taste*. Translated by Richard Nice. Cambridge, MA: Harvard University Press.

——. 1991. *Language and Symbolic Power*. Cambridge, MA: Harvard University Press.

Brady, Anne-Marie. 2003. *Making the Foreign Serve China: Managing Foreigners in the People's Republic*. Lanham, MD: Rowman and Littlefield.

Bucholtz, Mary, and Kira Hall. 2005. "Identity and Interaction: A Sociocultural Linguistic Approach." *Discourse Studies* 7 (4–5): 585–614.

Büscher, Karen, Sigurd D'Hondt, and Michael Meeuwis. 2013. "Recruiting a Nonlocal Language for Performing Local Identity: Indexical Appropriations of Lingala in the Congolese Border Town Goma." *Language in Society* 42 (5): 527–556.

Cameron, Deborah. 2000. "Styling the Worker: Gender and the Commodification of Language in the Globalized Service Economy." *Journal of Sociolinguistics* 4 (3): 323–347.

Campanella, Thomas. 2008. *The Concrete Dragon: China's Urban Revolution and What It Means for the World*. New York: Princeton Architectural Press.

Canagarajah, Suresh. 1999. *Resisting Linguistic Imperialism in English Teaching*. Oxford: Oxford University Press.

——. 2013. *Translingual Practice: Global Englishes and Cosmopolitan Relations*. New York: Routledge.

Carrico, Kevin. 2017. *The Great Han: Race, Nationalism, and Tradition in China Today*. Berkeley: University of California Press.

Cavanaugh, Jillian. 2005. "Accent Matters: Material Consequences of Sounding Local in Northern Italy." *Language and Communication* 25: 127–148.

——. 2012. *Living Memory: The Social Aesthetics of Language in a Northern Italian Town.* Chichester: Wiley-Blackwell.

Cavanaugh, Jillian R., and Shalini Shankar. 2014. "Producing Authenticity in Global Capitalism: Language, Materiality, and Value." *American Anthropologist* 116 (1): 51–64.

Certeau, Michel de. 1984. *The Practice of Everyday Life.* Berkeley: University of California Press.

Chang, Sen-Dou. 1977. "The Morphology of Walled Capitals." In *The City in Late Imperial China*, edited by G. William Skinner, 75–100. Stanford: Stanford University Press.

Chen, Xiaomei. 1995. *Occidentalism: A Theory of Counter-Discourse in Post-Mao China.* Oxford: Oxford University Press.

Cheng, Chin-Chuan. 1992. "Chinese Varieties of English." In *The Other Tongue: English across Cultures.* 2nd ed. Edited by Braj Kachru, 162–177. Urbana: University of Illinois Press.

Cheng, Liying. 1998. "Impact of a Public English Examination Change on Students' Perceptions and Attitudes toward Their English Learning." *Studies in Educational Evaluation* 24 (3): 279–301.

——. 2008. "The Key to Success: English Language Testing in China." *Language Testing* 25 (1): 15–37.

Cheng, Liying, and Christopher DeLuca. 2011. "Voices from Test-Takers: Further Evidence for Language Assessment Validation and Use." *Educational Assessment* 16 (2): 104–122.

Cheng, Liying, and Luxia Qi. 2006. "Description and Examination of the National Matriculation English Test." *Language Assessment Quarterly* 3 (1): 53–70.

Cheng, Liying, Yoshinori J. Watanabe, and Andy Curtis, eds. 2004. *Washback in Language Testing: Research Contexts and Methods.* Mahwah, NJ: Lawrence Erlbaum.

Cheng, Xiaotang. 2011. "The 'English Curriculum Standards' in China: Rationales and Issues." In *English Language Education across Greater China*, edited by Anwei Feng, 133–150. Bristol, UK: Multilingual Matters.

Cheng, Yinghong. 2011. "From Campus Racism to Cyber Racism: Discourse of Race and Chinese Nationalism." *China Quarterly* 207: 561–579.

Cho, John (Song Pae). 2012. "Global Fatigue: Transnational Markets, Linguistic Capital, and Korean-American Male English Teachers in South Korea." *Journal of Sociolinguistics* 16 (2): 218–237.

Christie, Dugald. 1914. *Thirty Years in Moukden: 1883–1913.* London: Constable.

Chubb, Andrew. 2015. "China's Shanzhai Culture: 'Grabism' and the Politics of Hybridity." *Journal of Contemporary China* 24 (92): 260–279.

Chumley, Lily Hope, and Nicholas Harkness. 2013. "Introduction: QUALIA." *Anthropological Theory* 13 (1–2): 3–11.

Chun, Allen. 2017. *Forget Chineseness: On the Geopolitics of Cultural Identification.* Albany: State University of New York Press.

Clifford, James. 1983. "On Ethnographic Authority." *Representations* 2: 118–146.

Cook, Vivian. 1999. "Going beyond the Native Speaker in Language Teaching." *TESOL Quarterly* 33 (2): 185–209.

Corder, S. P. (Pit). 1967. "The Significance of Learner's Errors." *International Review of Applied Linguistics in Language Teaching* 5 (4): 161–170.

Corsín Jiménez, Alberto. 2003. "On Space as a Capacity." *Journal of the Royal Anthropological Institute* 9 (1): 137–153.

Coupland, Nikolas. 2003. "Sociolinguistic Authenticities." *Journal of Sociolinguistics* 7 (3): 417–431.

Cowan, J. Ronayne. 1979. "English Teaching in China: A Recent Survey." *TESOL Quarterly* 13 (4): 465–482.

Crabb, Mary. 2010. "Governing the Middle-Class Family in Urban China: Educational Reform and Questions of Choice." *Economy and Society* 39 (3): 385–402.

Croll, Elisabeth. 2006. *China's New Consumers: Social Development and Domestic Demand.* New York: Routledge.

Crystal, David. 1997. *English as a Global Language.* Cambridge: Cambridge University Press.

Davidson, Deanna. 2007. "East Spaces in West Times: Deictic Reference and Political Self-Positioning in a Post-Socialist East German Chronotope." *Language and Communication* 27 (3): 212–226.

Davies, Alan. 2003. *The Native Speaker: Myth and Reality.* Clevedon, UK: Multilingual Matters.

Deng, Peng. 1997. *Private Education in Modern China.* Westport, CT: Praeger.

Derrida, Jacques. 1998. *Monolingualism of the Other; or, The Prosthesis of Origin.* Stanford: Stanford University Press.

Deterding, David. 2006. "The Pronunciation of English by Speakers from China." *English World-Wide* 27 (2): 175–198.

Dick, Hilary Parsons. 2010. "Imagined Lives and Modernist Chronotopes in Mexican Nonmigrant Discourse." *American Ethnologist* 37 (2): 275–290.

Dikötter, Frank. 1992. *The Discourse of Race in Modern China.* London: Hurst.

——. 2006. *Exotic Commodities: Modern Objects and Everyday Life in China.* New York: Columbia University Press.

Dirlik, Arif. 2005. *Marxism in the Chinese Revolution.* Lanham, MD: Rowman and Littlefield.

Divita, David. 2014. "From Paris to Pueblo and Back: (Re-)Emigration and the Modernist Chronotope in Cultural Performance." *Journal of Linguistic Anthropology* 24 (1): 1–18.

Doerr, Neriko Musha, ed. 2009. *The Native Speaker Concept: Ethnographic Investigations of Native Speaker Effects.* Berlin: Mouton de Gruyter.

Dong, Jie. 2009. "'Isn't It Enough to Be a Chinese Speaker': Language Ideology and Migrant Identity Construction in a Public Primary School in Beijing." *Language and Communication* 29 (2): 115–126.

——. 2010. "The Enregisterment of Putonghua in Practice." *Language and Communication* 30 (4): 265–275.

——. 2017. *The Sociolinguistics of Voice in Globalising China.* London: Routledge.

Dong, Madeleine Yue, and Joshua Lewis Goldstein. 2006. *Everyday Modernity in China.* Seattle: University of Washington Press.

Duara, Prasenjit. 2003. *Sovereignty and Authenticity: Manchukuo and the East Asian Modern.* Lanham, MD: Rowman and Littlefield.

Duchêne, Alexandre, and Monica Heller, eds. 2012. *Language in Late Capitalism: Pride and Profit.* New York: Routledge.

Duranti, Alessandro. 2015. *The Anthropology of Intentions: Language in a World of Others.* Cambridge: Cambridge University Press.

Ebrey, Patricia Buckley. 1991. *Confucianism and Family Rituals in Imperial China: A Social History of Writing about Rites.* Princeton, NJ: Princeton University Press.

Eckert, Penelope. 2008. "Variation and the Indexical Field." *Journal of Sociolinguistics* 12 (4): 453–476.

Eisenlohr, Patrick. 2004. "Temporalities of Community: Ancestral Language, Pilgrimage, and Diasporic Belonging in Mauritius." *Journal of Linguistic Anthropology* 14 (1): 81–98.

Esherick, Joseph, ed. 2000. *Remaking the Chinese City: Modernity and National Identity, 1900–1950.* Honolulu: University of Hawai'i Press.

Evans, Harriet. 2008. *The Subject of Gender: Daughters and Mothers in Urban China.* Lanham, MD: Rowman and Littlefield.

Evans, Stephen. 2006. "The Beginnings of English Language Teaching in China." *Asian Englishes* 9 (1): 42–63.

Farquhar, Judith. 2002. *Appetites: Food and Sex in Post-Socialist China.* Durham, NC: Duke University Press.

Fei, Xiaotong. 1992. *From the Soil: The Foundations of Chinese Society.* Translated by Gary Hamilton and Zheng Wang. Berkeley: University of California Press.

Feng, Anwei. 2009. "English in China: Convergence and Divergence in Policy and Practice." *AILA Review* 22 (1): 85–102.

Feng, Changrong. 2008. "Dongbeihua de tedian ji liuxing tese" [Dongbeihua's traits and popular characteristics]. *Dongbei shidi* [Northeastern history and geography] 2008 (1): 73–77.

Ferguson, James. 2006. *Global Shadows: Africa in the Neoliberal World Order.* Durham, NC: Duke University Press.

Feuchtwang, Stephan, ed. 2004. *Making Place: State Projects, Globalisation and Local Responses in China.* London: Routledge.

Fiskesjö, Magnus. 2006. "Rescuing the Empire: Chinese Nation-Building in the Twentieth Century." *European Journal of East Asian Studies* 5 (1): 15–44.

Fong, Emily Tsz Yan. 2009. "English in China: Some Thoughts after the Beijing Olympics." *English Today* 25 (1): 44.

Fong, Vanessa. 2004. *Only Hope: Coming of Age under China's One-Child Policy.* Stanford: Stanford University Press.

——. 2007. "SARS, a Shipwreck, a NATO Attack, and September 11, 2001: Global Information Flows and Chinese Responses to Tragic News Events." *American Ethnologist* 34 (3): 521–539.

——. 2011. *Paradise Redefined: Transnational Chinese Students and the Quest for Flexible Citizenship in the Developed World.* Stanford: Stanford University Press.

Fraser, David. 2000. "Inventing Oasis: Luxury Housing Advertisements and Reconfiguring Domestic Space in Shanghai." In *The Consumer Revolution in Urban China,* edited by Deborah Davis, 25–53. Berkeley: University of California Press.

Gal, Susan. 1988. "The Political Economy of Code Choice." In *Codeswitching: Anthropological and Sociolinguistic Perspectives,* edited by Monica Heller, 245–264. Berlin: Mouton de Gruyter.

——. 2013. "Tastes of Talk: Qualia and the Moral Flavor of Signs." *Anthropological Theory* 13 (1–2): 31–48.

Gal, Susan, and Judith Irvine. 1995. "The Boundaries of Languages and Disciplines: How Ideologies Construct Difference." *Social Research* 62 (4): 967–1001.

Gao, Jia, and Peter Pugsley. 2008. "Utilizing Satire in Post-Deng Chinese Politics: Zhao Benshan Xiaopin vs. the Falun Gong." *China Information* 22 (3): 451–476.

Gao, Shuang. 2012. "The Biggest English Corner in China." *English Today* 28 (3): 34–39.

Gao, Yihong, Jane Orton, and Joseph Lo Bianco, eds. 2009. *China and English: Globalisation and the Dilemmas of Identity.* Bristol, UK: Multilingual Matters.

Garcia, Ofelia, and Ricardo Otheguy. 1989. *English across Cultures, Cultures across English: A Reader in Cross-Cultural Communication.* Berlin: Mouton de Gruyter.

Gaubatz, Piper Rae. 1995. "Urban Transformation in Post-Mao China: Impacts of the Reform Era on China's Urban Form." In *Urban Spaces in Contemporary China: The Potential for Autonomy and Community in Post-Mao China,* edited by Deborah Davis, Richard Kraus, Barry Naughton, and Elizabeth Perry, 28–60. New York: Woodrow Wilson Center Press.

Giddens, Anthony. 1990. *The Consequences of Modernity*. Stanford: Stanford University Press.

Gil, Jeffrey. 2016. "English Language Education Policies in the People's Republic of China." In *English Language Education Policy in Asia*, edited by Robert Kirkpatrick, 49–90. Cham, Switzerland: Springer.

Gil, Jeffrey, and Bob Adamson. 2011. "The English Language in Mainland China: A Sociolinguistic Profile." In *English Language Education across Greater China*, edited by Anwei Feng, 23–45. Bristol, UK: Multilingual Matters.

Giles, John, Albert Park, and Fang Cai. 2006. "How Has Economic Restructuring Affected China's Urban Workers?" *China Quarterly* 185: 61–95.

Giroir, Guillaume. 2006. "A Globalized Golden Ghetto in a Chinese Garden: The Fontainebleau Villas in Shanghai." In *Globalization and the Chinese City*, edited by Fulong Wu, 208–225. London: Routledge.

Gladney, Dru. 2004. *Dislocating China*. Chicago: University of Chicago Press.

Goddard, Cliff. 2005. *The Languages of East and Southeast Asia: An Introduction*. Oxford: Oxford University Press.

Goebel, Zane. 2008. "Enregistering, Authorizing and Denaturalizing Identity in Indonesia." *Journal of Linguistic Anthropology* 18 (1): 46–61.

——. 2010. *Language, Migration, and Identity: Neighborhood Talk in Indonesia*. Cambridge: Cambridge University Press.

Goffman, Erving. 1959. *The Presentation of Self in Everyday Life*. New York: Doubleday Anchor.

——. 1983. "Felicity's Condition." *American Journal of Sociology* 89 (1): 1–53.

Gold, Thomas, Doug Guthrie, and David L. Wank, eds. 2002. *Social Connections in China: Institutions, Culture, and the Changing Nature of Guanxi*. Cambridge: Cambridge University Press.

Gorter, Durk, ed. 2006. *Linguistic Landscape: A New Approach to Multilingualism*. Bristol, UK: Multilingual Matters.

Green, Anthony. 2007. "Washback to Learning Outcomes: A Comparative Study of IELTS Preparation and University Pre-sessional Language Courses." *Assessment in Education: Principles, Policy and Practice* 14 (1): 75–97.

Gu, Mingyue (Michelle). 2009. "College English Learners' Discursive Motivation Construction in China." *System* 37 (2): 300–312.

Han, Ling. 2007. "'Zhongguo yingyu' xianzhuang fenxi" [An analysis of current research on "China English"]. *Waiyu yu waiyu jiaoxue* [Foreign languages and their teaching] 10: 28–32.

Han, Mei. 2007. "Cong dianshiju Liu Laogen kan Dongbei fangyan de tedian" [Examining the characteristics of the Dongbei dialect through the television drama *Liu Laogen*]. *Changchun shifan xueyuan xuebao (renwen shehui kexueban)* [Journal of Changchun Normal University (humanities and social sciences)] 26 (4): 77–81.

Han, ZhaoHong, and Elaine Tarone, eds. 2014. *Interlanguage: Forty Years Later*. Amsterdam: John Benjamins.

Hanks, William. 1999. "Indexicality." *Journal of Linguistic Anthropology* 9 (1–2): 124–126.

Hansen, Mette Halskov. 1999. *Lessons in Being Chinese: Minority Education and Ethnic Identity in Southwest China*. Seattle: University of Washington Press.

Hardt, Michael. 1999. "Affective Labor." *Boundary 2* 26 (2): 89–100.

Harkness, Nicholas. 2015. "The Pragmatics of Qualia in Practice." *Annual Review of Anthropology* 44 (1): 573–589.

Harrell, Stevan, ed. 1995. *Cultural Encounters on China's Ethnic Frontiers*. Seattle: University of Washington Press.

He, Deyuan, and David C. S. Li. 2009. "Language Attitudes and Linguistic Features in the 'China English' Debate." *World Englishes* 28 (1): 70–89.

He, Ping. 2002. *China's Search for Modernity: Cultural Discourse in the Late 20th Century.* Houndmills, UK: Palgrave.

Heller, Monica. 2001. "Legitimate Language in a Multilingual School." In *Voices of Authority: Education and Linguistic Difference,* edited by Marilyn Martin-Jones and Monica Heller, 381–402. Westport, CT: Ablex.

——. 2002. "Globalization and the Commodification of Bilingualism in Canada." In *Globalization and Language Teaching,* edited by Deborah Cameron and David Block, 47–63. London: Routledge.

——. 2003. "Globalization, the New Economy and the Commodification of Language and Identity." *Journal of Sociolinguistics* 7 (4): 473–492.

——. 2010. "The Commodification of Language." *Annual Review of Anthropology* 39 (1): 101–114.

Heller, Monica, and Bonnie McElhinny. 2017. *Language, Capitalism, Colonialism: Toward a Critical History.* Toronto: University of Toronto Press.

Hélot, Christine, ed. 2012. *Linguistic Landscapes, Multilingualism and Social Change.* Frankfurt: Peter Lang.

Henry, Eric. 2009. "The Beggar's Play: Poverty, Coercion, and Performance in Shenyang, China." *Anthropological Quarterly* 82 (1): 7–35.

——. 2012. "When Dragon Met Jasmine: Domesticating English Names in Chinese Social Interaction." *Anthropologica* 54 (1): 107–117.

——. 2013a. "Emissaries of the Modern: The Foreign Teacher in Urban China." *City and Society* 25 (2): 216–234.

——. 2013b. "Lending Words: Foreign Language Education and Teachers in Republican Peking." In *Foreigners and Foreign Institutions in Republican China,* edited by Anne-Marie Brady and Douglas Brown, 52–71. London: Routledge.

——. 2016. "The Local Purposes of a Global Language: English as an Intracultural Communicative Medium in China." In *The Cultural and Intercultural Dimensions of English as a Lingua Franca,* edited by Prue Holmes and Fred Dervin, 180–200. Bristol, UK: Multilingual Matters.

Higgins, Christina. 2009. *English as a Local Language: Post-Colonial Identities and Multilingual Practices.* Bristol, UK: Multilingual Matters.

Hill, Jane. 1985. "The Grammar of Consciousness and the Consciousness of Grammar." *American Ethnologist* 12 (4): 725–737.

——. 2008. *The Everyday Language of White Racism.* Oxford: Wiley-Blackwell.

Hoffman, Lisa. 2010. *Patriotic Professionalism in Urban China: Fostering Talent.* Philadelphia: Temple University Press.

Holborow, Marnie. 2015. *Language and Neoliberalism.* London: Routledge.

Hsu, Carolyn L. 2005. "A Taste of 'Modernity': Working in a Western Restaurant in Market Socialist China." *Ethnography* 6 (4): 543–565.

——. 2007. *Creating Market Socialism: How Ordinary People Are Shaping Class and Status in China.* Durham, NC: Duke University Press.

Hu, Guangwei. 2002a. "Potential Cultural Resistance to Pedagogical Imports: The Case of Communicative Language Teaching in China." *Language, Culture and Curriculum* 15 (2): 93–105.

——. 2002b. "Recent Important Developments in Secondary English Language Teaching in the PRC." *Language, Culture and Curriculum* 15 (1): 30–49.

——. 2005. "English Language Education in China: Policies, Progress, and Problems." *Language Policy* 4 (1): 5–24.

Hu, Guangwei, and Sandra Lee McKay. 2012. "English Language Education in East Asia: Some Recent Developments." *Journal of Multilingual and Multicultural Development* 33 (4): 345–362.

Hu, Shih. 1926. "The Renaissance in China." *Journal of the Royal Institute of International Affairs* 5 (6): 265–283.

Hu, Xiao. 2008. "Boundaries and Openings: Spatial Strategies in the Chinese Dwelling." *Journal of Housing and the Built Environment* 23 (4): 353–366.

Hu, Xiaoqiong. 2004. "Why China English Should Stand alongside British, American, and the Other 'World Englishes.'" *English Today* 20 (2): 26–33.

Hu, Yuanyuan. 2007. "China's Foreign Language Policy on Primary English Education: What's Behind It?" *Language Policy* 6 (3–4): 359–376.

——. 2008. "China's English Language Policy for Primary Schools." *World Englishes* 27 (3–4): 516–534.

Huang, Li-Shih. 2010. "The Potential Influence of L1 (Chinese) on L2 (English) Communication." *ELT Journal* 64 (2): 155–164.

Ingold, Tim. 2000. *The Perception of the Environment: Essays on Livelihood, Dwelling and Skill.* London: Routledge.

Inoue, Miyako. 2003. "The Listening Subject of Japanese Modernity and His Auditory Double: Citing, Sighting and Siting the Japanese Woman." *Cultural Anthropology* 18 (2): 156–193.

——. 2006. *Vicarious Language: Gender and Linguistic Modernity in Japan.* Berkeley: University of California Press.

Irvine, Judith. 1989. "When Talk Isn't Cheap: Language and Political Economy." *American Ethnologist* 16 (2): 248–267.

Jacka, Tamara. 2009. "Cultivating Citizens: Suzhi (Quality) Discourse in the PRC." *Positions: East Asia Cultures Critique* 17 (3): 523–535.

Jaffe, Alexandra. 1999. *Ideologies in Action: Language Politics on Corsica.* Berlin: Mouton de Gruyter.

Jameson, Fredric. 1991. *Postmodernism, or, The Cultural Logic of Late Capitalism.* Durham, NC: Duke University Press.

Janhunen, Juha. 2005. "Tungusic: An Endangered Language Family in Northeast Asia." *International Journal of the Sociology of Language* 173: 37–54.

Ji, Fengyuan. 2004. *Linguistic Engineering: Language and Politics in Mao's China.* Honolulu: University of Hawai'i Press.

Jiang, Yajun. 1995. "Chinglish and China English." *English Today* 11 (1): 51–56.

——. 2002. "China English: Issues, Studies and Features." *Asian Englishes* 5 (2): 4–23.

Johansson, Perry. 1999. "Consuming the Other: The Fetish of the Western Woman in Chinese Advertising and Popular Culture." *Postcolonial Studies* 2 (3): 377–388.

Johnstone, Barbara. 2009. "Pittsburghese Shirts: Commodification and the Enregisterment of an Urban Dialect." *American Speech* 84 (2): 157–175.

Kachru, Braj. 1986. *The Alchemy of English: Social and Functional Power of Non-Native Varieties.* Urbana: University of Illinois Press.

——, ed. 1992. *The Other Tongue: English across Cultures.* 2nd ed. Urbana: University of Illinois Press.

Kachru, Braj, Yamuna Kachru, and Cecil L. Nelson, eds. 2006. *The Handbook of World Englishes.* Malden, MA: Blackwell.

Keane, Webb. 2003. "Second Language, National Language, Modern Language, and Post-Colonial Voice: On Indonesian." In *Translating Cultures: Perspectives on Translation and Anthropology,* edited by Abraham Rosman and Paula Rubel, 153–175. New York: Berg.

———. 2007. *Christian Moderns: Freedom and Fetish in the Mission Encounter*. Berkeley: University of California Press.

Kelsky, Karen. 2001. *Women on the Verge: Japanese Women, Western Dreams*. Durham, NC: Duke University Press.

Kipnis, Andrew. 1995. "'Face': An Adaptable Discourse of Social Surfaces." *Positions: East Asia Cultures Critique* 3 (1): 119–148.

———. 1997. *Producing Guanxi: Sentiment, Self, and Subculture in a North China Village*. Durham, NC: Duke University Press.

———. 2006. "Suzhi: A Keyword Approach." *China Quarterly* 186: 295–313.

———. 2007. "Neoliberalism Reified: Suzhi Discourse and Tropes of Neoliberalism in the People's Republic of China." *Journal of the Royal Anthropological Institute* 13 (2): 383–400.

———. 2011. *Governing Educational Desire: Culture, Politics, and Schooling in China*. Chicago: University of Chicago Press.

———, ed. 2012. *Chinese Modernity and the Individual Psyche*. New York: Palgrave Macmillan.

Kirkpatrick, Andy, ed. 2010. *The Routledge Handbook of World Englishes*. London: Routledge.

Kirkpatrick, Andy, and Zhichang Xu. 2002. "Chinese Pragmatic Norms and 'China English.'" *World Englishes* 21 (2): 269–279.

Knapp, Ronald G. 2000. *China's Old Dwellings*. Honolulu: University of Hawai'i Press.

Knapp, Ronald, and Kai-Yin Lo. 2005. *House, Home, Family: Living and Being Chinese*. Honolulu: University of Hawai'i Press.

Knauft, Bruce, ed. 2002. *Critically Modern: Alternatives, Alterities, Anthropologies*. Bloomington: Indiana University Press.

Kockelman, Paul. 2006. "A Semiotic Ontology of the Commodity." *Journal of Linguistic Anthropology* 16 (1): 76–102.

Kondo, Dorinne. 1990. *Crafting Selves: Power, Gender, and Discourses of Identity in a Japanese Workplace*. Chicago: University of Chicago Press.

Kramer, Elise. 2011. "The Playful Is Political: The Metapragmatics of Internet Rape-Joke Arguments." *Language in Society* 40 (2): 137–168.

Kristeva, Julia. 1991. *Strangers to Ourselves*. New York: Columbia University Press.

Kwong, Julia. 2011. "Education and Identity: The Marginalisation of Migrant Youths in Beijing." *Journal of Youth Studies* 14 (8): 871–183.

Labov, William. 1972. *Language in the Inner City: Studies in the Black English Vernacular*. Philadelphia: University of Pennsylvania Press.

Lacan, Jacques. 1998. *The Four Fundamental Concepts of Psychoanalysis*. Edited by Jacques-Alain Miller. Translated by Alan Sheridan. New York: W. W. Norton.

LaDousa, Chaise. 2014. *Hindi Is Our Ground, English Is Our Sky: Education, Language, and Social Class in Contemporary India*. New York: Berghahn Books.

Latour, Bruno. 1993. *We Have Never Been Modern*. Translated by Catherine Porter. Cambridge, MA: Harvard University Press.

Lee, Benjamin, and Edward LiPuma. 2002. "Cultures of Circulation: The Imaginations of Modernity." *Public Culture* 14 (1): 191–213.

Lee, Haiyan. 2006. "Nannies for Foreigners: The Enchantment of Chinese Womanhood in the Age of Millennial Capitalism." *Public Culture* 18 (3): 507–529.

Lee, Leo Ou-fan. 1999. *Shanghai Modern: The Flowering of a New Urban Culture in China, 1930–1945*. Cambridge, MA: Harvard University Press.

Lefebvre, Henri. 1991. *The Production of Space*. Oxford: Blackwell.

Li, Chris Wen-Chao. 2004. "Conflicting Notions of Language Purity: The Interplay of Archaising, Ethnographic, Reformist, Elitist and Xenophobic Purism in the Perception of Standard Chinese." *Language and Communication* 24 (2): 97–133.

Li, Jingyan. 2009. "Motivational Force and Imagined Community in 'Crazy English.'" In *China and English: Globalisation and the Dilemmas of Identity*, edited by Yihong Gao, Jane Orton, and Joseph Lo Bianco, 211–123. Bristol, UK: Multilingual Matters.

Li, Minglin, and Richard Baldauf. 2011. "Beyond the Curriculum: A Chinese Example of Issues Constraining Effective English Language Teaching." *TESOL Quarterly* 45 (4): 793–803.

Li, Wei. 2016. "New Chinglish and the Post-Multilingualism Challenge: Translanguaging ELF in China." *Journal of English as a Lingua Franca* 5 (1): 1–25.

Li, Wenzhong. 1993. "Zhongguo yingyu yu zhongshi yingyu" [China English and Chinglish]. *Waiyu jiaoxue yu yanjiu* [Foreign language teaching and research] 4: 18–24.

Li, Xiaoguang, Zhan Ju, and Marinus van den Berg. 2016. "Urbanization, Education, and Language Behavior: The Case of Jilin University Students." *Journal of Asian Pacific Communication* 26 (1): 81–111.

Li, Yingzi. 2008. "Dongbei fangyan yanjiu zongshu" [A summary of research on the Dongbei dialect]. *Yuyan yingyong yanjiu* [Applied linguistics research] 10: 95–98.

Liang, Samuel. 2010. *Mapping Modernity in Shanghai: Space, Gender, and Visual Culture in the Sojourners' City, 1853–98*. New York: Routledge.

Liang, Sicheng. 1984. *A Pictorial History of Chinese Architecture: A Study of the Development of Its Structural System and the Evolution of Its Types*. Edited by Wilma Fairbank. Cambridge, MA: MIT Press.

Lin, Jing. 2007. "Emergence of Private Schools in China: Context, Characteristics, and Implications." In *Education and Reform in China*, edited by Emily Hannum and Albert Park, 44–63. New York: Routledge.

Lin, Yi-Chieh Jessica. 2011. *Fake Stuff: China and the Rise of Counterfeit Goods*. New York: Routledge.

Link, E. Perry, Richard Madsen, and Paul Pickowicz, eds. 1989. *Unofficial China: Popular Culture and Thought in the People's Republic*. Boulder, CO: Westview Press.

Liu, Fengshu. 2015. "The Rise of the 'Priceless' Child in China." *Comparative Education Review* 60 (1): 105–130.

Liu, Xin. 1997. "Space, Mobility, and Flexibility: Chinese Villagers and Scholars Negotiate Power at Home and Abroad." In *Ungrounded Empires: The Cultural Politics of Modern Chinese Transnationalism*, edited by Aihwa Ong and Donald Nonini, 91–114. New York: Routledge.

——. 2000. *In One's Own Shadow: An Ethnographic Account of the Condition of Post-Reform Rural China*. Berkeley: University of California Press.

——. 2002. *The Otherness of Self: A Genealogy of the Self in Contemporary China*. Ann Arbor: University of Michigan Press.

Lo, Ming-cheng, and Eileen Otis. 2003. "Guanxi Civility: Processes, Potentials, and Contingencies." *Politics and Society* 31 (1): 131–162.

Lu, Duanfang. 2006. *Remaking Chinese Urban Form: Modernity, Scarcity, and Space, 1949–2005*. London: Routledge.

Lu, Hanchao. 1999. *Beyond the Neon Lights: Everyday Shanghai in the Early Twentieth Century*. Berkeley: University of California Press.

Lu, Sheldon. 2000. "Soap Opera in China: The Transnational Politics of Visuality, Sexuality, and Masculinity." *Cinema Journal* 40 (1): 25–47.

Ma, Laurence, and Fulong Wu, eds. 2004. *Restructuring the Chinese City: Changing Society, Economy and Space*. London: Routledge.

Ma, Sizhou, and Guanghui Jiang, eds. 2005. *Dongbei fangyan cidian* [Dictionary of the Dongbei dialect]. Changchun: Jilin Literature and History Press.

Mair, Victor. 1991. "What Is a Chinese 'Dialect/Topolect'? Reflections on Some Key Sino-English Linguistic Terms." *Sino-Platonic Papers* 29: 1–31.

Makoni, Sinfree, and Alastair Pennycook, eds. 2007. *Disinventing and Reconstituting Languages*. Bristol, UK: Multilingual Matters.

Maley, Alan. 1983. "Xanadu—'A Miracle of Rare Device': The Teaching of English in China." *Language Learning and Communication* 2 (1): 97–104.

Manning, Paul. 2010. "The Semiotics of Brand." *Annual Review of Anthropology* 39 (1): 33–49.

Manning, Paul, and Ann Uplisashvili. 2007. "'Our Beer': Ethnographic Brands in Postsocialist Georgia." *American Anthropologist* 109 (4): 626–641.

Mao, Luming, and Yue Min. 2004. "Foreign Language Education in the PRC: A Brief Overview." In *Language Policy in the People's Republic of China: Theory and Practice since 1949*, edited by Minglang Zhou and Hongkai Sun, 319–330. Boston: Kluwer.

Mao, Zedong. 1977. "On the Correct Handling of Contradictions among the People." In *Selected Works of Mao Tsetung*, vol. 5, 384–421. Beijing: Foreign Languages Press.

Marx, Karl. 1978. *The Marx-Engels Reader*. 2nd ed. Edited by R. C. Tucker. New York: W. W. Norton.

Mattingly, Cheryl. 1994. "The Concept of Therapeutic 'Emplotment.'" *Social Science and Medicine* 38 (6): 811–822.

McCarthy, Susan K. 2009. *Communist Multiculturalism: Ethnic Revival in Southwest China*. Seattle: University of Washington Press.

McElhinny, Bonnie. 2006. "Written in Sand: Language and Landscape in an Environmental Dispute in Southern Ontario." *Critical Discourse Studies* 3 (2): 123–152.

McGill, Kenneth. 2013a. "No Magic Tricks: Commodity, Empowerment, and the Sale of StreetWise in Chicago." *Journal of Linguistic Anthropology* 23 (1): 1–20.

——. 2013b. "Political Economy and Language: A Review of Some Recent Literature." *Journal of Linguistic Anthropology* 23 (2): E84–101.

McIntosh, Janet. 2010. "Mobile Phones and Mipoho's Prophecy: The Powers and Dangers of Flying Language." *American Ethnologist* 37 (2): 337–353.

Meyer, Jeffrey. 1991. *The Dragons of Tiananmen: Beijing as a Sacred City*. Columbia: University of South Carolina Press.

MOE (Ministry of Education of the People's Republic of China). 2019. "Educational Statistics in 2018." http://en.moe.gov.cn/documents/statistics/2018/national/index_8.html.

Moore, Henrietta. 2004. "Global Anxieties: Concept-Metaphors and Pre-theoretical Commitments in Anthropology." *Anthropological Theory* 4 (1): 71–88.

Morgan, Marcyliena. 2002. *Language, Discourse, and Power in African American Culture*. Cambridge: Cambridge University Press.

Moskowitz, Marc. 2010. *Cries of Joy, Songs of Sorrow: Chinese Pop Music and Its Cultural Connotations*. Honolulu: University of Hawai'i Press.

Mu, Aili. 2004. "Two of Zhao Benshan's Comic Skits: Their Critical Implications in Contemporary China." *Concentric: Literary and Cultural Studies* 30 (2): 3–34.

Mufwene, Salikoko, John Rickford, Guy Bailey, and John Baugh, eds. 1998. *African-American English: Structure, History and Use*. London: Routledge.

Mullaney, Thomas. 2011. *Coming to Terms with the Nation: Ethnic Classification in Modern China*. Berkeley: University of California Press.

Mullaney, Thomas, James Leibold, Stéphane Gros, and Eric Vanden Bussche, eds. 2012. *Critical Han Studies*. Berkeley: University of California Press.

Munn, Nancy. 1986. *The Fame of Gawa: A Symbolic Study of Value Transformation in a Massim (Papua New Guinea) Society*. Durham, NC: Duke University Press.

Murphy, Rachel. 2004. "Turning Peasants into Modern Chinese Citizens: Discourse, Demographic Transition and Primary Education." *China Quarterly* 177: 1–20.

Nakano, Lynne. 2000. "Volunteering as a Lifestyle Choice: Negotiating Self-Identities in Japan." *Ethnology* 39 (2): 93–107.

Nakassis, Constantine V. 2012. "Brand, Citationality, Performativity." *American Anthropologist* 114 (4): 624–638.

National Bureau of Statistics. 2012. *Zhongguo 2010 nian renkou pucha ziliao* [Tabulation on the 2010 population census of the People's Republic of China]. Beijing: China Statistics Press.

Newell, Sasha. 2012. *The Modernity Bluff: Crime, Consumption, and Citizenship in Côte d'Ivoire*. Chicago: Chicago University Press.

Notar, Beth. 2006. "Authenticity Anxiety and Counterfeit Confidence: Outsourcing Souvenirs, Changing Money, and Narrating Value in Reform-Era China." *Modern China* 32 (1): 64–98.

Nunberg, Geoffrey. 1993. "Indexicality and Deixis." *Linguistics and Philosophy* 16 (1): 1–43.

Ochs, Elinor. 1992. "Indexing Gender." In *Rethinking Context: Language as an Interactive Phenomenon*, edited by Alessandro Duranti and Charles Goodwin, 335–358. Cambridge: Cambridge University Press.

Ochs, Elinor, and Lisa Capps. 2001. *Living Narrative: Creating Lives in Everyday Storytelling*. Cambridge: Harvard University Press.

Ong, Aihwa. 1997. "Chinese Modernities: Narratives of Nation and of Capitalism." In *Ungrounded Empires: The Cultural Politics of Modern Chinese Transnationalism*, edited by Aihwa Ong and Donald Nonini, 171–202. New York: Routledge.

——. 1999. *Flexible Citizenship: The Cultural Logics of Transnationality*. Durham, NC: Duke University Press.

Osburg, John. 2013. *Anxious Wealth: Money and Morality among China's New Rich*. Stanford: Stanford University Press.

Osella, Caroline, and Filippo Osella. 2006. "Once upon a Time in the West? Stories of Migration and Modernity from Kerala, South India." *Journal of the Royal Anthropological Institute* 12 (3): 569–588.

Ouyang, Huhua. 2000. "One-Way Ticket: A Story of an Innovative Teacher in Mainland China." *Anthropology and Education Quarterly* 31 (4): 397–425.

Oxfeld, Ellen. 2010. *Drink Water, but Remember the Source: Moral Discourse in a Chinese Village*. Berkeley: University of California Press.

Pan, Lin. 2010. "Dissecting Multilingual Beijing: The Space and Scale of Vernacular Globalization." *Visual Communication* 9 (1): 67–90.

——. 2015a. *English as a Global Language in China: Deconstructing the Ideological Discourses of English in Language Education*. Cham, Switzerland: Springer.

——. 2015b. "Glocalization and the Spread of Unequal Englishes: Vernacular Signs in the Center of Beijing." In *Unequal Englishes: The Politics of Englishes Today*, edited by Ruanni Tupas, 163–184. Houndmills: Palgrave Macmillan.

Pan, Lin, and David Block. 2011. "English as a 'Global Language' in China: An Investigation into Learners' and Teachers' Language Beliefs." *System* 39 (3): 391–402.

Park, Joseph Sung-Yul. 2009. *The Local Construction of a Global Language: Ideologies of English in South Korea*. Berlin: Mouton de Gruyter.

——. 2010. "Naturalization of Competence and the Neoliberal Subject: Success Stories of English Language Learning in the Korean Conservative Press." *Journal of Linguistic Anthropology* 20 (1): 22–38.

———. 2013. "Metadiscursive Regimes of Diversity in a Multinational Corporation." *Language in Society* 42 (5): 557–577.

———. 2014. "Cartographies of Language: Making Sense of Mobility among Korean Transmigrants in Singapore." *Language and Communication* 39: 83–91.

———. 2015. "Language as Pure Potential." *Journal of Multilingual and Multicultural Development* 37 (5): 453–466.

Park, Joseph Sung-Yul, and Lionel Wee. 2012. *Markets of English: Linguistic Capital and Language Policy in a Globalizing World*. New York: Routledge.

Park, So Jin, and Nancy Abelmann. 2004. "Class and Cosmopolitan Striving: Mothers' Management of English Education in South Korea." *Anthropological Quarterly* 77 (4): 645–672.

Peirce, Charles Sanders. 1974. *The Collected Papers of Charles Sanders Peirce*. Vol. 2, *Elements of Logic*. Edited by Charles Hartshorne, Paul Weiss, and Arthur Burks. Cambridge, MA: Harvard University Press.

Pennington, Martha, ed. 1998. *Language in Hong Kong at Century's End*. Hong Kong: Hong Kong University Press.

Pérez, Raúl. 2013. "Learning to Make Racism Funny in the 'Color-Blind' Era: Stand-Up Comedy Students, Performance Strategies, and the (Re)Production of Racist Jokes in Public." *Discourse and Society* 24 (4): 478–503.

Pérez-Milans, Miguel. 2012. "Beyond 'Safe-Talk': Institutionalization and Agency in China's English Language Education." *Linguistics and Education* 23 (1): 62–76.

———. 2013. *Urban Schools and English Language Education in Late Modern China: A Critical Sociolinguistic Ethnography*. New York: Routledge.

Perrino, Sabina. 2011. "Chronotopes of Story and Storytelling Event in Interviews." *Language in Society* 40 (1): 91–103.

Phillipson, Robert. 1992. *Linguistic Imperialism*. Oxford: Oxford University Press.

———. 2009. *Linguistic Imperialism Continued*. New York: Routledge.

Pieke, Frank. 1995. "Bureaucracy, Friends, and Money: The Growth of Capital Socialism in China." *Comparative Studies in Society and History* 37 (3): 494–518.

Pinkham, Joan. 2000. *Zhongshi yingyu zhijian* [The translator's guide to Chinglish]. Beijing: Foreign Language Teaching and Research Press.

Porter, Edgar. 1990. *Foreign Teachers in China: Old Problems for a New Generation*. New York: Greenwood Press.

Pow, Choon-Piew. 2009. *Gated Communities in China: Class, Privilege and the Moral Politics of the Good Life*. London: Routledge.

Pride, John B., and Ru-shan Liu. 1988. "Some Aspects of the Spread of English in China since 1949." *International Journal of the Sociology of Language* 74 (1): 41–70.

Proctor, Lavanya Murali. 2014. "English and Globalization in India: The Fractal Nature of Discourse." *Journal of Linguistic Anthropology* 24 (3): 294–314.

Qian, Suoqiao. 2011. *Liberal Cosmopolitanism: Lin Yutang and Middling Chinese Modernity*. Leiden: Brill.

Radtke, Oliver. 2007. *Chinglish: Found in Translation*. Layton, UT: Gibbs Smith.

———. 2009. *More Chinglish: Speaking in Tongues*. Layton, UT: Gibbs Smith.

Rafael, Vicente. 2005. *The Promise of the Foreign: Nationalism and the Technics of Translation in the Spanish Philippines*. Durham, NC: Duke University Press.

Raffles, Hugh. 1999. "'Local Theory': Nature and the Making of an Amazonian Place." *Cultural Anthropology* 14 (3): 323–360.

Rahman, Tariq. 2009. "Language Ideology, Identity and the Commodification of Language in the Call Centers of Pakistan." *Language in Society* 38 (2): 233–258.

Reyes, Angela, and Adrienne Lo, eds. 2009. *Beyond Yellow English: Toward a Linguistic Anthropology of Asian Pacific America*. Oxford: Oxford University Press.

Richard, Analiese, and Daromir Rudnyckyj. 2009. "Economies of Affect." *Journal of the Royal Anthropological Institute* 15 (1): 57–77.

Rofel, Lisa. 1999. *Other Modernities: Gendered Yearnings in China after Socialism.* Berkeley: University of California Press.

———. 2007. *Desiring China: Experiments in Neoliberalism, Sexuality, and Public Culture.* Durham, NC: Duke University Press.

Ross, Heidi. 1993. *China Learns English: Language Teaching and Social Change in the People's Republic.* New Haven, CT: Yale University Press.

Roth-Gordon, Jennifer. 2017. *Race and the Brazilian Body: Blackness, Whiteness, and Everyday Language in Rio de Janeiro.* Berkeley: University of California Press.

Ruan, Jiening, and Cynthia Leung, eds. 2012. *Perspectives on Teaching and Learning English Literacy in China.* Cham, Switzerland: Springer.

Rubdy, Rani, and Peter K. W. Tan. 2008. *Language as Commodity: Global Structures, Local Marketplaces.* London: Continuum.

Russell, Nancy Ukai. 1997. "Lessons from Japanese Cram Schools." In *The Challenge of Eastern Asian Education,* edited by Philip Altbach and William K. Cummings, 153–170. Albany: State University of New York Press.

Rutherford, Danilyn. 2003. *Raiding the Land of the Foreigners: The Limits of the Nation on an Indonesian Frontier.* Princeton, NJ: Princeton University Press.

Sangren, P. Steven. 2000. *Chinese Sociologics: An Anthropological Account of the Role of Alienation in Social Reproduction.* London: Athlone.

Santa Ana, Otto. 2009. "Did You Call in Mexican? The Racial Politics of Jay Leno Immigrant Jokes." *Language in Society* 38 (1): 23–45.

Saussure, Ferdinand de. 1959. *Course in General Linguistics.* New York: McGraw-Hill.

Schein, Louisa. 1994. "The Consumption of Color and the Politics of White Skin in Post-Mao China." *Social Text* 41: 141–164.

Scott, James C. 1985. *Weapons of the Weak: Everyday Forms of Peasant Resistance.* New Haven, CT: Yale University Press.

Seargeant, Philip. 2009. *The Idea of English in Japan: Ideology and the Evolution of a Global Language.* Bristol, UK: Multilingual Matters.

Seidlhofer, Barbara. 2011. *Understanding English as a Lingua Franca.* Oxford: Oxford University Press.

Selinker, Larry. 1972. "Interlanguage." *International Review of Applied Linguistics in Language Teaching* 10: 209–231.

Shankar, Shalini, and Jillian R. Cavanaugh. 2012. "Language and Materiality in Global Capitalism." *Annual Review of Anthropology* 41 (1): 355–369.

Shenyang Municipal Bureau of Statistics. 2014. *Shenyang tongji nianjian 2014* [Shenyang statistical yearbook 2014]. Shenyang: Shenyang Statistics Press.

Sherzer, Joel. 2002. *Speech Play and Verbal Art.* Austin: University of Texas Press.

Shin, Hyunjung. 2016. "Language 'Skills' and the Neoliberal English Education Industry." *Journal of Multilingual and Multicultural Development* 37 (5): 509–522.

Shin, Hyunjung, and Joseph Sung-Yul Park. 2016. "Researching Language and Neoliberalism." *Journal of Multilingual and Multicultural Development* 37 (5): 443–452.

Shohamy, Elana. 2001. *The Power of Tests: A Critical Perspective on the Uses of Language Tests.* Harlow, UK: Longman.

Silverstein, Michael. 1996. "Monoglot 'Standard' in America: Standardization and Metaphors of Linguistic Hegemony." In *The Matrix of Language: Contemporary Linguistic Anthropology,* edited by Ronald Macaulay and Donald Brenneis, 284–306. Boulder, CO: Westview Press.

———. 2003a. "Indexical Order and the Dialectics of Sociolinguistic Life." *Language and Communication* 23 (3–4): 193–229.

———. 2003b. "The Whens and Wheres—as Well as Hows—of Ethnolinguistic Recognition." *Public Culture* 15 (3): 531–557.

———. 2005. "Axes of Evals." *Journal of Linguistic Anthropology* 15 (1): 6–22.

———. 2015. "How Language Communities Intersect: Is 'Superdiversity' an Incremental or Transformative Condition?" *Language and Communication* 44: 7–18.

Silverstein, Michael, and Greg Urban, eds. 1996. "The Natural History of Discourse." In *Natural Histories of Discourse*, 1–17. Chicago: University of Chicago Press.

Simmons, Richard VanNess. 2016. "The Dōngběi Varieties of Mandarin." *Journal of Asian Pacific Communication* 26 (1): 56–80.

Simpson, William, and John O'Regan. 2018. "Fetishism and the Language Commodity: A Materialist Critique." *Language Sciences* 70: 155–166.

Skinner, G. William. 2001. *Marketing and Social Structure in Rural China*. Ann Arbor, MI: Association for Asian Studies.

Smart, Alan. 1993. "Gifts, Bribes, and Guanxi: A Reconsideration of Bourdieu's Social Capital." *Cultural Anthropology* 8 (3): 388–408.

Solinger, Dorothy. 2013. "Temporality as Trope in Delineating Inequality: Progress for the Prosperous, Time Warp for the Poor." In *Unequal China: The Political Economy and Cultural Politics of Inequality*, edited by Wanning Sun and Yingjie Guo, 59–76. London: Routledge.

Song, Geng. 2015. "Imagining the Other: Foreigners on the Chinese TV Screen." In *Chinese Television in the Twenty-First Century: Entertaining the Nation*, edited by Ruoyun Bai and Geng Song, 107–120. London: Routledge. ·

Spence, Jonathan. 1990. *The Search for Modern China*. New York: W. W. Norton.

Spolsky, Bernard. 2014. "Language Management in the People's Republic of China." *Language* 90 (4): e165–179.

Stafford, Charles. 1995. *The Roads of Chinese Childhood: Learning and Identification in Angang*. Cambridge: Cambridge University Press.

Stanlaw, James. 2004. *Japanese English: Language and Culture Contact*. Hong Kong: Hong Kong University Press.

Stanley, Phiona. 2013. *A Critical Ethnography of "Westerners" Teaching English in China: Shanghaied in Shanghai*. London: Routledge.

State Council. 2014. "Guanyu shenhua kaoshi zhaosheng zhidu gaige de shishi yijian" [Concerning the implementation of the suggestion to intensify the reform of the examination admissions system]. September 4. http://www.gov.cn/zhengce/content /2014-09/04/content_9065.htm.

Sun, Wanning. 2002. *Leaving China: Media, Migration, and Transnational Imagination*. Lanham, MD: Rowman and Littlefield.

———. 2013. "Inequality and Culture: A New Pathway to Understanding Social Inequality." In *Unequal China: The Political Economy and Cultural Politics of Inequality*, edited by Wanning Sun and Yingjie Guo, 27–42. London: Routledge.

Sun, Wanning, and Yingjie Guo, eds. 2013. *Unequal China: The Political Economy and Cultural Politics of Inequality*. London: Routledge.

Sung, Chit Cheung Matthew. 2013. "'I Would Like to Sound Like Heidi Klum': What Do Non-Native Speakers Say about Who They Want to Sound Like?" *English Today* 29 (2): 17–21.

Tam, Gina Anne. 2017. "'Orbiting the Core': Politics and the Meaning of Dialect in Chinese Linguistics, 1927–1957." *Twentieth-Century China* 41 (3): 280–303.

Tedlock, Barbara, and Dennis Tedlock. 1985. "Text and Textile: Language and Technology in the Arts of the Quiché Maya." *Journal of Anthropological Research* 41 (2): 121–146.

Theroux, Paul. 1988. *Riding the Iron Rooster: By Train through China*. New York: Putnam.

Thomassen, Bjørn. 2012. "Anthropology and Its Many Modernities: When Concepts Matter." *Journal of the Royal Anthropological Institute* 18 (1): 160–178.

Tomba, Luigi. 2009. "Of Quality, Harmony, and Community: Civilization and the Middle Class in Urban China." *Positions: East Asia Cultures Critique* 17 (3): 592–616.

Tu, Wei-Ming, ed. 1994. *The Living Tree: The Changing Meaning of Being Chinese Today.* Stanford: Stanford University Press.

Tupas, Ruanni, ed. 2015. *Unequal Englishes: The Politics of Englishes Today.* Houndmills: Palgrave Macmillan.

Urciuoli, Bonnie. 1985. "Bilingualism as Code and Bilingualism as Practice." *Anthropological Linguistics* 27 (4): 363–386.

——. 1991. "The Political Topography of Spanish and English: The View from a New York Puerto Rican Neighborhood." *American Ethnologist* 18 (2): 295–310.

——. 1996. *Exposing Prejudice: Puerto Rican Experiences of Language, Race, and Class.* Boulder, CO: Westview Press.

——. 2010. "Entextualizing Diversity: Semiotic Incoherence in Institutional Discourse." *Language and Communication* 30 (1): 48–57.

Van Leeuwen, Theo. 2007. "Legitimation in Discourse and Communication." *Discourse and Communication* 1 (1): 91–112.

Veeck, Ann. 2000. "The Revitalization of the Marketplace: Food Markets of Nanjing." In *The Consumer Revolution in Urban China*, edited by Deborah Davis, 107–123. Berkeley: University of California Press.

Vertovec, Steven. 2007. "Super-Diversity and Its Implications." *Ethnic and Racial Studies* 30 (6): 1024–1054.

Volosinov, V. N. 1986. *Marxism and the Philosophy of Language.* Cambridge, MA: Harvard University Press.

Waldram, James. 2012. *Hound Pound Narrative: Sexual Offender Habilation and the Anthropology of Therapeutic Intervention.* Berkeley: University of California Press.

Wan, Pengjie. 2005. "Zhongguo yingyu yu zhongshi yingyu zhi bijiao" [A comparison of China English and Chinglish]. *Shanghai fanyi* [Shanghai journal of translators] 2005: 41–44.

Wang, Labao. 2004. "When English Becomes Big Business." In *English and Globalization: Perspectives from Hong Kong and Mainland China*, edited by Timothy Weiss and Kwok-kan Tam, 149–168. Hong Kong: Chinese University Press.

Wang, Weihong. 2015. "Teaching English as an International Language in China: Investigating University Teachers' and Students' Attitudes towards China English." *System* 53: 60–72.

Wang, Wenfang, and Xuesong Gao. 2008. "English Language Education in China: A Review of Selected Research." *Journal of Multilingual and Multicultural Development* 29 (5): 380–399.

Wank, David L. 1999. *Commodifying Communism: Business, Trust and Politics in a Chinese City.* Cambridge: Cambridge University Press.

Watson, James. 1993. "Rites or Beliefs? The Construction of a Unified Culture in Late Imperial China." In *China's Quest for National Identity*, edited by Lowell Dittmer and Samuel Kim, 80–103. Ithaca, NY: Cornell University Press.

Wei, Rining, and Jinzhi Su. 2012. "The Statistics of English in China: An Analysis of the Best Available Data from Government Sources." *English Today* 28 (3): 10–14.

Wei, Yun, and Jia Fei. 2003. "Using English in China." *English Today* 19 (4): 42–47.

Wiedenhof, Jeroen. 2015. *A Grammar of Mandarin.* Amsterdam: John Benjamins.

Wirtz, Kristina. 2011. "Cuban Performances of Blackness as the Timeless Past Still among Us." *Journal of Linguistic Anthropology* 21 (s1): E11–34.

Woodward, Amber. 2008. "A Survey of Li Yang Crazy English." *Sino-Platonic Papers* 180: 1–71.

Woolard, Kathryn. 1985. "Language Variation and Cultural Hegemony: Toward an Integration of Sociolinguistic and Social Theory." *American Ethnologist* 12 (4): 738–748.

——. 2008. "Why Dat Now? Linguistic-Anthropological Contributions to the Explanation of Sociolinguistic Icons and Change." *Journal of Sociolinguistics* 12 (4): 432–452.

Woronov, T. E. 2008. "Raising Quality, Fostering 'Creativity': Ideologies and Practices of Education Reform in Beijing." *Anthropology and Education Quarterly* 39 (4): 401–422.

——. 2009. "Governing China's Children: Governmentality and 'Education for Quality.'" *Positions: East Asia Cultures Critique* 17 (3): 567–589.

Wortham, Stanton. 2000. "Interactional Positioning and Narrative Self-Construction." *Narrative Inquiry* 10 (1): 157–184.

——. 2006. *Learning Identity: The Joint Emergence of Social Identification and Academic Learning.* Cambridge: Cambridge University Press.

Wu, Fulong. 2010. "Gated and Packaged Suburbia: Packaging and Branding Chinese Suburban Residential Development." *Cities* 27: 385–396.

Xu, Yinong. 2000. *The Chinese City in Space and Time: The Development of Urban Form in Suzhou.* Honolulu: University of Hawai'i Press.

Xu, Zhichang. 2010. "Chinese English: A Future Power?" In *The Routledge Handbook of World Englishes,* edited by Andy Kirkpatrick, 282–298. London: Routledge.

Xu, Zhichang, and David Deterding. 2017. "The Playfulness of 'New' Chinglish." *Asian Englishes* 19 (2): 116–127.

Xu, Zhichang, Deyuan He, and David Deterding, eds. 2017. *Researching Chinese English: The State of the Art.* Cham, Switzerland: Springer.

Yan, Hairong. 2008. *New Masters, New Servants: Migration, Development, and Women Workers in China.* Durham, NC: Duke University Press.

Yan, Yunxiang. 1996. *The Flow of Gifts: Reciprocity and Social Networks in a Chinese Village.* Stanford: Stanford University Press.

——. 2005. "Making Room for Intimacy: Domestic Space and Conjugal Privacy in Rural North China." In *House, Home, Family: Living and Being Chinese,* edited by Ronald Knapp and Kai-yin Lo, 373–395. Honolulu: University of Hawai'i Press.

——. 2009. *The Individualization of Chinese Society.* Oxford: Berg.

Yang, Jie. 2007. "'Re-employment Stars': Language, Gender and Neoliberal Restructuring in China." In *Words, Worlds, and Material Girls: Language, Gender, Globalization,* edited by Bonnie McElhinny, 77–105. Berlin: Mouton de Gruyter.

Yang, Mayfair Mei-Hui. 1994. *Gifts, Favors, and Banquets: The Art of Social Relationships in China.* Ithaca, NY: Cornell University Press.

——. 2002. "The Resilience of Guanxi and Its New Deployments: A Critique of Some New Guanxi Scholarship." *China Quarterly* 170: 459–476.

Yang, Qingqing. 2015. *Space Modernization and Social Interaction: A Comparative Study of Living Space in Beijing.* Heidelberg: Springer.

Yeh, Wen-Hsin, ed. 2000. *Becoming Chinese: Passages to Modernity and Beyond.* Berkeley: University of California Press.

Yip, Virginia. 1995. *Interlanguage and Learnability: From Chinese to English.* Amsterdam: John Benjamins.

Yu, Chen-chung. 1984. "Cultural Principles Underlying English Teaching in China." *Language Learning and Communication* 3 (1): 29–40.

Zarrow, Peter, ed. 2006. *Creating Chinese Modernity: Knowledge and Everyday Life, 1900–1940.* New York: Peter Lang.

Zentz, Lauren. 2015. "'Is English Also the Place Where I Belong?' Linguistic Biographies and Expanding Communicative Repertoires in Central Java." *International Journal of Multilingualism* 12 (1): 68–92.

Zhang, Li. 2006. "Contesting Spatial Modernity in Late-Socialist China." *Current Anthropology* 47 (3): 461–484.

———. 2010. *In Search of Paradise: Middle-Class Living in a Chinese Metropolis*. Ithaca, NY: Cornell University Press.

Zhang, Li, and Aihwa Ong, eds. 2008. *Privatizing China: Socialism from Afar*. Ithaca, NY: Cornell University Press.

Zhang, Ping-yu. 2003. "Industrial Transformation of Shenyang City." *Chinese Geographical Science* 13 (3): 216–223.

Zhang, Qing. 2006. "Cosmopolitan Mandarin: Linguistic Practice of Chinese Waiqi Professionals." *Journal of Asian Pacific Communication* 16 (2): 215–235.

———. 2012. "'Carry Shopping through to the End': Linguistic Innovation in a Chinese Television Program." In *Style-Shifting in Public: New Perspectives on Stylistic Variation*, edited by Juan Manuel Hernandes-Campoy and Juan Antonio Cutillas-Espinosa, 205–224. Amsterdam: John Benjamins.

Zhang, Ripei. 2014. "The Improvement of the Language Environment for the Shanghai Expo 2010." In *The Language Situation in China*, vol. 2, edited by Yuming Li and Wei Li, 101–110. Berlin: Mouton de Gruyter.

Zhang, Zhen. 2000. "Mediating Time: The 'Rice Bowl of Youth' in Fin de Siècle Urban China." *Public Culture* 12 (1): 93–113.

Zhao, He-ping. 1987. "The Chinese Pronoun Zan and Its Person and Social Deictic Features." *Journal of Chinese Linguistics* 15 (1): 152–176.

Zhao, Junhai. 2016. "The Reform of the National Matriculation English Test and Its Impact on the Future of English in China." *English Today* 32 (2): 38–44.

Zheng, Xin-min, and Chris Davison. 2008. *Changing Pedagogy: Analysing ELT Teachers in China*. London: Continuum.

Zhou, Qingsheng, and Lei Wang. 2013. "Efforts of Creating a Good Language Environment for Beijing Olympic Games: A Brief Report." In *The Language Situation in China*, vol. 1, edited by Yuming Li and Wei Li, 171–179. Berlin: Mouton de Gruyter.

Zhu, Jianfei. 2004. *Chinese Spatial Strategies: Imperial Beijing, 1420–1911*. London: Routledge.

Zito, Angela. 1997. *Of Body and Brush: Grand Sacrifice as Text/Performance in Eighteenth Century China*. Chicago: University of Chicago Press.

Index

1911 Revolution 11, 45

accent: as guarantee of authenticity, 14, 15, 114–115, 131–132; and Chinglish, 129–130; of Dongbeihua (*see* Dongbeihua: accent of); erasure of, 40, 132; evaluations of, 39, 43, 53, 66, 72, 81; of foreigners, 107, 115; as indexical, 16, 33, 75; "thickness" of, 29, 36; and teaching, 105–106
African American English, 120–121
Agha, Asif, 15, 17–18, 34, 97
architecture, 56–57; modern, 62–66; traditional, 57–60

backwardness (*luohou*), 20, 74, 79, 87; and language, 30, 141, 143; of peasants, 31, 36, 138
Bakhtin, Mikhail, 15–17, 20, 48, 172
Basso, Keith, 23
BBC (British Broadcasting Corporation), 95, 131
Beijing, 11, 21, 58–60, 70, 173; and accent, 41, 43, 129; compared with Shenyang, 22, 87, 89
Beijing Olympics (2008), 4, 24, 119–120
Beijing Speaks Foreign Languages program, 119–120, 183n1
bilingualism, 27, 34, 69, 85, 98, 126, 170
Blommaert, Jan, 17, 52, 136, 176
Bourdieu, Pierre, 18–19, 96, 142
British Council, 153
buke, 108–110
bureaucracy, x, 111–113, 118

Cantonese, 17, 130
Cavanaugh, Jillian, 39
CCTV (China Central Television), 36–37, 170
Chaoji Nusheng (Super Girl), 51
China Central Television. *See* CCTV
China Daily 120
China English (*zhongguo yingyu*), 10, 122, 125–127, 143
Chinese language. *See* Mandarin Chinese
Chineseness: discourse of, 168–171
Chinese Revolution. *See* 1911 Revolution

Chinglish: campaign against, 119–121; and humor, 124, 137–139; as interlanguage, 122–123; legitimacy of, 125; views of, 126–137, 140–143
Christie, Dugald, 45
chronotope 16–24, 56–57; modernity as, 25–28, 41, 147, 175; and narrative, 79; and synchronicity 61–62, 73–75
code-switching, 51, 130, 133, 139
colonialism, 2, 5, 178
commodity: language as, 95–98, 117–118
Communist Party of China, 1, 45, 61
Confucianism, 60, 118
Corder, Pit, 121–122, 143
cosmopolitanism, 3, 69, 145, 169; and modernity, 18, 96, 104; as citizenship, 34, 36, 125, 151, 160; as identity, x, 14–15, 23, 54, 178
Crazy English (language program), 5, 173
cross-talk (*xiangsheng*), 30, 32
Cultural Revolution, 2, 11, 62, 106

deixis, 79
Deng Xiaoping, 4, 11, 62
dialogism, 16–17, 48
dirt (*tu*), 30, 67, 73, 87, 90; as form of talk, 29–30, 40
Dongbei (Northeast), 10, 42, 113; as regional identity, 38, 40, 43–44, 53, 177
Dongbeihua, xiii, 13–15, 33, 38, 41, 44–45, 176; accent of, 29–30, 36, 40–41, 106, 129; in conversation, 23–24, 29, 41, 73, 171, 176; description of, 36–38, indexicality of, 30–33, 40–44, 73; and Mandarin, 31–32, 35, 38–40; as performance, 13–14, 30; and space, 23, 66, 72, 75
Dongbeiren dou shi huo Lei Feng (song), 43–44
Dongbei yi jia ren (A Dongbei Family), 44

English as a lingua franca, 3–4, 134
English corner, 84, 115–116
English curriculum, 33–34, 109
English examinations, 3, 47–50, 76, 82. *See also* IELTS; NCEE

CPSIA information can be obtained
at www.ICGtesting.com
Printed in the USA
LVHW111720020421
683324LV00007B/204

9 781501 755163